Queer Stu

Series Editors

William F. Pinar
Department of Curriculum and Pedagogy
University of British Columbia
Vancouver, BC, Canada

Nelson M. Rodriguez
Department of Women's, Gender,
and Sexuality Studies
The College of New Jersey
Ewing, NJ, USA

Reta Ugena Whitlock
Department of Educational Leadership
Kennesaw State University
Kennesaw, Georgia, USA

LGBTQ social, cultural, and political issues have become a defining feature of twenty-first century life, transforming on a global scale any number of institutions, including the institution of education. Situated within the context of these major transformations, this series is home to the most compelling, innovative, and timely scholarship emerging at the intersection of queer studies and education. Across a broad range of educational topics and locations, books in this series incorporate lesbian, gay, bisexual, transgender, and intersex categories, as well as scholarship in queer theory arising out of the postmodern turn in sexuality studies. The series is wide-ranging in terms of disciplinary/theoretical perspectives and methodological approaches, and will include and illuminate much needed intersectional scholarship. Always bold in outlook, the series also welcomes projects that challenge any number of normalizing tendencies within academic scholarship, from works that move beyond established frameworks of knowledge production within LGBTQ educational research to works that expand the range of what is institutionally defined within the field of education as relevant queer studies scholarship.

International Advisory Board:

Louisa Allen, The University of Auckland, New Zealand
Edward Brockenbrough, University of Pennsylvania, USA
James Burford, Thammasat University, Thailand
Anna Carastathis, Independent Scholar, Greece
Rob Cover, The University of Western Australia, Perth, Australia
Cindy Cruz, University of California, Santa Cruz, USA
Xinyan Fan, The University of British Columbia, Canada
Anne Harris, RMIT University, Australia
Tiffany Jones, Macquarie University, Australia
Jón Ingvar Kjaran, University of Iceland, Reykjavík, Iceland
Kevin Kumashiro, Kevin Kumashiro Consulting, USA
Alicia Lapointe, Western University, Canada
Máirtín Mac an Ghaill, Newman University, UK
Paul Chamness Miller, Akita International University, Japan
sj Miller, University of Wisconsin-Madison, USA
Robert Mizzi, University of Manitoba, Canada
Thabo Msibi, University of KwaZulu-Natal, South Africa
Aoife Neary, University of Limerick, Ireland
Z Nicolazzo, University of Arizona, USA
Gul Ozyegin, William & Mary, USA
Moira Pérez, University of Buenos Aires, Argentina
Christine Quinan, Utrecht University, The Netherlands
Mary Lou Rasmussen, Australian National University, Australia
Eva Reimers, University of Gothenburg, Sweden
Emma Renold, Cardiff University, UK
Finn Reygan, Human Sciences Research Council, South Africa
Nick Rumens, Middlesex University, UK
Jacqueline Ullman, Western Sydney University, Australia

More information about this series at
https://www.palgrave.com/us/series/14522

sj Miller

Editor

Teaching, Affirming, and Recognizing Trans* and Gender Creative Youth

A Queer Literacy Framework

palgrave
macmillan

Editor
sj Miller
Santa Fe, New Mexico, USA

Queer Studies and Education
ISBN 978-1-137-56765-9 (hardcover)   ISBN 978-1-137-56766-6   (eBook)
ISBN 978-1-349-92939-9 (softcover)
DOI 10.1057/978-1-137-56766-6

Library of Congress Control Number: 2016942090

This Palgrave Macmillan imprint is published by Springer Nature
The registered company is Nature America Inc. New York

The world changes in direct proportion to the number of people willing to be honest about their lives.

Armistead Maupin

This work is dedicated to all trans*, queer, and gender creative youth whose lives have been lost in the war of misrecognition and misunderstanding. May your deaths not be in vain. May we draw hope from your darkest moments. May this work offer some attempt to heal your friends and families who lost you far too soon.

We are here. We hear you. And, we are so, so sorry.

FOREWORD

The relationship between realness and representation has been central to education for millennia. When Socrates discusses the divided line, he is critical of the act of representation for replacing the real with a pale copy. While we may not agree with his analysis, he does indicate to us the power of representation and the potential for reinscriptions to upset seemingly solid conceptions of what is real and by so doing to push us into new ways of thinking about truth, presence, and learning. Prof. sj Miller's wonderful edited collection pushes us to see the complex relationship between trans* people and other aspects of gendered and sexuality-related identity, authenticity, representation, recognition, and contestation. In a sense, this collection works a complex divided line of its own; it destabilizes gender identity and insists on the stabilization of justice by engaging the possibilities within literacy education. Reading (really, Socrates was right on this) is an interpretive task that shatters certainty but one also embedded in understandings that precede it. The circulation of meanings, in the best pedagogical and political contexts, opens possibilities for understandings, communities, and subjectivities. In its finest practice then, literacy is a transactional event, inviting students into meaning making and showing them that their intellect, lives, and bodies matter. Miller calls on us here to ensure we recognize trans* students and ensure their place in this energetic and challenging sort of learning community.

The authors in this collection aim to help us to think about how trans* innovations to teaching and learning can enhance student criticality and encourage equitable education. Encouraging students to understand the multiplicity of interpretations and experiences in their midst provides them not only with contexts for intellectual growth, but it also invites them into a world characterized in and through diverse perspectives and experiences. But schools may also be experienced as contexts that perpetually stress the right way to be, think, and act. In this sort of constrained institutional environment, perhaps too intent on accountability more than on students flourishing, the play of gender, the reversals of readings, and other resistant actions become suppressed by restrictive pedagogies, narrow curricula, and inequitable practices.

Queer and trans* theories have helped show us generative refusal of stability both in the context of meaning and subjectivity. This book shows how pedagogies based in those refusals can counter institutional omissions and welcome trans* students into schools, as well as encourage trans* allies to create equitable lessons and classrooms. Many educators are of course troubled by the exclusions written into school policy and practice. We can cite multiple examples of exclusions from the perpetual underserving of lower-income communities of color to more specific instances. We can cite the connections among exclusions; the outlawing of ethnic studies in Arizona; the fake prom in Mississippi held for queer kids and students with disabilities; and, the initial refusal of the principal of Sakia Gunn, who was African American and gender-nonconforming, to allow a moment of silence to mark her murder. Schools, all too often, are contexts for damaging refusals: refusal to recognize language and cultural diversity, refusal to mitigate divisive disciplinary policies, refusal to recognize gender identity diversity, and, the refusal to be inclusive of embodied and intellectual diversities. The added damage of these refusals of schools to sufficiently care for trans* and gender-nonconforming students may be seen in the disproportionate rates of bias and violence they experience, including especially the violence experienced by trans women of color. While schools will not solve everything, they are nonetheless institutions that can reflect the better hope for futures without violence through becoming more inclusive and welcoming places of and for difference.

This collection encourages educators to become more finely attuned to the play of meaning in texts and to the necessity for respect for the vast diversity of student identities. It encourages us to understand as well that trans* students are adept critical readers of social and embodied possibility, able to think at young ages about who they are and want to be. And one hopes that with more books like this groundbreaking collection, educators will be increasingly able to help young people negotiate what seems to be, sometimes, hopefully, a more welcoming society. Young trans people are coming out earlier and more often. Our task is to ensure that they are met with care and recognition of their complex work with and through genders, and to ensure they have access to educational contexts that encourage their flourishing, their creativity, and their potential to continue to help us all to think, read, and live gender better.

Cris Mayo
University of Illinois at Urbana-Champaign

Acknowledgments

I want to thank the contributors of this work for their care and compassion about creating classrooms that refuse to leave anyone out. I want to thank the inimitable Cris Mayo for being a silent strength and heartbeat that I knew I could always count on. We hardly *know* each other but I know we are kindred spirits. Thank you to Nicole Sieben, Sue Hopewell, Les Burns, Bettina Love, Cris Mayo, Nelson Graff, Kerryn Dixon, Meghan Barnes, and Stephanie Shelton for feedback on early drafts. I want to thank my chosen family Yolanda Sealey-Ruiz, Bettina Love, Darrell Hucks, Kerryn Dixon, Shirley Steinberg, Eelco Bultenhuis, Maryann Shaening, Mike Wenk, Penny Pence, Betsy Noll, Don Zancanella, Sue Hopewell, Diane and Todd Smith, Tara Star Johnson, Les Burns, Cynthia Tyson, Deb Bieler, Nicole Sieben, and Briann Shear, for their constant show of care and love and for never giving up on me. Each, in their own way, have encouraged me to keep writing and pushing boundaries, and to give voice to those in need of voice through the academy. Thank you for your unconditional love over the years and for supporting me to finally find home in my body.

Together, through the relationship between families and teachers, trans and gender creative youth *are* the hope for our future by embodying the change that can shift the genderscape of society.

The original version of this book was revised.

An erratum to this book can be found at
DOI 10.1057/978-1-137-56766-6_17

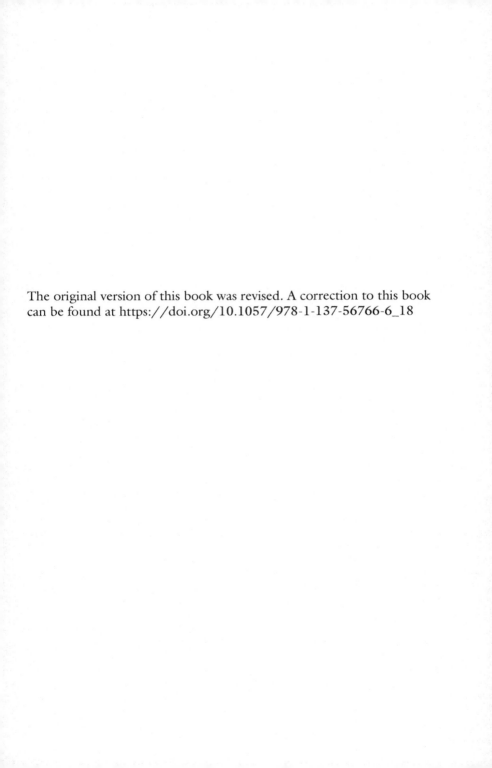

The original version of this book was revised. A correction to this book can be found at https://doi.org/10.1057/978-1-137-56766-6_18

CONTENTS

LIST OF FIGURES

LIST OF TABLES

CHAPTER 1

Introduction: The Role of Recognition

sj Miller

It is a peculiar sensation, this double-consciousness, this sense of always looking at one's self through the eyes of others, of measuring one's soul by the tape of a world that looks on in amused contempt and pity.

-W.E.B. Du Bois (1903)

I do not want to explain myself to others over and over again. I just want to be seen.

-sj

At one year of age, Blue is a curious and precocious pre-toddler, feeling her way through the world, putting everything in sight in her mouth, and grabbing spoons and using the family dog as a drum. Blue runs around *a lot*. In fact, Blue runs around so much, her family predicts Blue will become a phenomenal runner or some type of athlete. It is the early 1970s so Blue's parents dress her in gaudy suede jumpers with bling, pink socks, and clogs. Sort of a mismatch to the identity Blue has begun to exhibit.

At two, Blue's affinity for running has accelerated. Now, Blue runs after the dog, the neighbor, the birds, and right out of the door, into the yard,

sj Miller (✉)
Santa Fe, New Mexico, USA

© The Editor(s) (if applicable) and The Author(s) 2016
sj Miller (ed.), *Teaching, Affirming, and Recognizing Trans and Gender Creative Youth*, DOI 10.1057/978-1-137-56766-6_1

and even the street. Blue's mom supports these adventurous pursuits, but Blue's dad does not think it's appropriate for *his daughter* to behave this way, and even asserts, "I don't want my daughter to be a tomboy." Blue is just being Blue.

From ages three to five, Blue looks like a boy. Her hair fro'd, her now tube socks hiked up to her knees, her cutoffs pretty hideous even for the 1970s, and her appearance, masculine. Blue likes to watch her father pee standing up, and when alone, tries to emulate the behavior, but with limited success, and lots of splatter on the floor. Blue likes to watch her father shaving, and when alone, smears toothpaste on her face and traces it off with strokes of her toothbrush. She is far more successful with this task than the attempts at urinating. Blue likes to ride her Huffy BMX bike around the neighborhood and bring food home to her mom and sister when her dad is late home from work. Blue steps into a caregiving role, quite naturally, because it is just what feels *right*.

Blue loves playing football topless in the streets like the other boys do, and seems to be living life in a way that just *seems* right and normal. Then one day Blue runs into the house screaming, "I want to be a boy!" Blue's parents do not understand these words, but actually maybe they do. In response, Blue's dad begins to gender Blue by reminding her of her gender in passive-aggressive ways. For special events, he wrestles Blue into dresses and heels, only for Blue to then throw her body into dog shit and roll around in it. Then Blue's dad beats Blue and dresses her up again. Helpless and in tears, Blue's mom, watched passively as her only recourse. To different degrees, this family battle would play out for the next forty years.

At the age of five, Blue enters school. Blue has mostly boys as friends and enacts behavior typical of other boys. Blue plays sports during recess, sits with the boys at lunch, *tries* to pee in the boy's restroom, and only wants to be in classroom groups with other boys. The only gender marker to reveal that Blue is a girl is her clothing and the colors, those that typically demarcate girls' identities. Blue doesn't understand when the class is separated into groups based on gender and why she is put into the groups with other girls. After all, Blue feels like a boy, thinks she is a boy, and is treated like a boy by other boys in school.

As Blue goes through her primary and secondary schooling years, gender was not on the radar in her teachers' classrooms. Music, dating, film, and athletics are the only aspects of her life, outside of her family, that gives Blue sources to understand her gender confusion. Blue is drawn to musicians for unconscious reasons. For Blue, the artists and bands she is most drawn to, like Morrissey (the Smiths), Adam Ant, David Byrne, Tracy Chapman, Boy George, Depeche Mode, the Talking Heads, Kate Bush, Pet Shop Boys, Erasure, Trio, Oingo Boingo, New Order, Yaz, and David Bowie seem to express challenges to the gender binary through both looks *and* lyrics. Blue's favorite musician is Robert Smith, lead singer of The Cure. Smith dresses in black, has disheveled hair, wears lipstick, and occasionally even dresses. Smith's lyrics are poetic, dark, and forlorn but they bring meaning, order, and respite to Blue. Blue listens to everything produced by The Cure until it drowns out the negative thoughts about Blue's internal gender struggle. The Cure *is* the cure.

Throughout high school, Blue dates males. Blue doesn't understand her feelings but is drawn to boys, as if she herself is one. She has many close female friends and is attracted to some of them, but not from the identity of female; she is drawn to them as if she *is* male. So she continues to live her life, dates males, acquires friends along a continuum of genders and with queered identities—gay, lesbian, bisexual, and straight. All of this just feels *normal* to Blue. The unconscious urges to be with males, as a male, remain unremitting but she does not know how to talk about them. None of her teachers address gender or sexual identity in her classes. She reads no texts, sees no examples of herself or others that could possibly help her understand who she is. Even with friends and teachers she adored, she is lost at school.

Blue turns to film for reasons similar to music. Films assuage a curiosity that gives visual recognition to different identities in the world. Without the language to support the unconscious emotionality Blue feels, films such as *The Unbearable Lightness of Being, The Rocky Horror Picture Show, I've Heard the Mermaid Singing,* and all films by Ivory Merchant Productions become running stills that shape and inform who Blue is becoming. Many of the characters in the films, and the actors who illuminate them, give calm to the raging storm brewing inside Blue.

Soccer and swimming, two stabilizing factors for Blue's identity development throughout secondary school, provide critical spaces and opportunities to release pain and confusion. Again, without the language to know what Blue feels inside, these sports calm the inner rage. Blue is a better-than-average swimmer and often places in the top five at meets in both freestyle and butterfly sprints. Blue's natural talent as a runner is channeled into soccer, and Blue is a *star*. As a forward, Blue breaks district and state records, leads her team to compete at the state level, and becomes the first female All-American in her state. Six top academic and

Division 1 schools offer her scholarships. She chooses Cal-Berkeley. With memories of her family, music, friends, teachers, school, and film, Blue leaves for college—it is 1988. The future is unknown, and it would take Blue until age forty, twenty-two years later, to come to terms with her gender confusion....

RECOGNITION

The struggle for recognition is at the core of human identity. With social positioning as the presumed or "normative" condition, those whose gender identities fall outside of the binary tend to be misrecognized and misunderstood and suffer from what I call a *recognition gap*, much as I did in my childhood and adolescence, when I was *Blue*.

Misrecognition subverts the possibility to be made credible, legible, or to be read and/or truly understood. When one is misrecognized, it is altogether difficult to hold a positive self-image, knowing that others may hold a different or negative image (Harris-Perry 2011). When the presumed normative condition is challenged though, a corollary emerges; this suggests that at the base of the human condition, people are in search of positive recognition, to be seen as "normal," because it validates their humanity.

Looking back into *my* youth, there was no common language for society to help people understand gender confusion, or if there was it was not brought into my life. This leaves me little room to wonder why a core group of my peers in high school and even in college—many who felt similar to me—have only come to identify themselves as trans*[1] or gender creative[2] later in their lives. As language and understanding around trans* and gender creative identities have become part of the social fabric of society, youth have had more access to recent changes in health care and therapeutic services that have supported them in their processes of becoming and coming to terms with their true selves. These opportunities for visibility have galvanized a movement fortifying validation and generating opportunities for both personal and social recognition. Now, we see more trans* and gender creative people portrayed positively in the media. With individuals such as Laverne Cox, Janet Mock, Chaz Bono, Aydian Dowling, Scott Turner Schofield, Ian Harvey, and Caitlyn Jenner, and TV shows such as *Transparent, Becoming Us, Orange Is the New Black, The Fosters,* and *I am Jazz*, just to name a few, we see a growing media presence. With an estimated 700,000 trans* people now living in the USA, there is even the "Out Trans 100," an annual award given to individuals who demonstrate courage through their efforts to promote visibility in their professions and communities. But, where teacher education still falls short is in how to support pre-K-12 teachers about how to integrate and normalize instruction that affirms and recognizes trans* and gender creative youth. These identities are nearly invisible in curriculum and in the Common Core Standards. That is why this book was written, as an attempt to bring trans* and gender creative recognition and legibility into schools. In this collection, authors model exciting and innovative approaches for teaching, affirming, and recognizing trans* and gender creative youth across pre-K-12th grades.

To understand the role of recognition in school, this work draws inspiration from W.E.B. Du Bois who, in *The Souls of Black Folk*, wrote about the struggle for Black recognition and validation in USA. In this book, Du Bois (1903) describes a double consciousness, that sense of simultaneously holding up two images of the self, the internal and the external, while always trying to compose and reconcile one's identity. He concerns himself with how the disintegration of the two generates internal strife and confusion about a positive sense of self-worth, just as I shared in my story.

Similar to what Du Bois names as a source for internal strife, youth who live outside of the gender binary and challenge traditionally entrenched forms of gender expression, such as trans* and gender creative youth, experience a double consciousness. As they strive and yearn to be positively recognized by peers, teachers, and family members, they experience macroaggressions, because of their systemic reinforcement, and are forced to placate others by representing themselves in incomplete or false ways that they believe will be seen as socially acceptable in order to survive a school day. Such false fronts or defensive strategies are emotionally and cognitively exhausting and difficult (Miller et al. 2013), otherwise known as *emotional labor* (Hochschild 1983; Nadal et al. 2010; Nordmarken 2012); trans* and gender creative youth are thereby positioned by the school system to sustain a learned or detached tolerance to buffer the self against the countless microaggressions experienced throughout a typical school day. In fact while research from Gay, Lesbian & Straight Educators Network (GLSEN) (2008, 2010, 2014) reveals that at the secondary level trans* youth experience nearly the *highest* rates of bullying in schools, even more startling, painful, and of grave concern is that trans* youth of color, when combined with a queer sexual orientation, experience *the* highest rates of school violence.

When school climates support and privilege the normalization of het-erosexist, cisgender, Eurocentric, unidimensional (i.e., non-intersectional), or gender normative beliefs—even unconsciously—it forces students who fall outside of those dominant identifiers to focus on simple *survival* rather than on *success and fulfillment in* school (Miller 2012; Miller and Gilligan 2014). When school is neither safe nor affirming, or lacks a pedagogy of recognition, it leaves little to the imagination why trans* and gender creative youth are suffering. As potential remedy to disrupt this double consciousness and an erasure of such youth, a trans* pedagogy emerges from these urgent realities and demands for immediate social, educational, and personal change and transformation. Such legitimacies of the human spirit, when affirmed by and through a trans* pedagogy, invite trans* and gender creative youth to see their intra, inter, and social value mirrored, and to experience (a)gender[3] self-determination and justice. My hope for the millennial generation of trans* and gender creative youth is that they can start living the lives they were meant to have from an early age, be affirmed and recognized for who they are, and not wait a lifetime to find themselves. Educating teachers (and parents) and school personnel across grade levels is an intervention and potential remedy. For schooling to truly integrate and embed gender justice into curriculum, it is important to understand the history of gender injustice that led us to the present day. When Edmund Burke spoke the words "Those who don't know history are doomed to repeat it," little did he know the importance of how their potential prophecy would manifest for specific populations of humanity.

ATTEMPTS AT TRANS* ERASURE

While nearly thirty years of research about the criticality of bridging lesbian, gay, bisexual, transgender, and questioning issues (Quinn and Meiners 2011) to school curriculum has been well documented, educa-tion remains without a large-scale study of how schools of education are preparing preservice teachers to address and incorporate topics for the *mil-lennial* generation lesbian, gay, bisexual, transgender, intersex, agender/asexual, gender creative, and questioning youth (LGBTIAGCQ[M])[4] (Miller 2015). There is, however, a growing body of pre-K-16 LGBTIAGCQ research across various geographical contexts of preservice teacher pre-paredness. Studies include teachers' personal beliefs (Meyer 2007; Miller 2014; Robinson and Ferfolja 2001a, b; Schmidt et al. 2012); teach-ing and queering disciplinary literacy (Athanases 1996; Blackburn and

Buckley 2005; Clark and Blackburn 2009; Ryan and Hermann-Wilmarth 2013; Schmidt 2010); preparing teachers to teach queer youth of color (Blackburn and McCready 2013; Cammarota 2007; McCready 2007); program effectiveness on preparing teachers to teach LGBTQGV issues (Griffin and Ouellett 2003; Szalacha 2004); and of key relevance to this book, challenges to gender norms (Miller 2009; Martino and Pallotta-Chiarolli 2003; Mayo 2004, 2007; Robinson 2005; Savage and Harley 2009). Absent from this list is both glaring and recognizable—supporting teachers who work with or will work with trans* and gender creative youth. While previous work has been concerned with gender normativity and has focused on trans* issues in the midst as part of LGBTQ work, this book takes supporting trans* and gender creative students as its primary and concerted function.

Historically, society has tried to erase trans* people but in this attempt at erasure, trans* identities and visibility (Namaste 2000) have actually been produced. In this production though, society writ large has experienced a grand anxiety (Miller 2015), and trans* and gender creative youth are the resultant victims of this anxiety. In schools therefore, such youth experience inurement because of this larger lack of systemic recognition and legibility. This production of invisibility of trans* and gender creative youth has generated a movement toward greater visibility, and such visibility is where this work asserts that a trans* pedagogy must be produced to sustain the personal and social legitimacy of trans* and gender creative youth as both recognizable and validated.

Such polemics usher in the urgent concern about what schools and teachers can do to not only recognize the presence of trans* and gender creative students in their classrooms, but how to sustain safe, affirming, and inclusive classrooms across myriad sociocultural and linguistic contexts. Through a *queer literacy framework* (QLF) (Miller 2015, 2016, forthcoming), a framework guided by ten principles and subsequent commitments about how to recognize, honor, and affirm trans* and gender creative youth, the next chapter presents how teachers can use *trans** pedagogy and sustain curriculum in order to mediate safe, inclusive, and affirming classroom contexts. Drawing then from parts of the QLF, the book offers pre-K-12 teachers a select sample of strategies that cut across social, economic, cultural, and linguistic contexts to support their students about how to understand and read (a)gender through a queer lens; how to rework social and classroom norms where bodies with differential realities in classrooms are legitimated and made legible to self and other; how to shift classroom contexts for reading (a)gender; and how to support classroom students toward personal, educational, and social legitimacy through understanding the value of (a)gender self-determination and justice.[5]

A Trans* Pedagogy and a Theory of Trans*ness

First, we begin with why a trans* pedagogy matters? We know that in schools, trans* and gender creative youth have identities that are "made" vulnerable to incurring the highest rates among their peers of bullying, harassment, truancy, dropping out, mental health issues (Kosciw et al. 2010; Miller et al. 2013), and suicidal ideation (Ybarra et al. 2014). Such deleterious realities beget a deeper and more systemic issue that unearths how underprepared teachers and schools are equipped to mediate learning that affirms and creates and then *sustains* classrooms of recognition and school spaces *for all* (Jennings 2014; Quinn and Meiners 2011). While many tropes about trans* and gender creative youth focus on their suffering, this project hopes to advance a different narrative that calls for recognition, stemming from a misrecognition. Some argue that we cannot have pedagogy without theory but in this case, I operate from the premise that youth need recognition in classrooms and schools, and from within that indeterminate context, a theory of trans*ness emerges. By creating a pedagogy for *trans*ness*, a pedagogy built upon and by rhizomatic (Deleuze and Guittari 1987; Miller 2014), spatiality and hybridity, and geospatial (Miller 2014; Soja 2010) theories, this work seeks to inspire a school climate that advances and graduates self-determined youth whose bodies become *spatially agentive* (Miller 2014), who can shift deeply entrenched binary opinions about gender through a deepening of human awareness, thus revealing that identities are multitudinous and on an ever-changing path in search of love and recognition.

A trans* pedagogy first and foremost presumes axioms (see Table 1.1) that can both validate trans* and gender creative youth and support their legibility and readability in schools and form the foundation for a trans* pedagogy. For instance:

What Does Trans Mean?*

The word trans* infers to cut across or go between, to go over or beyond or away from, spaces and/or identities. It is also about integrating new ideas and concepts and new knowledges. Trans* is therefore comprised of multitudes, a moving away or a *refusal* to accept essentialized constructions of spaces, ideas, genders, or identities. It is within this confluence or mash-up that the self can be made and remade, always in perpetual construction and deconstruction, thereby having agency to create and draw the self into identity(ies) that the individual can recognize. But self-recognition is not enough because, as Butler (2004) suggests, human value is context based, and one's happiness and success are dependent on social legibility (p. 32). Therefore, the possibility of becoming *self-determined* presumes the right to make choices to self-identify in a way that authenticates one's self-expression and self-acceptance, rejects an imposition to be externally controlled, defined, or regulated, and can unsettle knowledge to generate new possibilities of legibility.

Self-determination resides in the rhetorical quality of the "master's" discourse (Butler 2004, p. 163). This is problematic when the "master's" (i.e., in this case the teacher or the school) discourse lacks deep under-standing about how to integrate new knowledges that affirm trans* and gender creative youth. Therefore, this theory of trans*ness suggests that for new knowledges to emerge, classrooms must be thought of and taught rhizomatically, or as a networked space where relationships intersect, are concentric, do not intersect, can be parallel, non-parallel, perpendicular, obtuse, and fragmented (Miller 2014). Arising from this plan then, trans* as a theoretical concept connects to spatiality and hybridity studies that have focused on how literacy practices position student identities (Brandt and Clinton 2002; Latour 1996; Leander and Sheehy 2004; McCarthey

Table 1.1   Axioms for a trans* pedagogy

➤ We live in a time we never made, gender norms predate our existence;
➤ Nongender and sexual "differences" have been around forever but norms operate to pathologize and delegitimize them;
➤ Children's self-determination is taken away early when gender is inscribed onto them. Their bodies/minds become unknowing participants in a roulette of gender norms;
➤ Children have rights to their own (a)gender legibility;
➤ Binary views on gender are potentially damaging;
➤ Gender must be dislodged/unhinged from sexuality;
➤ Humans have agency;
➤ We must move away from pathologizing beliefs that police humanity;
➤ Humans deserve positive recognition and acknowledgment for who they are;
➤ We are all entitled to the same basic human rights; and,
➤ Life should be livable for all.

---

and Moje 2002), and to other studies which have focused on how histories have spatial dimensions that are normalized with inequities hidden in bodies whereby bodies becomes contested sites that experience social injustice temporally and spatially (Miller and Norris 2007; Nespor 1997; Slattery 1992, 1995). This book offers readers insight on how teachers mediate these axioms that bodies are not reducible to language alone because language continuously emerges from bodies as individuals come to know themselves. Bodies can thereby generate and invent new knowledges or as Butler (2004) suggests, "The body gives rise to language and that language carries bodily aims, and performs bodily deeds that are not always understood by those who use language to accomplish certain conscious aims" (p. 199). Similarly, Foucault (1990) reminds us that the self constitutes itself in discourse with the assistance of another's presence and speech. Therefore, when trans* and gender creative youth experience the simultaneity of both self and social recognition, they are less likely to experience the psychic split or double consciousness that DuBois (1903) called debilitating.

Building upon these frames, a theory of trans*ness aligns with geospatial theory mediated by a "spatial turn" (Soja 2010), or a rebalancing between social, historical, and spatial perspectives, whereby none of these domains is privileged when reading and interpreting the world (p. 3), rather, they are viewed in simultaneity. This connection between these theories therefore presumes that geographies are beholden to geohistories (Miller 2014), or the ideological practices that shape a collective history of a people and a place, revealing a society's dominant view through acts of social justice and injustice, reinforced through policy and patterned absences of language (Massey 2005; Soja 2010). Combined, such theories inform a critical consciousness about how we read and are read by the world (Freire 1970).

TEACHERS APPLYING A TRANS* PEDAGOGY: CLASSROOM AS SPACE FOR RECOGNITION

The classroom as a space, encumbered by the inheritance of myriad geohistories, is shaped by the deployment of policies that typically affirm or negate the body's drive for true expression and recognition. When policies, or a lack thereof, are made visible through discussion or units of study, such as banning a gay–straight alliance, or states that have no promo homo laws, or do not enumerate specific kinds of bullying, or share with students that their country lacks federal anti-bullying laws, studying these macroaggressions through schools' codes of conduct and examining school climate through the eyes of students, teachers can begin to enact what I see as the strongest mediator of a trans* pedagogy: *refusal*. Refusal is a strategy that teachers can take up to support their students in developing positive identities. Through models of refusal that will be explored in subsequent chapters throughout the book, the teachers, in drawing from the axioms, disrupt binary constructions of gender and introduce new tools that support students in their critique of the world.

SETTING THE STAGE FOR WORKING THROUGH THE BOOK

Across the millennial generation of pre-K-12 in myriad school contexts, both nationally and internationally, we see a growing number of youth who eschew gender and sexual labels, who embody what seems to them to be self-determined authentic identities, and who are proleptically changing the landscape of school and society writ large by pushing back on antiquated gender norms. Faced with these realities, teachers across all grade levels and disciplines are challenged to mediate literacy learning that affirms these differential realities in their classrooms. That said, how can teachers move beyond discussions relegated to only gender and sexuality and toward an understanding of a continuum that also includes the (a)gender complexities students embody? How *can* teachers undo restrictively normative conceptions of sexual and gendered life, unhinging one from the other, and treat them as separate and distinct categories? Even more critical, how can we support emerging literacy professionals and in-service literacy teachers to develop and embody the knowledge, skills, and dispositions necessary to help *all* students learn while simultaneously supporting them to remain open to redefinition and renegotiation when they come up against social limits?

This affirming book forges a pathway for teachers who work with or will work with trans* and gender creative youth as they address such fundamental questions and provide literacy teacher educators and subsequent researchers examples for future study through models of a flexi-sustainable[6] curriculum design (some aligned to standards), pedagogical knowledge and applications, and assessments across pre-K-12 literacy contexts, either/or in and out of school, by highlighting affirming texts across genres, media representations, models for inclusion and differentiation, and applications for technology. The QLF frames the book as a model for how literacy teacher educators can support their preservice teachers to support classroom students to develop and embody life-affirming and deeply layered identities that map out across classroom practices. Each chapter incorporates how the QLF is expressed throughout their lessons while mapped onto subsequent principles. Through these expressions, chapters demonstrate successful models by practicing classroom teachers about how literacy teacher educators can show preservice and in-service teachers how to understand and teach students that they are entitled to (a)gender self-determination and how that can generate (a)gender justice.

To not challenge current understandings of gender norms, we are left with a myopic and vulnerabilized understanding of the evolving lived realities of people. If we ascribe to a recurrence of sameness, it creates a flattening and unidimensional perspective of gender, while it continues to delegitimize those who do not ascribe to gender norms by relegating them to an ongoing inferior status. In the literacy classroom (and eventually for schools writ large), the absence of recognition reinscribes gender norms in schooling practices and enhances policies of exclusion at the same time it obscures voices from rising and having power to change and shift social spaces. Most critically, such an absence condones an anxiety that emerges from the unknown and which can produce and reproduce systemic forms of violence. Teachers who do not affirm differential bodied realities become co-conspirators in not only reproducing current understandings of gender but also in reproducing rationales that can lead to gender-based violence.

THE QLF AND CHAPTERS IN THE BOOK

The book is spread across 16 chapters and some cut across disciplines and multiple grade levels, especially at the secondary level where the use of some texts can be taught at either the middle school or high school level. In each chapter, aside from my own, authors note which QLF principles are taken up or align with their research studies or lessons. Next, they introduce their approaches to teaching to or about trans* and/or gender creative youth through unique varieties of theoretical and conceptual framings. For their chapters, they provide a rationale (i.e., why the lesson mattered) and pedagogy, introduce any key terms or ideas, and take readers through the research study or lesson itself, some of which include the study of different genres of texts, dramatics, art, and/writing. Lastly, authors discuss their findings or what students learned, how lessons were assessed, and conclude with implications or suggestions.

In Chap. 2, "Why a Queer Literacy Framework Matters: Models for Sustaining (A)Gender Self-Determination and Justice in Today's Schooling Practices," Miller deepens the book's focus about how to teach, affirm, and recognize trans* and gender creative youth by connecting it to and introducing the QLF and shows how authors mediated lessons by drawing upon aspects of the QLF. Miller historicizes the production of gender and details its legacy of prejudicial and biased views to frame the rationale for the QLF. Miller then provides an overview of the importance of disruption of gender production in school and society writ large and discusses how the role of fostering external and internal safety in classrooms can promote and instantiate a trans* and gender creative legibility for self and other. Ending with sample strategies of applications using the QLF, Miller demonstrates how recognition of self and other can lead to (a)gender self-determination and promote justice in schools and society writ large.

In Chap. 3, "Teaching Our Teachers: Trans* and Gender Education in Teacher Preparation and Professional Development," Cathy A.R. Brant introduces an analysis of two research studies that address preservice and practicing teachers' sense of self-efficacy, across different grade levels and disciplines in working with and working for trans* and gender creative youth, and ends with a moving discussion about normalizing how queer inclusive pedagogies can be infused into the teacher preparation classroom and professional development. Ashley Lauren Sullivan then picks up in Chap. 4, "Kindergartners Studying Trans* Issues Through *I am Jazz*," by sharing a unique, relevant, and momentous lesson plan. Sullivan expertly weaves together the QLF and early childhood pedagogical structured read aloud approaches with the children's text *I am Jazz*. Founded in the theoretical frameworks of Judith Butler and Michel Foucault, this Common Core aligned lesson utilizes the autobiography of a young transgender girl to instruct preschoolers and kindergartners about trans* youth. Via the integration of research-based vocabulary instruction techniques, including the incorporation of a character splash, students are drawn into Jazz's compelling story. This social justice approach emphasizes inclusion in an interactive, rigorous, and student-centered manner. Preschool and elementary teachers, scholars, and preservice teacher educators can utilize the pedagogical techniques presented with a variety of pertinent audiences. Then benjamin lee hicks in Chap. 5, "BEYOND THIS OR THAT: Challenging the Limits of Binary Language in Elementary Education

Through Poetry, Word Art and Creative Book Making," provides practical tools and detailed lesson plans to help elementary school teachers use free-form poetry, word art, and creative book construction to challenge the supposed rules of language and absolutes of identity in both form and content. hicks suggests that these projects offer opportunities to restimulate creative thinking in students who have been limited by false binaries and to positively reexperience these constructs in beauty-full ways.

Moving up into grade levels where these lessons can be applied for 7th–12th grades, Kate E. Kedley in Chap. 6, "The Teacher as a Text: Uncentering Normative Gender Identities in the Secondary English Language Arts Classroom," suggests that the Secondary English Language Arts classroom can serve as a crucial site for perpetuating or challenging normative gender categories. The teacher's presence is one way students learn about gender—they "read" the teacher's presumed gender before they read novels and short stories. Kedley suggests that well-intentioned Secondary English Language Arts teachers subconsciously risk underscoring the gender binary; when they don't critically complicate themselves as a text that students read, they contribute to a social and educational environment which is at present risky and even dangerous for trans* and (a)gender diverse students. In illustrating the thesis of this chapter, Kedley utilizes the QLF to provide concrete suggestions for teachers to be "text" as a pedagogical strategy that supports students to understand how (a)gender functions in the classroom as a jumping off point for texts writ large. Katherine Mason Cramer and Jill Adams follow with a wonderful discussion about the inclusion of young adult literature in Chap. 7, "The T* in LGBT*: Disrupting Gender Normative School Culture Through Young Adult Literature," for middle through high school English classrooms. Cramer and Adams demonstrate that the field of young adult literature offers opportunities in a variety of genres for teens and teachers alike to learn more about trans* and gender creative identities and/or to have their own experiences mirrored back to them. After sharing a brief history of the portrayal of trans* youth in Young Adult Literature (YAL), they describe specific contemporary texts, learning activities, and assessments that aim to help high school students become more knowledgeable about, welcoming toward, and appreciative of all gender identities. Next, Stephanie Shelton and Aryah O'Tiss S. Lester transport us to the rural south in Chap. 8, "Risks and Resiliency: Trans* Students in the Rural South," where they examine the risks that secondary (9–12) students in the

American Southeast—a politically and religiously conservative region—and particularly in rural areas of the South, face, with increased bullying and decreased school support. Through personal narratives and education research, this chapter explores the challenges faced and the incredible resiliency demonstrated by trans* students in the South, as well as possible means through which ally teachers might support trans* students in rural Southern communities. Closing this section, Paul Chamness Miller and Hidehiro Endo take us overseas to Japan and into their research study about the education of second language students, in Chap. 9, "Introducing (A)gender into Foreign/Second Language Education." They illustrate how, through short readings and art-based activities, second and foreign language middle and high school teachers can use language to introduce the concept of (a)gender. One of the challenges that language teachers face is that language learners often do not possess the vocabulary, linguistic skills, or knowledge to express their ideas about gender creativity. This chapter reveals that whether at a beginning or more advanced level of linguistic ability, art-based activities, coupled with appropriate reading materials and in-class discussion, will equip language learners with the tools and skills to engage in important topics that challenge gender normativity. The authors demonstrate how to achieve these goals through several samples of their own intermediate-level English language learners' work.

Moving into high school curriculum, Paula Greathouse in Chap. 10, "Exploring Gender Through *Ash* in the Secondary English Classroom," offers secondary English Language Arts teachers a thematic unit that employs literature as a pedagogical tool for teaching and discussing gender and identity in a tenth grade high school classroom. Focusing on the tale of *Cinderella* across time periods and cultures, the chapter draws on texts as both revision and evolution by exploring and dialoging with youth about trans* and gender creative identities and gender expressions. Through the exploration of beliefs and values about gender, gender expectations, gender norms, and those that express gender outside the cisnormative, Greathouse shows how students can gain insight into their own and others' beings. Summer Pennell in Chap. 11, "Transitional Memoirs: Reading Using a Queer Cultural Capital Model," provides a unit plan for high school English teachers centered on two memoirs written by transgender teens: *Some Assembly Required* and *Rethinking Normal*. Using a queer cultural capital model, students will read the memoirs and analyze moments of strength exemplified by Andrews and Hill as they transition during high school. By reading these memoirs as a pair, students are prevented from thinking there is only one way to be transgender. The unit plan includes definitions of the forms of queer cultural capital, examples from each text, and a unit assessment. Following this chapter, Judith A. Hayn, Karina R. Clemmons, and Heather A. Olvey in Chap. 12, "Trans* Young Adult Literature for Secondary English Classrooms: Authors Speak Out," describe how Standard VI, the new standard for social justice in Secondary English Language Arts teacher preparation, informs how to plan instruction responsive to students' individual identities based on gender expression. The chapter provides an essential motivation for teachers to prioritize and advocate for including trans*young adult literature in the Secondary English Language Arts high school curriculum. They advocate for examining the beliefs, experiences, and understandings of YA authors who write texts that will serve as a conduit for changing student perceptions, attitudes, and behaviors. The writers select key trans* texts and include suggestions for engagement with their authors on a personal level, thus giving teachers strategies to build a trans*accepting classroom with their students.

Turning toward the inclusion of drama, Toby Emert in Chap. 13, "Puncturing the Silence: Teaching *The Laramie Project* in the Secondary English Classroom," describes a collaborative research project in which he partnered with four grade 9–12 English teachers who were introducing an explicitly queer text in their classrooms for the first time. The teachers developed instructional units on *The Laramie Project* (Kaufman 2001), a documentary-style play about the brutal 1998 attack on gay college student Matthew Shepard in Laramie, Wyoming. The compelling narrative engaged and moved the students and invited them to converse about the sociocultural constructions of identity, society's expectations regarding gender, and issues of justice and personal responsibility. The chapter details the teachers' experiences, offers an exemplar assignment, and summarizes reflections written by the participating teachers and their students. Then Mike Wenk in Chap. 14, "Making Space for Unsanctioned Texts: Teachers and Students Collaborate to Trans*form Writing Assignments," describes this part of his dissertation study which formed a Curriculum Design Team, where teachers and students collaborated in the construction of writing assignments that offered opportunities to explore queer issues and identities in school. Participants examined how non-normative identities were materialized or foreclosed in their school's curriculum, and developed writing assignments that promoted visibility, exploration, critique, and affirmation of discourses (Gee 2010) that affect queer youth. Kathryn Cloonan closes the author chapters in Chap. 15, "Using Queer Pedagogy and Theory to Teach Shakespeare's *Twelfth Night*," by exploring Early Modern constructions and conventions of both gender and theater. Cloonan offers high school teachers of 11th and 12th graders who teach Shakespeare's plays, particularly *Twelfth Night* (2005), activities and discussion points that will illuminate students' readings. Through the provided unit, which includes dramatic performances, writing activities, and textual analysis, teachers and their students use queer theory and queer pedagogy to ultimately challenge gender norms.

Lastly, in Chap. 16, "The Non-Conclusion: Trans*ing Education into the Future-This Cannot Wait," Miller synthesizes prior chapters and reviews suggestions for systemic changes that affirm, enhance, and recognize the identities of trans* and gender creative youth, and which can mediate personal, educational, and social legitimacy. This chapter concludes with recommendations about the urgency for research about how teacher education, school districts, professional development, curriculum specialists, community organizations, families, and policy makers must come together to support the psychosocial and emotional needs of trans* and gender creative youth. Miller finalizes these recommendations by introducing what a proleptic trans*/post trans* schooling system could look like, and how that can potentially change humanity.

BLUE TODAY

At forty years old, and after drawing upon the courage from the youth of our world, I decided to medically transition from female *toward* male—as I name it. I am (a)pronounced and (a)gender. For most of my life, I could not look in the mirror because I hated what I saw- and experienced a double consciousness. I *hated* having breasts, a vagina, and a body that produced estrogen. So to remedy my inner rage and because I needed to walk from potential suicide for the third time, I started taking testosterone (T), the day *after* I received tenure. This medical transition was planned in collaboration with my therapist and it was a very *conscious* decision. Within six weeks of starting T, I had a double mastectomy, and within six weeks of my mastectomy, I had a hysterectomy and oophorectomy.[7] A year later, I had a metoidioplasty,[8] scrotoplasty,[9] and pelvic release.[10] I will inject T weekly for the rest of my life so that I can continue to appear male, and that is how I want to be read by the world. I am a transsexual[11] and have become comfortable and happy, finally in my body. Now, after fully healing from these surgeries, I can look in the mirror and *recognize* the person I always felt I was on the inside. Now, they are in synch with each other. The next step in this journey is determining how to be read and recognized by and in the world around me. That is still my process in becoming the human I always knew I was and *am*.

It has taken nearly a lifetime of inner struggle to understand myself as Blue. Had teachers understood Blue's gender confusion and introduced dialog and development of safe spaces, and any of the lessons modeled by these authors, it is likely Blue would have grown up with an affirmed and more stable sense of self. Blue still struggles and will likely always struggle with a vulnerabilized self, with a frailty that cannot be reversed, and even fractured relationships. Had the world been more kind, compassionate, and prepared to meet the needs of trans* and gender creative youth while Blue was growing up, Blue would not still be playing catch-up. This book hopes to inspire all literacy teacher educators and teachers who will have a Blue in their classroom and can support Blue into becoming *gold*.

NOTES

1. I refer to trans* a prefix or adjective used as an abbreviation of transgender, derived from the Greek word meaning "across from" or "on the other side of." Many consider trans* to be an inclusive and useful umbrella term. Trans (without the asterisk) is most often applied to trans men and trans women, and the asterisk is used more broadly to refer to all non-cisgender gender identities, such as (a)gender, cross-dresser, bigender, genderfluid, gender**k, genderless, genderqueer, non-binary, non-gender, third gender, trans man, trans woman, transgender, transsexual and two-spirit.
2. Expressing gender in a way that demonstrates individual freedom of expression and that does not conform to any gender.
3. I refer to (a)gender as a rejection of gender as a biological or social construct altogether and refusing to identify with gender. The lower case (a) in parenthesis does not nullify gender, it is a way of combining the terms so both gender refusal and gender are collapsed into one word.

4. While the acronym as cited originally in Miller 2015 drew from the conventional use of *transgender* without the asterisk, from here on out it is replaced with trans* and thereby reflected as such in the acronym LGBT*IAGCQ.

5. This work focuses only on (a)gender, for a discussion of *both* (a)gender and (a)sexuality self-determination and justice, see original printing, Miller (2015).

6. Flexi-sustainable means models of lessons with affordances that broker spaces for emerging identities that students may proleptically embody. It also means that the sustainability is in process because these models are new and the results are indeterminate.

7. The removal of the ovaries which means the body no longer produces estrogen.

8. The process of cutting the outer labia and fissuring it around the clitoris in order to create a neo-phallus.

9. The process of creating a scrotum by implanting testicles from the outer labia.

10. An incision made in order to reposition the surgically created phallus.

11. While not all trans* people have surgeries or take T, as there is no single trans* story, it was important for me. Trans* people are on a spectrum of identities just as are cisgender people.

REFERENCES

Athanases, S. Z. (1996). A gay-themed lesson in an ethnic literature curriculum: Tenth graders' responses to "Dear Anita". *Harvard Educational Review, 66*(2), 231–256.

Blackburn, M. V., & Buckley, J. F. (2005). Teaching queer inclusive English language arts. *Journal of Adolescent and Adult Literacy, 49*(3), 202–212.

Blackburn, M., & McCready, L. (2013). Lesbian, gay, bisexual, transgender, queer, and questioning people and issues in urban education. In R. Milner & K. Lomotey (Eds.), *Handbook of urban education* (pp. 129–146). New York: Routledge.

Brandt, D., & Clinton, K. (2002). Limits of the local: Expanding perspectives on literacy as a social practice. *Journal of Literacy Research, 34*(3), 337–356.

Butler, J. (2004). *Undoing gender*. New York: Routledge.

Cammarota, J. (2007). A social justice approach to achievement: Guiding Latina/o students toward educational attainment with a challenging, socially relevant curriculum. *Equity & Excellence in Education, 40*, 87–96.

Clark, C., & Blackburn, M. (2009). Reading LGBT literature. *English Journal, 98*(4), 25–32.

Deleuze, G., & Guittari, F. (1987). *A thousand plateaus: Capitalism and schizophrenia*. Minneapolis: University of Minnesota Press.

Du Bois, W. E. B. (1903). *Souls of black folks*. Chicago: A.C. McClurg & CO.

Foucault, M. (1990). *The history of sexuality*. New York: Vintage.

Freire, P. (1970). *Pedagogy of the oppressed*. New York: Herder and Herder.

Gee, J. (2010). *An introduction to discourse analysis: Theory and method* (3rd ed.). New York: Routledge.

Griffin, P., & Ouellett, M. (2003). From silence to safety and beyond: Historical trends in addressing lesbian, gay, bisexual, transgender issues in k-12 schools. *Equity & Excellence in Education, 36*, 106–114.

Harris-Perry, M. (2011). *Sister citizen: Shame, stereotypes, and black women in America*. New Haven: Yale University Press.

Hill, K. (2014). *Rethinking normal: A memoir in transition*. New York: Simon and Schuster.

Hochschild, A. (1983). *The managed heart: The commercialization of human feeling*. Berkeley: University of California Press.

Jennings, T. (2014). Is the mere mention enough? Representation across five different venues of educator preparation. In L. Meyer & D. Carlson (Eds.), *Gender and sexualities in education: A reader* (pp. 400–412). New York: Peter Lang.

Kaufman, M. (2001). *The Laramie project*. New York: Vintage.

Kosciw, J., Greytak, E., & Diaz, E. (2008). *The 2007 National School Climate Survey: The experiences of lesbian, gay, bisexual and transgender youth in our nation's schools*. New York: GLSEN.

Kosciw, J., Greytak, E., Diaz, E., & Bartkiewicz, M. (2010). *The 2009 National School Climate Survey: The experiences of lesbian, gay, bisexual and transgender youth in our nation's schools*. New York: GLSEN.

Kosciw, J. G., Greytak, E. A., Palmer, N. A., & Boesen, M. J. (2014). *The 2013 National School Climate Survey: The experiences of lesbian, gay, bisexual and transgender youth in our nation's schools*. New York: GLSEN.

Latour, B. (1996). On interobjectivity (trans: Bowker, G.). *Mind, Culture, and Activity: An International Journal, 3*, 228–245.

Leander, K., & Sheehy, M. (Eds.). (2004). *Spatializing literacy research and practice*. New York: Peter Lang.

Martino, W., & Pallotta-Chiarolli, M. (2003). *So what's a boy? Addressing issues of masculinity and schooling*. Buckingham: Open University Press.

Massey, D. (2005). *For space*. London: Sage Publications.

Mayo, C. (2004). *Disputing the subject of sex: Sexuality and public school controversies*. Lanham: Rowman & Littlefield.

Mayo, J. B. (2007). Negotiating sexual orientation and classroom practice(s) at school. *Theory & Research in Social Education, 35*, 447–464.

McCarthey, S., & Moje, E. (2002). Identity matters. *Reading Research Quarterly*, *37*(2), 228–238.

McCready, L. T. (2007). Queer urban education: Curriculum and pedagogy for LGBTQI youth in the city. *Journal of Curriculum and Pedagogy*, *4*(2), 71–77.

Meyer, E. (2007). But I'm not gay: What straight teachers need to know about queer theory. In N. Rodriguez & W. Pinar (Eds.), *Queering straight teachers: Discourse and identity in education* (pp. 15–29). New York: Peter Lang.

Miller, s. (2009). (Dis)embedding gender diversity in the preservice classroom. In S. Steinberg (Ed.), *Diversity and multiculturalism: A reader* (pp. 193–209). New York: Peter Lang.

Miller, s. (2012). Mythology of the norm: Disrupting the culture of bullying in schools. *English Journal*, *101*(6), 107–109.

Miller, s. (2014). Cultivating a disposition for sociospatial justice in English teacher preparation. *Teacher Education and Practice*, *27*(1), 44–74.

Miller, s. (2015). A queer literacy framework promoting (a)gender and (a)sexuality self- determination and justice. *English Journal*, *104*(5), 37–44.

Miller, s. (2016). Reading YAL queerly: A queer literacy framework for inviting (a)gender and (a)sexuality self- determination and justice. In D. Carlson & D. Linville (Eds.), *Beyond borders: Queer eros and ethos (ethics) in LGBTQ young adult literature* (pp. 153–180). New York: Peter Lang.

Miller, s. (forthcoming). Queer literacy framework. In E. Brockenbrough, J. Ingrey, W. Martino & N. Rodriquez (Eds.), *Queer studies and education: Critical concepts for the 21st century.* New York: Palgrave Macmillan.

Miller, s., & Gilligan, J. (2014). Heteronormative harassment: Queer bullying and gender non-conforming students. In D. Carlson & E. Meyer (Eds.), *Handbook of gender and sexualities in education* (pp. 217–229). New York: Peter Lang.

Miller, s., & Norris, L. (2007). *Unpacking the loaded teacher matrix: Negotiating space and time between university and secondary English classrooms.* New York: Peter Lang.

Miller, s., Burns, L., & Johnson, T. S. (2013). *Generation BULLIED 2.0: Prevention and intervention strategies for our most vulnerable students.* New York: Peter Lang.

Nadal, K. L., River, D. P., & Corpus, M. J. H. (2010). Sexual orientation, and transgender microaggressions: Implications for mental health and counseling. In D. W. Sue (Ed.), *Microaggressions and marginality: Manifestation, dynamics, and impact* (pp. 217–240). Hoboken: Wiley.

Namaste, V. (2000). *Invisible lives: The erasure of transsexual and transgendered people.* Chicago: University of Chicago Press.

Nespor, J. (1997). Tangled up in school: Politics, space, bodies and signs in the educational process. Mahwah: Lawrence Erlbaum Associates.

Nordmarken, S. (2012). *Everyday transgender emotional inequality: Microaggressions, micropolitics, and minority emotional work.* Unpublished paper presented at The American Sociological Association Annual Meeting, Denver.

Quinn, T., & Meiners, E. R. (2011). Teacher education, struggles for social justice, and the historical erasure of lesbian, gay, bisexual, transgender, and queer lives. In A. Ball & C. Tyson (Eds.), *Studying diversity in teacher education* (pp. 135–151). Maryland: Rowman & Littlefield.

Robinson, K. H. (2005). "Queerying" gender: Heteronormativity in early childhood education. *Australian Journal of Early Childhood, 30*(2), 19–28.

Robinson, K. H., & Ferfolja, T. (2001a). 'What are we doing this for?' Dealing with lesbian and gay issues in teacher education. *British Journal of Sociology of Education, 22*(1), 121–133.

Robinson, K. H., & Ferfolja, T. (2001b). A reflection of resistance. Discourses of heterosexism and homophobia in teacher training classrooms. *Journal of Gay & Lesbian Social Services, 14*(2), 55–64.

Ryan, C., & Hermann-Wilmarth, J. (2013). Already on the shelf; Queer readings of award-winning children's literature. *Journal of Literacy Research, 45*(2), 142–172.

Savage, T. A., & Harley, D. A. (2009). A place at the blackboard: Including lesbian, gay, bisexual, intersex, and queer/questioning issues in the education process. *Multicultural Education, 16*, 2–9.

Schmidt, S. J. (2010). Queering social studies: The role of social studies in normalizing citizens and sexuality in the common good. *Theory & Research in Social Education, 38*, 314–335.

Schmidt, S. J., Chang, S., Carolan-Silva, A., Lockhart, J., & Anagnostopoulos, D. (2012). Recognition, responsibility, and risk: Pre-service teachers' framing and reframing of lesbian, gay, and bisexual social justice issues. *Teaching and Teacher Education, 28*(8), 1175–1184.

Shakespeare, W. (2005). *Twelfth Night.* (B. Mowat & P. Werstine, Eds.). New York: Simon & Schuster, Inc.

Slattery, P. (1992). Toward an eschatological curriculum theory. *JCT: An Interdisciplinary Journal of Curriculum Studies, 93*(3), 7–21.

Slattery, P. (1995). *Curriculum development in the postmodern era.* New York: Garland.

Soja, E. (2010). *Seeking spatial justice.* Minneapolis: University of Minnesota Press.

Szalacha, L. A. (2004). Educating teachers on LGBTQ issues: A review of research and program evaluations. *Journal of Gay & Lesbian Issues in Education, 1*(4), 67–79.

Ybarra, M. L., Mitchell, K. J., & Kosciw, J. G. (2014). The relation between suicidal ideation and bullying victimization in a national sample of transgender and non-transgender adolescents. In P. Goldblum, D. Espelage, J. Chu, & B. Bognar (Eds.), *Youth suicide and bullying: Challenges and strategies for prevention and intervention* (pp. 134–147). New York: Oxford University Press.

CHAPTER 2

Why a Queer Literacy Framework Matters: Models for Sustaining (A)Gender Self-Determination and Justice in Today's Schooling Practices

sj Miller

The gender lenses and (a)gender experiences that students bring with them into schooling may either be affirmed or challenged by "normative" positions of gender by classroom teachers, others in the school, or even by peers. Typically, the schooling process intercepts students' *in situ* understanding of gender in all of its varying representations. Instances where youth may learn about how gender is represented along a continuum by friends, family, media, and culture; schooling can interfere with broadening perspectives and instead reindoctrinate and transmit gender-normative definitions, relations, social norms, and differences, while "disguising" itself objectively in curriculum (Apple 2002; Arnot 2002). In schools then, normative gender categories tend to reinforce dominant gender ideologies and illuminate "arbitrary social constructs" (Arnot 2002, p. 118). While it is true that many teachers try to understand students' out-of-school lived experiences and even build upon their "funds of knowledge" (Moll

sj Miller (✉)
Santa Fe, New Mexico, USA

© The Editor(s) (if applicable) and The Author(s) 2016
sj Miller (ed.), *Teaching, Affirming, and Recognizing Trans and Gender Creative Youth*, DOI 10.1057/978-1-137-56766-6_2

et al. 1992) to make classrooms more authentic, students today challenge teachers to understand their emerging identities, including a matrix of (a)genders, gender identities, gender nonconformities, gender creativities, and gender expressions that have unfamiliar discourses, contexts, social roles, and support systems that pose challenges for recognition within and by curriculum. Such vicissitudes challenge classroom teachers then to remain aware and current about their students and learn about unveiled representations of these traditionally marginalized and unrecognized selves. So, as schools, parents, communities, and the nation writ large educate themselves on shifting representations of (a)gender in all its grand facets, we can reposition youth as agentive subjects within multiple contexts and collectively become better equipped to unveil and advance shifting discourses. So the question then emerges how *do* we help teachers see and affirm and recognize the true lived (a)genders of students? How can teachers learn from students' discourses and lived experiences and yet wrestle with possibly their own discomforts that may challenge dominant and "normative" gender ideologies that have acted as long-standing traditions and pillars across myriad classroom practices?

Furthermore, the classroom space holds contemporaneous plurality and teachers have great agentive possibility to rupture dangerous dichotomies and myths about (a)gender while educating adolescence/ts about how all students (and others) can be rendered legible. For students who have differential bodied realities, they are highly attuned to prevailing gender norms and typically feel unsafe from the moment they cross onto school property. Gaps in codes of conduct, posters that do not reflect their realities, gendered and heteronormative school events, locker rooms, gendered bathrooms, notes home that reinforce heteronormative or gender norms, and an undemocratic, unidimensional, non-intersectional, or Eurocentric, classroom curriculum that ignore students' lived truths, delegitimize their realities, and can absent a sense of communal belonging. Such macro-aggressions, day after day, and year after year, legitimize that students don't matter and can systemically destabilize their abilities to ever feel or experience safety at school, and even in their lives, writ large. These contextual realities, however, can be shifted by a deeper and more informed understanding of how gender normativity vulnerabilizes students in schools, which can lead toward *contexts* shifting.

As described, gender norms, conscribed under heteropatriarchy have established violent and unstable social and educational climates for trans* and gender creative youth (Miller 2015). Therefore, as possible intervention and disruption to what could potentially damage one's sense of self over a lifetime, the QLF provides a possible remedy to interrupt, from early on in a child's academic span, inurement. Inurement can lead students down a pathway and away from the selves that are both inter- and intrapersonally recognizable. A primary goal of the chapters in this book is to foster within a school environment, vis-a-vis pre-K-12 classrooms, (a)gender[1] self-determination which can lead to (a)gender justice. However, understanding the historicity of modern gender roles and expressions requires a dive back into their geohistories.

Understanding a Historicity of Gender Production

Deeply ingrained by ideologies present within a historicity of Western Capitalism (which predates industrial capitalism in the mid-eighteenth century), gender categories and roles were set in motion long before our existence, mostly due to women's primary dependence on men's income and as primary care taker in, and of, the home (Rose 1993). The continuance of this power differential into Industrial Capitalism subordinated women and played out in "sexual segregation of jobs, machines, household responsibilities, and unequal political rights and activities" (Rose 1993, p. 192). In these ways then, not only was women's sexuality regulated and controlled by men, but gender differences were *produced* both ideologically and materially (Rose 1993). The role of the mother to raise children both prior to and during her entrance into the labor force continued to conscribe masculine and feminine characteristics and gender roles (Marx et al. 1992). Therefore, ideologies within early Industrial Capitalism and women's inurement into a classed and labored society continued to *also* chattel them as the primary care taker at home. Consequently, women and men's roles and how they expressed their roles continued to produce and recognize gender through a rigid casting and division of labor. Fortunately, as evidenced in the three waves of feminism beginning in the late 1700s and continuing through today, subsequent research about women's rights and the production of gender and gender roles, society is now witness to both de jure and de facto practices that place women on equal footing—those not always practiced—with men socially, materially, intersectionally, and culturally (for further reading on these topics, see Chesir-Teran and Hughes 2009; Crenshaw 1989; de Beauvoir 1973; Hill-Collins 1990; Irigaray 1985; Tharinger 2008; Wittig 1983).

As a result of these advancements, children are coming to terms with themselves in a redesigned postindustrial, neo-capitalist context. In this new era, women's place, expressions, and (a)gender performances have released women's dependence, roles, and traditional notions of reproductivity within the family structure. With this widening gap and a dislodging of gender from sex and even the family structure, the production of women's gender in relationship to men has been reframed and reconstituted as has the freedom of women to occupy their bodies with multitudinous (a)gender expressions and sex.

The separation of women from men and their release of once normative gender expressions and roles have also permitted men to redefine and reconstitute themselves and be recognized along a multitude of masculine and feminine identities. Though women incur varying types of bullying and harassment still for challenges to deeply entrenched beliefs about feminine expressions and roles, men too, incur varying types of bullying and harassment when they perform gender or roles outside of socially expected norms. While we do see forms of intersectional and cultural masculine expressions and roles more vast and widespread than times past (Butler 2004; Dieser 2008; Kirkland 2013; McCready 2007; Miller et al. 2013), these expressions are often discouraged in schooling practices and reinforced through pressure to enact hegemonic masculinities. Sadly, we tend to see males emotionality silenced and marginalized and forced to repress their true feelings, selves, and even desires (Connell 1995; Dieser 2008; Duncanson 2015; Kirkland 2013; Martino 2000; McCready 2007; Messerschmidt 2000; Renold 2004; Robinson 2005). Certainly, not to fault teachers for how they (microaggress) unknowingly educate youth and reinforce hetero-gender-normative ideologies hidden and embedded deeply in curriculum, this book demonstrates models for true *change*. Collectively, as we educate ourselves on shifting gender norms, the spatial agentivenes (Miller 2014a) embodied by students and teachers and the like, can, over time, and across multiple contexts, unveil shifting discourses and identities.

Although several prior feminist theories on gender have been fundamental in shaping dominant perspectives on gender, this book reflects on (a)gender as premised in Butler's (1990, 2004) works—that gender is *performance*. Butler suggests that the given identity of the individual is illuminated by the gender that one performs. Butler (1990) offers: "… gender is an identity tenuously constituted in time, instituted in an exterior space through a *stylized repetition of acts*" [sic] (p. 140) and a "surface signification...," "...created through sustained social performances" (p. 141). Butler essentially argues that the individual is a subject, capable of action—not an object to be constructed or produced. *Connecting a theory of trans*ness to Butler then, I proffer that people have agency in how they invite in, embody, and can thereby be recognized by the self and the other as they perform multitudinous identities that can be perpetually reinvented.*

Disruption of Uneven Bodied Realities

As we reflect on students in classrooms today, we know that traditional gender norms have spilled into schooling practices and created an inequitable treatment of bodies. This complicates how teachers might try to disrupt its continuance, when humanity, for the most part, is still dependent on norms and external forces for social acceptance and worth. These norms, which are put on psyches from birth, maintain status quo beliefs and make identities both legible and readable. One's legibility is therefore socially mediated and constituted in any context. One cannot exist without drawing on the sociality of norms that precede one's existence, so from inception, personhood is constituted outside the self, leaving little space for a person to organically *know* what the true self could be or look like. Such norms, which construct ways to read and understand the other, maintain uneven social realities, and the ability to become an (a)gender self-determined, autonomous agent. So based on these complex realities, how can teachers and schools disrupt the conscription of these dangerous gender norms?

(A)gender self-determination is one way to create such disruption. Drawing from Moses (2002), who draws from Kymlicka (1991) and Raz's (1979) work, Moses integrates their ideas to support a conceptualization of personal autonomy and self-determination. Moses's concept of "autonomy as self-determination" provides a framework to analyze race-conscious education policies that mitigate the racism and oppression often experienced by students of color in US educational institutions.[2] Moses conceptualizes the ideal or possible realization of self-determination through two specific conditions: favorable social contexts of choice and authenticity. Leonardi and Saenz (2014) take up these concepts and apply them to how queer youth can become self-determine,[3] as they experience *internal safety*, or the embodied trust that galvanizes individuals to take risks and be their authentic selves. Building from Moses, they proffer that internal safety requires "both autonomy and self-determination and that these components are contingent upon favorable social contexts of choice" (p. 207). Drawing from the combined works of Moses, and Leonardi and Saenz, I extend these concepts to how to create and sustain classrooms that can generate (a)gender self-determination.

Though families and communities play a determinate role in how youth perceive and are perceived by the world, classrooms typically shape how youth think inwardly about themselves and others. Classrooms that fail to affirm students' (a)gender diversity can contribute to students' disconnection from and desire to participate in learning (Hagood 2002; Moje and van Helden 2004; Miller 2009, 2014b; Miller and Gilligan 2014). However, in classrooms and schools that normalize and integrate favorable social conditions inclusive of favorable social contexts and authentic identity-affirming choices with activities that foster independence, agency, integrity, an adequate range of options, and that authenticate cultural identity (Moses 2002), students can develop and embody internal safety (Leonardi and Saenz 2014; Leonardi and Meyer, forthcoming). With internal safety, combined with *external safety*, such as a classroom or an entire school, that mirrors students' identities or identities that are affirming or relatable—such as through posters, books, classroom and school libraries, bulletin boards, gay-straight alliances, guest speakers, or even teachers whose identities are nonconforming, students may come to experience (a)gender self-determination (see Picture 2.1). Combined, internal and external safety present limitless possibilities for students to be "read" or "made" legible both to themselves and others (Butler 2004).

Fostering conditions that can lead to (a)gender self-determination, schools must strive to rid the environment of "unsafety" (e.g., all forms of bullying; see Miller et al. 2013) by eliminating all enactments of domination and oppression (Young 1990) from the micro- to the macrolevel across practices and policies. When schools are predicated on democratic values that inspire independence, integrity, and an adequate range of options, the prevailing schooling environment *can* shift. The QLF was developed as a mediator for that very purpose. The question before us now is how can teachers "do" this work in schools?

As the authors in the book draw from and apply the QLF across literacy-focused pre-K-12 classrooms, the presented concerns and specified conditions are taken up in models that demonstrate how to develop safety. The QLF proffers that students must be allowed to self-identify however

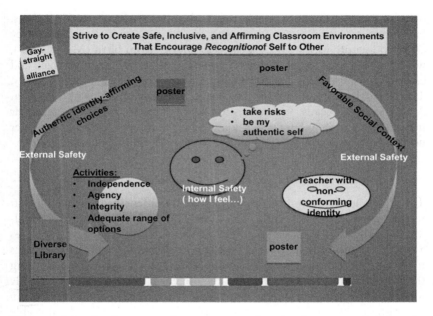

Picture 2.1 A classroom that supports the development of (a)gender self-determination

they choose and be provided opportunities to see themselves reflected back in a positive manner. Such legitimacy can foster a student's ability to experience safety at school. As adolescents thereby come to see their realities reflected, affirmed, and made legible both through literacy practices in the classroom and society writ large, (a)gender self-determination and the actualized freedom of youth to be self-expressive, without redress of social, institutional, or political violence, they can move toward a realization of a spatialized queer autonomy.

WHY A QLF MATTERS

The QLF is a critical interventionist and political strategy to challenge the taken-for-granted value of hegemonic demarcations of (a)gender assumed under patriarchy and hidden within and by curriculum. It is a strategy for literacy teachers to reinscribe, instate, affirm, and recognize differential bodied realities and give voice to those who experience illegibility and delegitimization. Because social norms, and in this case binary gender norms, have great structural power in shaping the lived realities of people as they come to identify with a set of social conventions from birth (Miller 2012), when they are fixed and rigid, people are made vulnerable to internalized and external oppressions that can destroy self-love, acceptance, and internal safety. Therefore, the QLF as tool for legitimization affirms all forms of (a)gender. A QLF *matters* because it positions teachers as agentive, who, through their teaching, can affect and influence adolescence/ts to not only expand gender norms but to also potentially influence changes in school policy en route.

Why Not Using a QLF Matters

To not challenge current understandings of gender norms, society is left with a myopic and vulnerabilized understanding of the evolving lived realities of people. If we ascribe to a recurrence of gender sameness, it creates a flattening and unidimensional perspective of gender, while it continues to delegitimize those who do not ascribe to gender norms by relegating them to ongoing inferior status. In the literacy classroom (and eventually for schools writ large), the absence of a QLF reinscribes gender norms in schooling practices. It also enhances policies of exclusion for the invisible and marginalizes the possibility of change. Most critically, its absence condones a gender anxiety that can produce and reproduce systemic forms of violence. Teachers who elect not to employ a QLF become co-conspirators in reproducing not only current understandings of gender but also rationales that can lead to gendered violence.

The Queer Literacy Framework

The QLF is comprised of ten principles with ten subsequent commitments for educators to queer literacy practices. The framework is underscored by the notion that our lives have been structured through an inheritance of a political, gendered, economic, social, religious, linguistic system we never made and with indissoluble ties to heteropatriarchy. This is not to suggest that we should do away with (a)gender categories altogether, but that we pivot into an open-ended paradigm that refuses to close itself or be narrowly defined, and which strives to shift and expand norms that account for a continuum of evolving (a)gender identities and differential bodied realities. In this trans* space, and the yet to be defined, a QLF can shift norms that operationalize our lives.

The framework is intended to be an autonomous, ongoing, nonhierarchical tool within a teaching repertoire; it is not something someone does once and moves away from. Rather, the principles and commitments should work alongside other tools and perspectives within a teacher's disposition and curriculum. *An intention of the framework is that it can be applied and taken up across multiple genres and disciplines within literacy acquisition, as it was not intended for any sole literacy purpose.*

Nuanced Language for Activating the QLF

As teachers begin to work within the framework, it is important to unpack the key language within. First, we begin with the term *queer*, which refers to a suspension of rigid gender and sexual orientation categories (Jagose 1996). Through its application to disrupt what is perceived as normative, queer is underscored by attempts to interrogate and interrupt heteronormativity by acknowledging diverse people across gender, sex, and desires (e.g., emotional and/or sexual) (Blackburn and Clark 2011). Queer also embraces the freedom to not be boxed into any one-identity category or to be positioned based on an identity category during a space-time (Miller and Norris 2007). It embraces the freedom to move beyond, between, or even away from, yet even to later return to, myriad identity categories, that supports the perpetual reinvention of the self (Britzman 1997). Queer is therefore not relegated to just lesbian, gay, bisexual, trans*, intersex, agender/asexual, gender creative, and questioning youth (LGBT*IAGCQ), but is inclusive of any variety of experience that transcends socially and politically accepted categories for gender and sexual orientation. The use of the word queer in the framework is enveloped by a continuum for (a)gender expressions.

Another key term for the QLF is *literacy*. Conventional literacy practices mean myriad forms of communication, and even the yet to emerge, as applied across any discipline that inherently develops students' speaking, reading, writing, and technological skills in order to interact and engage with the self and the world around. As individuals develop multiple forms of literacy throughout schooling practices, it can travel with them across spaces and time, and potentially impact, shift, and advance contexts. For this book though, connecting literacy to a theory of trans*ness means that literacy can move back and forth, between, over, beyond, away from, into, and be fragmented, as students come to understand and recognize that, as their bodied communications are made legible, they become legible to others. In other words, their bodies become emerging forms of and for understanding and teaching literacy.

Next, the term (a)*gender self-determination* provides an understanding for the main goal of the QLF. Building upon the definition of self-determination in the introduction which presumes an individual's right for self-identification, rejects external control, and can unsettle knowledge, *(a)gender self-determination* is the inherent right to both occupy one's (a)gender and make choices to self-identify in a way that authenticates self-expression. It is also a type of self-granted or inherited permission that can help one refute or rise above social critique; it presumes choice and rejects an imposition to be defined or regulated; it presumes that humans are entitled to unsettle knowledge, which can generate new possibilities of legibility; and, it means that any representation of (a)gender deserves the same inalienable rights and the same dignities and protections as any other human. This de 'factoness' grants individuals ways of intervening in and disrupting social and political processes because one's discourse and self-determined ways of being demonstrate placement as a viable stakeholder in society, revealing that no one personhood is of any more or less value than any other. Consider this, were (a)gender self-determination broadly actualized, perhaps transphobia, gender typing, and hence, compulsory gender labeling, would be deemed as systemic forms of violence, and they would be considered worthy of consequence. In sum, teachers who take up a QLF can be agents for social, political, and personal transformations which can move society toward (a)gender justice.

Lastly, it is important to unpack what *refusal* can look like as a trans* pedagogical tool. First, teachers, in drawing from the axioms in the Introduction, can refuse to accept that gender is biologically based or that gender-based answers are only understood through a new critic's approach to reading, thinking, and problem solving—that is, that ideas and answers are approached only superficially when they could be critiqued through grade-level specific practices and applications of critical literacy. However, by taking up such disruptions to binary constructions of gender and introducing new tools through the application of the QLF that support students in their critique of (a)gender in the world, teachers can disrupt a re-conscription of a hetero-gender-normative society. Refusal can thereby be a support for students to develop the embedded awareness that they are entitled to (a)gender self-determination, and should be autonomous beings.

But How Do I *Apply* a Trans* Pedagogy? Classroom as Space for Recognition

It is important, when working with the QLF, that teachers avoid using offensive language (see at the end of the Glossary "Best to Avoid"), which can shut students down from engaging in the classroom. Mindfully creating activities that foster external safety and that draw upon independence, agency, integrity, and an adequate range of options (Raz 1979), the authors in this book demonstrate amazing and powerful examples that support students in being internally safety. The QLF is intended to be modified for different grade levels, and teachers should discern how to adapt the language that is suitable for their students. This adaption can be done in collaboration with peers, mentors, community members, parents, and even by asking students if they understand certain concepts and terminology. I have always believed that classroom teachers are truly amazing and resourceful experts and instinctually know what works best for their students (see Fig. 2.1).

Model Lessons Drawing from the QLF

Principle 1
Here, I introduce three very different examples for different grade levels about how the QLF can be applied by drawing on the notion of refusal, though I do not provide an entire lesson plan as the authors do. In the first example, if someone were teaching a second grade class, drawing on Principle 1: *Refrains from possible presumptions that students ascribe to a gender*, teachers can approach students as tabula rasa, and refrain from inscribing gender onto them or characters in texts. While gender is always operating, a teacher can invite dialog about the importance of the self and wanting others to see and recognize them as they are and to develop empathy and appreciation for others (see Fig. 2.2). The following list provides multiple pathways to achieve that purpose.[4]

Principle 5
In the second example, if someone were teaching in a middle school language arts classroom they could draw on Principle 5: *Opens up spaces for students to self-define with chosen (a)genders, (a)pronouns, or names.* For this lesson, teachers could hand out a slip of paper that allows students

Principles	Commitments of Educators who Queer Literacy
1. Refrains from possible presumptions that students ascribe to a gender	Educators who use queer literacy never presume that students have a gender.
2. Understands gender as a construct which has and continues to be impacted by intersecting factors (e.g., social, historical, material, cultural, economic, religious)	Educators who employ queer literacy are committed to classroom activities that activelypush back against gender constructs and provide opportunities to explore, engage and understand how gender is constructed.
3. Recognizes that masculinity and femininity constructs are assigned to gender norms and are situationally performed	Educators who engage with queer literacy challenge gender norms and gender-stereotypes and actively support students' various and multiple performances of gender.
4. Understands gender as flexible	Educators who engage with queer literacy are mindful about how specific discourse(s) can reinforce gender and norms, and they purposefully demonstrate how gender is fluid, or exist on a continuum, shifting over time and in different contexts.
5. Opens up spaces for students to self-define with chosen (a)genders, (a)pronouns,or names	Educators who engage with queer literacy invite students to self-define and/or reject a chosen or preferred gender, name, and/or pronoun.
6. Engages in ongoing critique of how gender norms are reinforced in literature, media, technology, art, history, science, math, etc.,	Educators who use queer literacy provide ongoing and deep discussions about how society is gendered and, and thus invite students to actively engage in analysis of cultural texts and disciplinary discourses.
7. Understands how Neoliberal principles reinforce and sustain compulsory heterosexism, which secures homophobia; andhow gendering secures bullying and transphobia	Educators who employ queer literacy understand and investigate structural oppression and how heterosexism sustains (a)gendered violence, generate meaningful opportunities for students to become embodied change agents and to be proactive against, or to not engage in bullying behavior.
8. Understands that (a)gender intersects with other identities (e.g. sexual orientation, culture, language, age, religion, social class, body type, accent, height, ability, disability, and national origin) that inform students' beliefs and thereby, actions	Educators who engage with queer literacy do not essentialize students' identities, but recognize how intersections of sexual orientation, culture, language, age, religion, social class, body type, accent, height, ability, disability, and national origin, inform students' beliefs and thereby, actions.
9. Advocates for equity across all categories of (a)gender performances	Educators who employ queer literacy do not privilege one belief or stance, but advocate for equity across all categories of (a)gender performances.
10. Believes that students who identify on a continuum of gender identities deserve to learn in environments free of bullying and harassment	Educators who use queer literacy make their positions known, when first hired, to students, teachers, administrators and school personnel and take a stance when any student is bullied or marginalized, whether explicitly or implicitly, for their (a)gender identities.

Fig. 2.1 A queer literacy framework promoting (a)gender and self-determination and justice (Modified but originally printed as Miller (2015). Copyright 2015 by the National Council of Teachers of English. Reprinted with permission)

to privately reveal their chosen and preferred name, (a)pronouns, and (a)gender, and with an option if they want any of these categories publically acknowledged. For the student who does not want others to know but

Pre-reading strategies
Explore characteristics of gender markers

- Ask students where notions of gender arise. Ask them how such notions are reinforced. Ask, do people have to "be" or "have a gender."
- Ask students what ideas, concepts, behaviors, mannerisms, activities, dress, feelings, occupations, seem to be identified with gender. Ask them for examples in society where gender seems fluid and non-descript. Ask for examples where people seem agender or gender flexible.
- Ask students what makes gender matter?
- Ask, what happens to people who are gender flexible or who seem to behave in a gender that is different than their assigned sex.
- Ask students how gender and sex are different.
- Ask students to consider why and which authors try to reinforce binary gender behaviors and performances. If so, which authors have they observed enacting this? What have they learned from those texts?

Comprehension strategies:

- Ask, how are characters in the text treated because of gender?
- Ask, are there any characters who seem to transcend gender markers?
- Ask, for the characters in the text, are there any personal, social, familial, cultural, economic, linguistic, political, or religious consequences for transcending gender markers?
- What sort of support (if any) is given to elements or characters who question the gender binary? What happens to those elements/characters?
- Ask, how does the author resolve any conflict incurred by characters that transcend gender orientation markers?
- Ask, for any characters, how does the author treat healing? Remorse? Redemption? The future?
- Ask students in what ways these self-identified characters acted as change agents in their lived worlds. Who, what, and/or how were they impacted?

Cultural Connections:

Ask students to make connections between characters and artists, musicians, athletes, media personalities, religious figures, politicians, friends, or family, etc., who do not ascribe to expected gender markers. What are their stories? How were/are they treated? What have they experienced? How are their lives today? What have you learned about gender markers from those individuals? What can you now teach others about those who do not ascribe to expected gender markers?

Fig. 2.2 Examples of pathways for Principle 1

is comfortable sharing that part of the self with the teacher, the teacher can respond on assignments with comments that recognize the students true (a)gender, preferred name, and (a)pronoun. With the initial slip of paper, the teacher sends a clear message to the class about the importance of affirmation and legibility, and thereby recognition. In addition, to this strategy, the teacher can post placards in the classroom that affirm gender identity, and inclusivity (see Picture 2.2) and make (a)gender recognition part of the classroom norms.

The following list provides even more additional pathways to achieve Principle 5 (see Fig. 2.3)

Principle 6
The last example might be used in a twelfth grade language arts classroom. Drawing from Principle 6: *Engages in ongoing critique of how gender norms are reinforced in literature, media, technology, art, history, science, math, and so on,* teachers can ask students over a 24-hour period to do a (a)gender and cisgender audit and make notes about how one's own gender is reinforced as well as how (a)gender/cisgender is reinforced/policed in society writ large. Observations can range from images in the

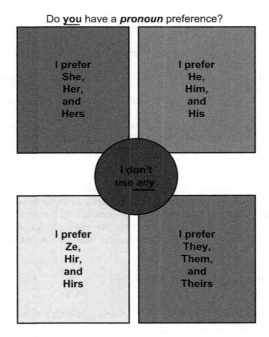

Picture 2.2   Example of Principle 5

Pre-reading strategies:

- Ask students if they like their names. Why or why not? Ask them if they have a right to change their name or prefer to be called by a different name.
- Ask students which pronouns the English language has for gender. Ask them if they like those. If not, what other suggestions do they have. Ask, have they ever considered that some people don't feel certain pronouns fit their identities.
- Ask students if people have a right to refuse to be pronounced. Are there any "real" rules that keep a person from selecting pronouns that fit more appropriately. Are there any "real" rules that keep a person from refuting to be identified by a pronoun?
- Ask students what it feels like to have something private about themselves revealed.
- Ask students why respecting privacy is important.
- Ask students why some people might be uncomfortable sharing aspects of their (a)gender or with others.
- Ask students in what ways teachers can demonstrate respect for students' privacy related to (a)gender and (a)pronoun choice (refusal to be pronounced).
- Ask students in what ways schools, doctors, dentists, coaches, etc., can demonstrate respect for students' privacy related to (a)gender and (a)pronoun choice.
- Ask students to consider which authors explore issues of chosen (a)gender, (a)pronouns and naming. What have they learned from those texts?

Comprehension strategies:

- Ask students if textual characters revealed private information to anyone about (a)gender, chosen names or (a) pronouns.
- Ask students if any of the textual characters had private information related to (a)gender publically revealed.
- Ask students how the textual characters responded to the breach of information.
- Ask students if there were any consequences or redress about the breach.
- Ask students why the textual characters were uncomfortable sharing aspects of their (a)gender with others.
- Ask students in what ways teachers, parents, peers, family, social circles, others demonstrated respect for textual characters characters' privacy related to (a)gender and (a)pronoun choice (refusal to be pronounced).
- Ask students in what ways the textual characters who revealed their (a)gender, and chosen name or (a)pronoun choice felt normalized in school, home, with family, peers, etc.,
- Ask students in what ways these self-defined characters acted as change agents in their lived worlds. Who, what, and/or how were they impacted?

Cultural Connections

Ask students to make connections and draw inferences between textual characters and artists, musicians, athletes, media personalities, religious figures, politicians, friends, or family, etc., who have had private aspects of their (a)gender revealed publically. What are their stories? What have they experienced? How were/are they treated? Was there an apology? How did they respond? How are their lives today? What have you learned about the ways they perform their identities? What can you now teach others about respecting one's right to self disclose?

Fig. 2.3   Examples of pathways for Principle 5

media to institutional gender division, family talk, after school activities, and beyond. The classroom discussions that ensue can draw from these findings and help students see the visibility and invisibility of particular forms of gender expression and how they are privileged. A recognition of the privileging of certain types of gender expression as seen in classroom dialog, while it may feel or seem oppressive to those who fall outside of the binary, has great potential to invite deeper dialog about (a)gender inequities and about striving for (a)gender justice (for more examples, see Miller 2009 *(Dis)Embedding gender diversity in the preservice classroom)*. Teachers can remind students that through acquiescence to status quo gender norms it is in fact larger *society* that suffers from gender perception dysphoria, not the people who inhabit it. The following list provides additional pathways to achieve Principle 6 (see Fig. 2.4).

The Transformative Power of Recognition

Students, when affirmed and made legible to self and others, have the power for not only self-recognition but to be truly spatially agentive. Such recognition can cut across borders of space, time, technology, the futurities of the children yet to be born, and possibly shape and inform future contexts. Through an integration of a conscious curriculum, not only can trans* and gender creative youth be recognized, but their peers can begin to mirror back their lived realities in affirming, inclusive and then possibly over time, sustaining ways. Youth don't always know why they are driven to be particular identities or even why those identities change over time, but if teachers can maintain that mindset, they are likely to impact the future of humanity.

An ultimate hope for the QLF is for researchers and teacher education programs to take up this work and modify it to their social, racial, linguistic, and geographic contexts. As researchers, teacher educators, and pre- and in-service teachers study, unpack, and practice the QLF, they can supplement their repertoire of resources that they, in turn, can use concomitantly in classroom practice. Such practices can instill in their dispositions a confidence to address trans* and gender creative youth and a continuum of (a)gender experiences in the classroom. Teacher education and professional development for teachers, that remain open to evolving understandings of (a)gender, can generate a stabilized futurity for (a)gender justice; in other words, as individuals leave schools and move into the world, their embodied autonomy, recognizable by self as they navigate their life, truly has great agentive potential for social shifts as they impact others' perspectives.

Pre-reading strategies:

- Ask students to log how gender norms are reinforced in a chosen movie, talk show, TV show. How is gender policed?
- Ask students to log how gender norms are reinforced in school (other classes, school policies, messages, posters, sports, etc.,). How are gender norms socially policed?
- Ask students to log how gender norms are reinforced in different disciplines and genres/sub genres within technology, art, history, radio, music, literature, science, math, sports, policy., etc. How are gender norms socially policed?
- Ask students to provide examples about where in these disciplines there is push back against gender norms. Ask, what have they learned from the push back?
- Ask students to consider which authors explore social policing and reinforcement of (a)gender
- What have they learned from those texts?

Comprehension strategies:

- Ask students to log how gender norms are reinforced in a texts across different aspects of characters' lives. How are gender norms socially policed in the text?
- What messages do the characters receive? How are they interrupted and disrupted?
- Ask students to provide examples about who pushes back against these gender norms. Ask, what have they learned from the push back?
- Ask, how was gender interrupted? What impact does this have on the characters or social environment. How do people come to read each other differently?
- Ask students in what ways these characters acted as change agents in their lived worlds. Who, what, and/or how were they impacted?

Cultural Connections:

Ask students to make connections and draw inferences between textual characters and artists, musicians, athletes, media personalities, religious figures, politicians, friends, or family, and in any academic discipline, etc., who have pushed back against gender norms and embrace (a)gender presentation. What are their stories? What have they experienced? How were/are they treated? How are their lives today? What have you learned about the ways they perform their identities? What can you now teach others about challenging gender norms and embracing (a)gender presentations?

Fig. 2.4 Examples of Principle 6

Over time, as more literacy educators continue to use the QLF across different disciplines, and work to align academic standards along with queer-inclusive curriculum, integrating a theory of trans*ness and a trans* pedagogy, while both affirming and supporting recognition of students' differential bodied realities, its effect can have real-time generative consequences for students, who, as stewards with expanding mindsets, can

INCLUSIVE SPACE

This space

RESPECTS

all aspects of people including age, gender, race,
ethnicity, religion/no religion, national origin,
language, education, marital status, body size,
political affiliation/philosophy, (a)sexual
orientation, (a)gender identity/expression and
creativity, physical and mental ability, social-
economic status, genetic information, HIV, and
veteran status.

Picture 2.3   Example of Principle 5

begin to create even more equitable and accepting spaces. Hence, (a)gen-
der self-determination and a queer autonomy have real time possibility for
becoming a normalized and integrated curricular piece—and that would
be the *ultimate* justice.

NOTES

1. As mentioned in Chap. 1, (a)gender is a rejection of gender as a biological
   or social construct altogether and refusal to identify with gender. The lower
   case (a) in parenthesis does not nullify gender, it is a way of combining the
   terms so both gender refusal and gender are collapsed into one word.
2. See Moses for a robust discussion of autonomy as self-determination, which
   is characterized by Raz's (1979) concepts of integrity, independence, and

adequate range of options, and so on. Herein, these terms are thoroughly defined.
3. For an extended discussion on "internal safety" see Leonardi and Saenz's (2014) conceptualization.
4. For original printing of examples of Principle 1, 5, and 6, see: Miller, 2016.

REFERENCES

Apple, M. (2002). *Official knowledge*. New York: Routledge.
Arnot, M. (2002). Cultural reproduction: The pedagogy of sexuality. In *Reproducing gender? Essays on educational theory and feminist politics* (pp. 41–53). London: Routledge-Falmer.
Blackburn, M., & Clark, C. T. (2011). Becoming readers of literature with LGBT themes in and out of classrooms. In S. Wolf, K. Coats, P. Enciso, & C. Jenkins (Eds.), *The handbook of research on children's and young adult literature* (pp. 148–163). New York: Routledge.
Brandt, D., & Clinton, K. (2002). Limits of the local: Expanding perspectives on literacy as a social practice. *Journal of Literacy Research, 34*(3), 337–356.
Britzman, D. P. (1997). What is this thing called love new discourses for understanding gay and lesbian youth. In S. de Castell & M. Bryson (Eds.), *Radical interventions: Identity politics and difference/s on educational praxis* (pp. 183–207). Albany: State University of New York.
Butler, J. (1990). *Gender trouble: Feminism and the subversion of identity*. New York: Routledge.
Butler, J. (2004). *Undoing gender*. New York: Routledge.
Chesir-Teran, D., & Hughes, D. (2009). Heterosexism in high school and victimization among lesbian, gay, bisexual, and questioning students. *Journal of Youth and Adolescence, 38*(7), 963–975.
Collins, P. H. (1990). *Black feminist thought: Knowledge, consciousness, and the politics of empowerment*. New York: Routledge.
Connell, R. W. (1995). *Masculinities*. Berkeley: University of California Press.
Crenshaw, K. (1989). Demarginalizing the intersection of race and sex: A black feminist critique of antidiscrimination doctrine, feminist theory and antiracist politics. *Chicago Legal Forum, Special Issue: Feminism in the Law: Theory, Practice and Criticism, 5*, 139–167.
de Beauvoir, S. (1973). *The second sex* (trans: Parshley, E. M.). New York: Vintage Books.
Dieser, R. (2008). Tales from grades 1 through 12: Understanding the complex web of multiple life forces located in schools. *Alberta Journal of Educational Research, 54*(3), 293–308.
Duncanson, C. (2015). Hegemonic masculinity and the possibility of change in gender Relations. *Men and Masculinities, 18*(2), 231–248.

Hagood, M. (2002). Critical literacy for whom? *Reading Research and Instruction,* *41*(3), 247–266.

Irigaray, L. (1985). *The sex which is not one* (trans: Porter, C., & Brooke, C.). Ithaca: Cornell University Press.

Jagose, A. (1996). *Queer theory: An introduction.* Melbourne: University of Melbourne Press.

Kirkland, D. (2013). *A search past silence: The literacy of young Black men.* New York: Teachers College Press.

Kymlicka, W. (1991). *Liberalism, community, and culture.* New York: Oxford University Press.

Leonardi, B., & Meyer, E. (forthcoming). Internal safety. In E. Brockenbrough, J. Ingrey, W. Martino, & N. Rodriquez (Eds.), *Queer studies and education: Critical concepts for the 21st century* (pp. xx–xx). New York: Palgrave Macmillan.

Leonardi, B., & Saenz, L. (2014). Conceptualizing safety from the inside out: Heteronormative spaces and their effects on students' sense of self. In L. Meyer & D. Carlson (Eds.), *Gender and sexualities in education: A reader* (pp. 202–229). New York: Peter Lang.

Martino, W. (2000). Mucking around in class, giving crap and acting cool: Adolescent boys enacting masculinities at school. *Canadian Journal of Education, 25*(2), 102–112.

Marx, K., Engels, F., Moore, S., & McLellan, D. (1992). *The Communist manifesto.* Oxford: Oxford University Press.

McCready, L. (2007). Making space for diverse masculinities in "Urban" education. *Orbit, 36*(3), 16–20.

Messerschmidt, K. (2000). Becoming "real men"; Adolescent masculinity, challenges and sexual violence. *Men and Masculinities, 2*(3), 286–307.

Miller, s. (2009). (Dis)embedding gender diversity in the preservice classroom. In S. Steinberg (Ed.), *Diversity and multiculturalism: A reader* (pp. 193–209). New York: Peter Lang.

Miller, s. (2012). Mythology of the norm: Disrupting the culture of bullying in schools. *English Journal, 101*(6), 107–109.

Miller, s. (2014a). Cultivating a disposition for sociospatial justice in English teacher preparation. *Teacher Education and Practice, 27*(1), 44–74.

Miller, s. (2014b). Hungry like the wolf: Gender non-conformity in young adult literature. In C. Hill (Ed.), *The critical merits of young adult literature: Coming of age* (pp. 55–72). New York: Routledge.

Miller, s. (2015). A queer literacy framework promoting (a)gender and (a)sexuality self-determination and justice. *English Journal, 104*(5), 37–44.

Miller, s. (2016a). Reading YAL queerly: A queer literacy framework for inviting (a)gender and (a)sexuality self- determination and justice. In D. Carlson & D. Linville (Eds.), *Beyond borders: Queer eros and ethos (ethics) in LGBTQ young adult literature* (pp. 153–180). New York: Peter Lang.

Miller, s., & Gilligan, J. (2014). Heteronormative harassment: Queer bullying and gender non-conforming students. In D. Carlson & E. Meyer (Eds.), *Handbook of gender and sexualities in education* (pp. 217–229). New York: Peter Lang.

Miller, s., & Norris, L. (2007). *Unpacking the loaded teacher matrix: Negotiating space and time between university and secondary English classrooms.* New York: Peter Lang.

Miller, s., Burns, L., & Johnson, T. S. (2013). *Generation BULLIED 2.0: Prevention and intervention strategies for our most vulnerable students.* New York: Peter Lang.

Moje, E. B., & van Helden, C. (2004). Doing popular culture: Troubling discourses about youth. In J. A. Vadeboncoeur & L. P. Stevens (Eds.), *Re/constructing "the adolescent": Sign, symbol, and body* (pp. 211–248). New York: Peter Lang.

Moll, L., Amanti, C., Neff, D., & Gonzalez, N. (1992). Funds of knowledge for teaching: Using a qualitative approach to connect homes and classrooms. *Theory Into Practice, 31,* 132–141.

Moses, M. S. (2002). *Embracing race: Why we need race-conscious education policy.* New York: Teachers College Press.

Raz, J. (1979). *The morality of freedom.* New York: Oxford University Press.

Renold, E. (2004). Other' boys: Negotiating non-hegemonic masculinities in the primary school. *Gender and Education, 16*(2), 247–265.

Robinson, K. (2005). Reinforcing hegemonic masculinities through sexual harassment: Issues of identity, power and popularity in secondary schools. *Gender and Education, 17*(1), 19–37.

Rose, J. (1993). *Limited livelihoods: Gender and class in nineteenth-century England.* Berkeley: University of California Pres.

Tharinger, D. J. (2008). Maintaining the hegemonic masculinity through selective attachment, homophobia, and gay-baiting in schools: Challenges to interventions. *School Psychology Review, 37*(2), 221–227.

Wittig, M. (1983). The point of view: Universal of particular? *Feminist Issues, 3*(2), 63–69.

Young, I. M. (1990). *Justice and the politics of difference.* Princeton: Princeton University Press.

CHAPTER 3

Teaching Our Teachers: Trans* and Gender Education in Teacher Preparation and Professional Development

Cathy A.R. Brant

Queer Literacy Framework Principles:

2. Understands gender as a construct that has and continues to be affected by intersecting factors (e.g. social, historical, material, cultural, economic and religious); and,
6. Engages in ongoing critique of how gender norms are reinforced in literature, media, technology, art, history, science, math, and so on.

When I was an elementary school teacher, one of my colleagues had a student in his classroom who was born as a biological male. This child wore pink, princess crowns, and loved to play with the girls. He even told his teacher that when he grew up he was going to be a woman and a mommy. I remember the discussions in the teachers' room about this child. Colleagues asked the teacher how he "dealt" with the issue. They were shocked that a parent would "let" their child dress and act that way. Other teachers blatantly made fun of the child. I was appalled by the

C.A.R. Brant (✉)
University of South Carolina, Columbia, USA

© The Editor(s) (if applicable) and The Author(s) 2016   47
sj Miller (ed.), *Teaching, Affirming, and Recognizing Trans and Gender Creative Youth*, DOI 10.1057/978-1-137-56766-6_3

discussion. At the time, I did not have the understanding of terms such as trans*, gender nonconforming, or gender creative, but I knew that I had never addressed these types of gender issues in my teacher preparation program. The gender issues we addressed involved making sure classrooms were equitable for both boys and girls. We had never discussed gender existing outside the gender binary.

Since then, I have made addressing issues of homophobia and transphobia a component of all of my teacher preparation courses, whether it is an introduction to education course, a social studies methods course, or a multicultural education course for elementary or middle school preservice teachers. As a cisgender, heterosexual woman who has a history and belief system that had demonstrated care that has and continues to recognize and affirm all identities in my courses, I actually thought that I was doing a pretty decent job including and teaching about these topics. In fact, over the past several weeks, I have watched many of my former teacher preparation students comment about how Caitlyn Jenner's "coming out" as a transgender woman has played out in social media. Most of the responses I have seen across social media have been positive, yet at the same time, I have seen several posts from former students of mine asking questions as to why anyone should care about Caitlyn's gender identity. It appears I have missed the mark as a teacher educator. My former students, most of whom are now teachers employed in Pre-K-8 public schools, have failed to see the consequences of why understanding gender identity and the needs of trans* and gender creative youth is important.

With this book's focus on recognizing, teaching, and affirming trans* and gender creative youth, it is critical to not only discuss the experiences of these students in schools and the specific practices teachers can employ to make school spaces more inclusive, but to also include a discussion on the preparation of teachers to work with these amazing populations of youth. In this chapter, I present a discussion of the experiences of trans* youth in schools, followed by an analysis of two studies that address preservice and practicing teachers' sense of self-efficacy in working with and working for trans* and gender creative youth, and end with a discussion of the ways in which queer inclusive pedagogies can be infused into the teacher preparation classroom. The goal is to avoid situations such as the two presented above and to make all spaces trans* inclusive spaces.

STATE OF SCHOOLS FOR TRANS* AND GENDER CREATIVE YOUTH

The biennial GLSEN report (Kosciw et al. 2014) indicates some startling realities for trans* and gender creative youth. Out of the 7,898 students between the ages of 13 and 21 surveyed:

- 37.8% felt unsafe because of their gender expression.
- 56.4% heard negative remarks about gender expression (not acting "masculine enough" or "feminine enough") frequently or often.
- 33.1% heard negative remarks specifically about transgender people, like "tranny" or "he/she," frequently or often.
- 55.5% reported hearing negative remarks about gender expression from teachers or other school staff.
- 55.2% were verbally harassed (e.g. called names or threatened) in the past year because of their gender expression.
- 22.7% were physically harassed (e.g. pushed or shoved) in the past year because of their gender expression.
- 11.4% were physically assaulted (e.g. punched, kicked, injured with a weapon) in the past year because of their gender expression.

Additionally, most school policies and curricula are not inclusive for trans* youth.

- 42.2% of transgender students had been prevented from using their preferred name (10.8% of LGBT students overall).
- 59.2% of transgender students had been required to use a bathroom or locker room of their legal sex (18.7% of students overall).
- 31.6% of transgender students had been prevented from wearing clothes considered inappropriate based on their legal sex (19.2% of students overall) (Kosciw et al. 2014).

These experiences in schools can lead to a number of negative effects for trans* and gender creative youth, including isolation from friends and family (Beam 2007), drug and/or alcohol use and addiction (Beam 2007; Holmes and Cahill 2004), low self-esteem (Beam 2007), lack of engagement in school (Holmes and Cahill 2004; Kosciw et al. 2010, 2012, 2014) academic failure (Kosciw et al. 2010, 2012, 2014), fighting (Beam 2007), and suicide (Ybarra et al. 2014).

As Miller discusses in Chap. 2 of this book, using a Queer Literacy Framework (QLF) is essential because it legitimizes all students, regardless of their (a)gender, and it can begin to combat the negative experiences that trans* students experience in schools. In order for teachers to be able to engage in a QLF in their classrooms, they must be trained to do so effectively so that their students can "as individuals leave schools [and] can remain autonomous and embodied by an internalized safety as they navigate their life pathways" (Miller 2015, pp. 42–43). Not only do teachers need this training as a part of their teacher education and professional development opportunities, but teachers also need to have self-efficacy in order to effectively implement a QLF pedagogy in their classrooms.

SELF-EFFICACY IN WORKING WITH TRANS* AND GENDER CREATIVE YOUTH

Teacher efficacy can be defined as a teacher's belief in his or her ability to accomplish a specific teaching task (Tschannen-Moran et al. 1998). The concept of teacher efficacy can be applied to teaching specific content (e.g. teaching fractions, covering the civil war, etc.), from classroom management practices, to working with specific populations of students. Teachers' sense of self-efficacy in the different areas of classroom instruction, interactions with students, and classroom management impacts why and how they engage in the various elements of classroom life (Friedman and Kass 2002). These topics are reflected by two larger studies which focused on teachers' sense of their own ability to work with and work for LGBTQ students and their families (Brant 2014; Brant and Tyson, In Press).

As a part of the larger studies, prompts were focused specifically on teachers' sense of self-efficacy when working with and working for trans* and gender creative youth using Likert-style items. Study one (Brant 2014) surveyed 69 preservice teachers at a large Mid-Western institution. This study focused on the preservice teachers' understanding of terms relevant to multicultural education and LGBTQ issues in addition to their sense of self-efficacy in working with and working for LGBTQ youth and families. Specifically, the Likert prompts relating to (a)gender in this study were as follows:

- I can work with gender nonconforming, transgender, or queer students.

- I can work with gender nonconforming, transgender, or queer parents.
- I can plan instructional activities to reduce prejudice about gender nonconforming, transgender, or queer people in my current of future classroom.
- I can identify biases against gender nonconforming, transgender, or queer people in commercial materials used in teaching.
- I can identify school practices that may be harmful for those who identify as gender nonconforming, transgender, or queer.

The participants in this study were preservice teachers in Early Childhood, Middle Childhood Education, Physical Education, and Art Education.[1] The preservice teachers ranged in age from 21 to 50, with an average age of 26, and a median age of 23. Two-thirds of these participants were in the ages of 21 and 25. The surveys in study one were administered in person during the participants' student teaching seminar.

Study two (Brant and Tyson, under review) grew out of study one and surveyed a smaller sample (48 participants). Since study one was a dissertation covering a variety of topics, study two's focus was solely on teachers' sense of self-efficacy in working with and working for LGBTQ students and families. The Likert prompts used in study two discussed in this chapter include:

- I can teach students who are gender nonconforming.
- I can teach students who are transgender.
- I can work with parents/caregivers who are gender nonconforming.
- I can work with parents/caregivers who are transgender.
- I can implement instructional activities to reduce prejudice about gender nonconforming people.
- I can implement instructional activities to reduce prejudice about transgender people.
- I can identify commercial materials, textbooks, and curriculum with biases against transgender people.
- I can identify commercial materials, textbooks, and curriculum with biases against gender nonconforming people.
- I can identify school practices and/or policies that may be harmful for those who identify as transgender or gender nonconforming.

The participants in study two ranged in age from 21 to 63 years, with an average of 28 and a median age of 25. The participants came from a total of 17 states. When this project was initially conceived, we wanted to only survey preservice and novice (5 years or less) teachers. We received a number of responses from more seasoned teachers, and we decided to deepen the scope of our data to include them as well.

In this chapter, I provide the data from the two studies relevant to the participants' sense of self-efficacy in various (a)gender issues. The self-efficacy prompts from the two studies addressed the following topics:

1. Working with trans* and gender creative students;
2. Working with trans* and gender creative parents and guardians;
3. Implementing instructional activities to reduce prejudice about trans* and gender creative individuals;
4. Identifying commercial materials, textbooks, and curricula with biases against trans* and gender creative individuals; and
5. Identifying school practices and/or policies that may be harmful for those who identify as trans* or gender creative.

Taken together, the two studies yielded results that are especially relevant for teacher educators when addressing gender issues in their teacher preparation coursework or within professional development for teachers. The first two Likert Scale prompts assessed participants' self-efficacy in working with trans* and gender creative parents and/or guardians. Some of the examples from the Likert Scale prompts included ratings on *I can work with transgender and gender nonconforming students* and *I can work with transgender and gender nonconforming parents and/or guardians*. In both studies, the participants reported a high sense of self-efficacy in working with trans* youth as well as working with trans* parents. Results from study one (69 preservice teachers) demonstrated that 84% of respondents reported a high sense of self-efficacy (e.g. *I am confident I could do this*, or *believe that I could do this reasonably well, if I had time to prepare*) in working with students and 90% demonstrated readiness to work with parents and guardians. For the participants in study two (48 preservice and in-service teachers), 87% reported a high sense of self-efficacy in working with students and 89% in working work parents and guardians. These findings are very encouraging because teachers should be comfortable working with all their students as well as with different types of parents and guardians. When individuals have a high sense of self-efficacy while working with trans* and gender creative youth, it provides a gateway for teachers to be able to enact change in their classrooms about topics related to (a)gender issues.

Regardless of participants' self-efficacy in working with trans* youth, it is critical that teacher preparation and professional development provide preservice and in-service teachers with information regarding the realities of the experiences of trans* and gender creative youth. Teachers need to understand how this group of students may experience schools in ways that are different from their cisgender and LGB peers. The goal is to prepare teachers to establish positive, productive relationships with their trans* and gender creative students. Most importantly, teachers need to understand that gender is a social construction and that for many individuals gender identity and gender expression are fluid and flexible (Miller 2015). Teachers need to support the students in their classroom regardless of their gender identity or expression within both the formal classroom setting and the school community at large.

In the final three Likert Scale prompts, there was a shift in the self-efficacy from predominantly high self-efficacy (e.g. *I am confident I could do this*, or *I believe that I could do this reasonably well, if I had time to prepare*) to a mix of both high and medium self-efficacy. The third prompt assessed the participants self-efficacy in engaging in lessons that reduce (a)gender prejudice (e.g. *I can implement instructional activities to reduce prejudice about those who are trans* or gender nonconforming*). In study one (69 preservice teachers), 80% of participants reported a high sense of self-efficacy, and 15% a medium sense of self-efficacy. In study two (48 preservice and in-service teachers), 50% reported having a high sense of self-efficacy, and 44% reported a medium sense of self-efficacy. It is interesting that there is such a significant discrepancy between the two studies. There are several reasons why this may have occurred. The first may be that study one was administered face-to-face with the participants' professor present. While they were told that their answers would not be shared with their instructor, many of them may have wanted to please them or me. Another difference may be attributed that study two involved in-service teachers. Given the realities of their particular contexts, they may feel less able to do this effectively than those who are still preparing to become teachers.

Despite these differences in self-efficacy, these results have some clear implications for what teachers need to be prepared to do in their classrooms. They need to explore their own biases and prejudices about trans* and gender creative students, understand the ways in which this prejudice manifests itself in society, and be given the tools about how to address these issues with Pre-K-12 students. The acceptance of all individuals, regardless of gender identity and gender expression, can be addressed in schools at any grade level; the ways in which this is done, though, will vary. Teachers need to learn developmentally appropriate ways to do so. As Miller (2015) suggests, drawing on the QLF as a pedagogical tool for recognizing, teaching, and affirming equality across all categories of (a)gender, teachers have endless potential to impact the contexts which their students will inhabit.

The fourth Likert prompt in the study, *How can I can identify commercial materials, textbooks, and curriculum with biases against transgender people,* assessed self-efficacy in identifying bias in commercial materials, textbooks, and curriculum against trans* and gender creative individuals. In study one (69 preservice teachers), 81% reported a high sense of self-efficacy (e.g. *I am confident I could do this*) and 13% reported a medium sense of self-efficacy (e.g. *I could probably do this*). In study two (48 preservice and in-service teachers), 47%, reported a high sense of self-efficacy, and 38% reported a medium sense of self-efficacy. Results from these findings clearly indicate that teacher preparation and professional development programs should be in place to help teachers recognize the ways in which trans* and gender creative individuals can be marginalized within the materials mass produced for schools. Once individuals understand their own and others' biases and prejudice toward trans* and gender creative individuals, they can then begin to unlearn the ways that biases and prejudices can manifest themselves in the curriculum. Teachers who are taught to recognize that when trans* and gender creative youths' identities are absent in textbooks and commercial teaching materials (Miller 2015), they are vulnerabilized from experiencing both internal and external recognition (Miller, this volume, Chap. 1), and they are susceptible to becoming part of the statistics revealed by GLSEN (2014).

The final Likert prompt, *How can I identify school practices and/or policies that may be harmful for those who identify as transgender or gender nonconforming,* measured self-efficacy in identifying school practices and/or policies that may be harmful for those who identify as trans* or gender creative. The findings revealed a large discrepancy between the two studies for this prompt. In study one, 82% of the 69 preservice teachers reported a high sense of self-efficacy and 13% reported a medium sense of self-efficacy, while for study two, 66% of the 48 preservice and in-service teachers reported a high sense of self-efficacy and 30% reported a medium

Leilah Babirye — Visual Artist

sense of self-efficacy. These findings indicate that the first step in practicing teachers' classroom is to make teachers aware of the ways in which school practices and policies can be harmful to trans* and gender creative youth. In fact, the study indicates that schools need to have antibullying and harassment policies enumerating language that includes protection for trans* and gender creative youth. Such a policy will permit teachers and schools to take action when students are discriminated against. Secondly, findings from the study indicate that schools must acknowledge trans*and gender creative students, allow them to go by their chosen names, and use bathrooms or locker rooms that reflect their gender identities. Lastly, findings indicate that dress codes need to be revised so trans* and gender creative youth can dress in the way that reflects their chosen gender expression and identity.

While these statistics are in fact quite encouraging such that for almost every Likert prompt, over 90% of the participants had either a high or medium self-efficacy, this is not yet enough. For change to be truly sustained, 100% of all teachers should have a high sense of self-efficacy in all of the five areas indicated by the two studies. The way to do this is *through* teacher education, both during the teacher preparation process and well as professional development opportunities for in-service teachers. The remainder of this chapter will focus on a method to teach preservice teachers about trans* and gender issues and will conclude with an example of how the QLF can be applied to teaching teachers about these important issues.

Trans* Inclusion in the Teacher Education Curriculum

Just as teacher education programs are taking up issues of race, ethnicity, and class as a part of the teacher preparation process, issues of sexuality and gender should be addressed across all content areas as well. It is clear, from the aforementioned statistics, that trans*, gender creative, and (a)gender youth have difficulties in schools and their teachers and school administrators must take action. Such preparation should begin in the teacher preparation classroom and be scaffolded from the first class taken and then across all subsequent coursework. This raises the following questions: Are trans* and other related gender issues being addressed in teacher education programs? If so, how are they addressed?

Issues of heterosexuality and homophobia are topics that are minimized or omitted from multicultural teacher education coursework (Gorski et al. 2013) and textbooks (Gorski 2009; Macgillibray and Jennings 2008; Sherwin and Jennings 2006). In fact, Gorski, David, and Reiter reported that during an average of 45 hours of college level instructions, LGBTQ issues were only addressed for 1.7 hours. Even if that time were split equally between issues of gender and sexuality, less than an hour would likely be focused on trans*, gender expression, and gender identity issues. These studies, spanning the past 9 years, show that issues of (a)gender are not being addressed for the amount of time they could be or should be.

Using a QLF in Teacher Preparation Programs

Throughout this chapter, I have provided statistics that demonstrate the importance of the preparedness for both pre- and in-service teachers and professional development to address trans* and gender creative issues in the classroom and schools writ large. In this section, I apply the QLF and two salient principles to this task. More specifically, this lesson will focus on the following QLF principles:

- Principle 2: Understands gender as a construct that has and continues to be affected by intersecting factors (e.g. social, historical, material, cultural, economic, and religious)
- Principle 6: Engages in ongoing critique of how gender norms are reinforced in literature, media, technology, art, history, science, math, and so on.

Addressing these principles as a part of a teacher preparation program can ostensibly enable preservice teachers to see the ways in which gender not only impacts them, but also their future classroom students.

Rationale

In my ongoing work as a preservice teacher educator, I find that discussing issues of sexuality and gender is more difficult for my students than talking about race or class. When I bring up (a)gender in my college classrooms, I experience resistance from my students for a number of reasons. Many students argue that there are only two genders, male and female and believe that gender is immutable. They also argue that these "controversial" topics are best left for parents to address at home and fear being fired if they take up these "controversial" issues. They also proffer that it is inappropriate to address these issues in early childhood classrooms because it will confuse children about their own gender identity, and that there is no need for them to address these types of issues because they do not have students in their classes that identify as trans*, gender creative, or (a)gender. In my work with my students, I try to acknowledge and validate their reservations, but push them further to understand why addressing these topics is so critical, not only for trans* youth but for their cisgender peers.

Lesson

To address these two principles in a teacher preparation classroom, just as in a Pre-K-12 classroom, requires a great deal of scaffolding. The figures below show the activities teacher educators can engage in with their pre- and in-service teachers, and critical questions they can be asking along with those activities. First, in an attempt to help preservice teachers understand the ways in which gender is socially constructed, they can look at how the gender norms have changed over the years. We look at sources such as television shows, movies, and magazines. I engage the students in critical discussion about what changes have occurred, but also why those changes occurred (see Fig. 3.1).

My goal is to help them understand that our gender expectations are based on society and culture. I also work with them to recognize the ways in which these gender roles are reinforced through the media. I find it especially effective to look at holiday toy catalogs and commercials from some of the major retailers. They are often shocked to see how gendered they are. From there, I ask the students to go to one of their local stores and walk down the toy aisles and baby aisles. Once again, students return to the teacher preparation classroom surprised at the sharp divide between "boy" toys and clothes and "girl" toys and clothes. Figure 3.2 presents some of the questions I ask my students.

Once the preservice teachers have a strong understanding about the ways in which society creates and reinforces gender roles and norms, we can then have a serious discussion about the ways in which trans*, gender creative, and (a)gender students experience the classroom and the world. One of the ways that I find effective in discussing these types of issues with my students is through the use of children's literature (see Appendix),

Critical Questions When Analyzing Gender Norms Over the Years
• How are men/women and boys/girls represented?
• What things can someone do/not do because of his or her gender during this time period?
• How were gender norms policed/enforced?
• What were the consequences of someone not meeting gender norms/expectations?
• How and why have things changed?
• What are/were the consequences of things changing?
• How have those changes brought us to where we are today?

Fig. 3.1   Critical questions when analyzing gender norms over the years

Critical Questions For Analysis of Children's Clothing & Toys
• What toys are being specifically marketed to girls? Boys? How do you know?
• Why are those toys being marketed in that way?
• What did you notice about the ways that stores lay out gendered clothing and toys for children?
• What happens in schools and society when boys play with "girl" toys or girls play with "boy" toys?
• Is there a difference in how they are treated? Why do you think this is?
• What is problematic about the ways in which these stores are laid out of for children who may not identify with their assigned gender?

Fig. 3.2   Critical questions for analysis of children's clothing and toys

regardless of discipline or preservice grade level focus. There are a growing number of children's picture books, in particular, that address trans* and gender creative youth. After reading the books to the class, I have my students react both as a listener/reader and as a teacher. I begin to encourage them to think about whether they would use the book in their classroom and how they would do so. We discuss the benefits of using texts such as these in their classroom for both trans* youth and their cisgender peers. Often, during these discussions I am able to let the students discuss and debate the issues on their own.

Assessment

While it is difficult, as a teacher educator, to know which of my students will engage in a QLF in their classrooms, I can, by the end of the semester, have a deeper awareness about who is open to engaging in socially just pedagogies. This is most evidenced when I let the students talk and debate issues with one another. It is always interesting to see who becomes quiet during these discussions and who is willing to stand up for trans* kids against their peers.

To Conclude or Not to Conclude

The need for the inclusion of trans* issues in Pre-K-12 classrooms is critical for trans* and cisgender youth alike. In order for teachers to engage in a QLF in their classrooms they must have the appropriate amount of self-efficacy to do so. Supporting pre-and in-service teachers, and school personnel to develop the dispositions that can travel with them across contexts and across space and time can truly impact the future and normalization for trans* and gender creative youth to live life without fear of harassment or negative self-worth. Every human is entitled to the same inalienable rights and as Miller (this volume, Chap. 2) suggests, a life worthy of dignity and respect. Teacher education and professional development must challenge the recognition gap (Miller, this volume, Chap. 1) that is still so pervasive. I, however, am confident, that change is in the making and as changes are made, we can move ourselves into more inclusive spaces for all. The teacher preparation program is the *key place* to help trans* and gender creative youth become recognized and its efficacy can and will make schools a safe and inclusive space for all.

APPENDIX

Children's Picture Books Addressing (A)Gender Topics

dePaola, T. (1979). *Oliver Button Is a Sissy* (Reissue edition). S.l.: HMH Books for Young Readers.

Ewert, M. (2008). *10,000 dresses*. New York: Triangle Square.

Fierstein, H. (2005). *The sissy duckling*. New York: Simon & Schuster Books for Young Readers.

Herthel, J., & Jennings, J. (2014). *I am Jazz*. New York, New York: Dial Books.

Hoffman, S., & Hoffman, I. (2014). *Jacob's new dress*. Chicago, Illinois: Albert Whitman & Company.

Kilodavis, C. (2010). *My princess boy* (1 edition). New York: Aladdin.

*List adapted from:

http://www.therainbowtimesmass.com/2013/03/21/transgender-parent-friendly-picture-books-for-young-children/ & https://www.goodreads.com/list/show/20314.Transgender_Friendly_Young_Children_s_Books_

NOTES

1. Each study cited was approved by IRB.

REFERENCES

Beam, C. (2007). *Transparent: Love, family, and living the T with transgender teenagers.* Orlando: Harcourt Books.

Brant, C. A. R. (2014). *Preservice teachers' perspectives on methods, pedagogy and self-efficacy related to gender and sexuality as a part of their multicultural teacher education* (Doctoral dissertation). Retrieved from ProQuest Dissertations and Theses (Accession Order No. 3671810).

Brant, C. A. R., & Tyson, C.A. (in press). *LGBTQ self-efficacy in the Social Studies, Journal of Social Studies Research.*

Friedman, I. A., & Kass, E. (2002). Teacher self-efficacy: A classroom-organization conceptualization. *Teaching and Teacher Education, 18*(6), 675–686. doi:10.1016/S0742-051X(02)00027-6.

Gorski, P. (2009). What we're teaching teachers: An analysis of multicultural teacher education coursework syllabi. *Journal of Teaching and Teacher Education, 25*(2), 309–318.

Gorski, P. C., Davis, S. N., & Reiter, A. (2013). An examination of the (in)visibility of sexual orientation, heterosexism, homophobia and other LGBTQ concerns in U.S. multicultural teacher education coursework. *Journal of LGBTQ Youth, 10,* 224–248.

Holmes, S. E., & Cahill, S. (2004). School experiences of gay, lesbian, bisexual and transgender youth. *Journal of Gay & Lesbian Issues in Education, 1*(3), 53–66.

Kosciw, J. G., Greytak, E. A., Diaz, E. M., & Bartkiewicz, M. J. (2010). *The 2009 National School Climate Survey: The experiences of lesbian, gay, bisexual and transgender youth in our nation's schools.* New York: GLSEN.

Kosciw, J. G., Greytak, E. A., Diaz, E. M., & Bartkiewicz, M. J. (2012). *The 2011 National School Climate Survey: The experiences of lesbian, gay, bisexual and transgender youth in our nation's schools.* New York: Gay, Lesbian & Straight Education Network.

Kosciw, J. G., Greytak, E. A., Palmer, N. A., & Boesen, M. J. (2014). *The 2013 National School Climate Survey: The experiences of lesbian, gay, bisexual and transgender youth in our nation's schools.* New York: GLSEN.

Macgillibray, I. K., & Jennings, T. (2008). A content analysis exploring lesbian, gay, bisexual and transgender topics in foundations of education textbooks. *Journal of Teacher Education, 59*(2), 170–188.

Meyer, E. (2010). *Gender and sexual diversity in schools.* New York: Springer.

Miller, s. (2015). A queer literacy framework promoting (a)gender and a(sexuality) self-determination and justice. *English Journal, 104*(5), 37–44.

Sherwin, G., & Jennings, T. (2006). Feared, forgotten or forbidden: Sexual orientation topics in secondary teacher preparation programs in the USA. *Teaching Education, 17*(3), 207–233.

Tschannen-Moran, M., Woolfolk-Hoy, A., & Hoy, W. K. (1998). Teacher efficacy: Its meaning and measure. *Review of Educational Research, 68*(2), 202–248.

Ybarra, M. L., Mitchell, K. J., & Kosciw, J. G. (2014). The relation between suicidal ideation and bullying victimization in a national sample of transgender and non-transgender adolescents. In P. Goldblum, D. Espelage, J. Chu, & B. Bognar (Eds.), *Youth suicide and bullying: Challenges and strategies for prevention and intervention* (pp. 134–147). New York: Oxford University Press.

CHAPTER 4

Kindergartners Studying Trans* Issues Through *I Am Jazz*

Ashley Lauren Sullivan

Queer Literacy Framework Principles:

3. Recognizes that masculinity and femininity constructs are assigned to gender norms and are situationally performed;
6. Engages in ongoing critique of how gender norms are reinforced in literature, media, technology, art, history, science, math, and so on;
9. Advocates for equity across all categories of (a)gender performance; and,
10. Believes that students who identify on a continuum of gender identities deserve to learn in environments free of bullying and harassment.

INTRODUCTION TO KINDERGARTEN STRUCTURED READ ALOUD LESSON: *I AM JAZZ*

Transgender children live their lives within narratives of difference (Butler 2006). These differences, as beautiful and powerful as they may be, are rarely displayed in children's literature (Rowell 2007). As transgender children learn within hegemonic, heteronormative, gender-normative, and transphobic early childhood education environments, they are forced to do so with minimal representations of themselves (Butler 2004; DePalma and Atkinson 2009). Despite increased visibility and understanding of this resilient, diverse, and marginalized group, transgender children continue to

A.L. Sullivan
The Behrend College, Erie, USA

© The Editor(s) (if applicable) and The Author(s) 2016
sj Miller (ed.), *Teaching, Affirming, and Recognizing Trans and Gender Creative Youth*, DOI 10.1057/978-1-137-56766-6_4

experience bullying and "gender policing" (Butler 2006). Lack of exposure to transgender narratives in classroom texts can cause gender nonconforming children to feel alone, strange, and exposed (Sullivan 2009). As more and more children transition during early childhood, there is an even greater need for literary examples of this transformation (Sullivan 2009). This lack of exposure to books with identifiable characters is oppressive and marginalizing, regardless of how mundane and silent the discrimination (Rowell 2007). There is a great need of exposure to these narratives both for transgender as well as cisgender children (DePalma and Atkinson 2009). As early childhood educators, we have a responsibility to create welcoming and inclusive environments for all of the children in our care (Cannella and Viruru 2004).

The educational system in the USA is dominated by upper-middle class, white, Christian male values (Cannella and Viruru 2004). In this system (a microcosm of the larger society), children who deviate from ethnic, gender, sexual orientation, or language norms are frequently unsupported, ridiculed, discriminated against, ostracized, and/or physically harmed (Baker 2002). Transgender children are particularly likely to experience these ills due to heterosexist worldviews and the influence of rigid gender role dichotomies that disallow for gender variations (Baker 2002; DePalma and Atkinson 2009). In reality, the "binary of heterosexual-homosexual is…a regulatory fiction, with the consequence that normative assumptions underpinning the 'naturalness' of heterosexuality are themselves merely fictions" (Kitchin and Lysaght 2003, p. 491). Michel Foucault proposes that "subject identities are not given, but are created through representations, practices, and performances, with the placing of people into particular sexual categories dependent on the predominant discourse and power relations operating at any time" (Kitchin and Lysaght 2003, p. 491).

In addition to enduring a heterosexist learning environment, transgender children are also faced with transphobic educational systems. Transphobia is defined as the "fear and hatred of transgender persons" (Norton 1997, p. 139). Norton explains that transphobia is a "variant of homophobia understood as hatred of the queer, where 'queer' means any formation of sexuality and/or gender that deviates from the norm of reproductive heterosexuality" (1997, p. 139). In addition to external transphobia faced by transgender individuals, some struggle with internalized transphobia as well (Morrow 2004). This occurs when a transgender human being internalizes "the negative messages perpetrated by society relative to their transgender identity status" (Morrow 2004, p. 94). Transgender children are exposed to the same pejorative terms (sissy, girly boy, fag etc.) and misinformation that is projected to the rest of US society. Frequently transgender children have to "unlearn much of that harmful rhetoric. Doing so can be difficult in a social context that is so overwhelmingly heterocentric and traditional in the appointing of rigid gender roles" (Morrow 2004, p. 94).

As a former kindergarten teacher, this unit plan was specifically designed to help early childhood teachers to begin to increase visibility of transgender children, include diverse narratives, and reduce body normalization and transphobia. The lessons align to the Common Core literacy standards, and aid teachers to draw from and blend the Queer Literacy Framework (QLF) into classroom curriculum. Although one text is used for the lessons in this chapter, the framework below can be utilized with other picture books that contain transgender main characters. The development of an entire unit on this subject will help develop kindergartners into true ambassadors and allies for transgender persons. Some examples of other titles for use with this lesson include *When Kayla Was Kyle, 10,000 Dresses, My Princess Boy,* and *Be Who You Are.*

Situated Within Research Findings

The framework for this unit plan was developed based on the findings of a study titled, *Hiding in the Open, Navigating Education at the Gender Poles-A Study of Transgender Children in Early Childhood* (Sullivan 2009).[1] This qualitative study of transgender children and internalized body normalization in early childhood education settings was steeped in critical methodologies including poststructuralism, queer theory, and feminist approaches. As a means to gain insight into the internalizing effects of body normalization on young children, ten transsexual adults were interviewed about their educational experiences. The inquiry focused on their reflections on schooling from the ages of three through eight years. From their narratives, multiple themes arose regarding navigating transphobic social interactions. Most interviewees befriended peers who held the same gender identity and/or were considered "outcasts." There were barriers to friendship that stemmed from nonconforming behavior, and these seemed to increase with age. All were teased and assaulted, and each found different ways to cope with being bullied (including self-induced isolation, retaliation, building relationships with allies, and providing beneficial services to peers). When reflecting on interactions with teachers, the interviewees (known as research partners) recalled double the amount of negative interactions than positive ones. Included in these narratives were discussions of maximum control over the physical body, restrictive curriculum methods, and public humiliation.

The research partners also recalled the effects of gender-normative physical spaces and typically regarded the music classroom, art room, auditorium and library as safe and empowering spaces and the gymnasium, cafeteria, bathrooms, and principal's office as unsafe and disempowering locations. Foucault's normalization of body theory was explored in relationship to the studied population (1995 [1975]). The findings suggest that gender performativity, gender segregation, and gender normalization/gender role conformity are of particular concern for transgender children in early childhood education. The study concludes with suggestions for creating more inclusive classrooms for diverse students including allowing children to be themselves, abandoning assumptions, eliminating gender segregation, involving parents, creating a safe environment, and supporting/protecting transgender children.

Starting the Unit Plan: Notes to the Teacher

Be sure to post the entire layout below on a wall in your classroom (from title through enduring understandings) so that the students may reference the material throughout the lessons. Then show students how to refer to this information when they are completing their writing activities. In addition to providing students with open access to important concepts, the layout of the unit plan will help guide the lessons and demonstrate to all who enter your classroom exactly what the students will be learning.

The character splashes created during the lessons should be displayed and accessible to the children. For those who are unfamiliar with the terms, tier 2 vocabulary words are more sophisticated words with high utility that can replace a word with a lower Lexile score or provide nuanced meaning. They appear in a variety of contexts/situations (e.g., the word disinterested appears in an assortment of texts about different subjects). Tier 3 vocabulary words are words that children may not know that are uniquely related to certain content areas (e.g., the word pollinate is specific to the field of biology).

Gender creative is a tier 3 term that is included below. The term gender creativity refers to the process by which "every child uniquely and expansively constructs from many different sources their own authentic gender...It is not static, creativity never is, it is something that can grow over the course of a lifetime" (Ehrensaft 2012). Understanding this term is essential to understanding the experiences of the main character. Throughout the lessons, be sure to reference this concept in a manner that is accessible for your kindergartners.

I Am Jazz *Classroom Display Layout*

Title-I Am Jazz

Authors- Jessica Herthel and Jazz Jennings
Illustrator- Shelagh McNicholas
Genre- Nonfiction/Autobiography
Unit Length- Four days
Tier 2 Vocabulary- convince, normal, tease, ignore, crummy
Tier 3 Vocabulary- girl brain, boy body, transgender, gender creative
Inferred Feelings- uncomfortable, thrilled, devastated, supported, and relieved
Character Traits- authentic, brave, playful, imaginative, and artistic

Student Learning Objectives (based on Common Core Standards)-

1. **Identify** the main character in the story. **(K.RL.3)**
2. **Describe** how a character looks, what the character does, and how the character feels. **(K.RL.3) (K.W.3)**
3. **Understand** question words (e.g., who, what, when, where, why, how). **(K.L.1d)**
4. **Describe** how the illustrations match the words in a story. **(K.RL.7)**
5. **Compose** opinion (combination of drawing, dictating, and writing) pieces to include your feeling about an event in the story or the story. (My favorite part of the story was _____. My favorite book is _____.**(K.W.1)**
6. **Understand** new vocabulary words. (K.L.K4)

Essential Questions-

1. What does it mean to be transgender?
2. How can we be friends with all people, including people who are transgender?

Enduring Understandings-

1. It is okay to be different.
2. People with boy bodies are not always boys. People with girl bodies are not always girls.
3. You cannot tell if a person is a boy or a girl just by looking at them.
4. All kids should be able to play with the toys they want, choose the colors they like, and wear what they want. (QLF Principle 3)
5. It is not true that there are "boy things" and "girl things." (QLF Principle 6)
6. No one should ever be teased because they are transgender. (QLF Principle 10)
7. Gender creative means being yourself, not just acting in a way that people think boys and girls are supposed to act. (QLF Principle 3)

Note to Preschool Teachers

Although this lesson was designed for kindergartners, it is possible to modify it for use with preschoolers. In order to do so, follow the same sequence but shorten the sessions. Simplify the character splash by including fewer items. It is not necessary to eliminate the more complex! I successfully utilized similar structured read aloud lesson plans with preschoolers. They are quite capable of accessing more difficult content if presented in an age appropriate way.

LESSON PLAN—FOUR SESSIONS, EACH LESSON 30 MINUTES WITH 15 MINUTE FOLLOW-UP ACTIVITY

For preschool students or younger kindergartners, these sessions can be split in half, as long as the sequence is followed.

Session 1

Prepare For this lesson, markers or crayons should be used to complete the character splash outline on chart paper (see Chart 4.1-this is a blank chart that will be filled in by the students throughout the subsequent lessons), and blank sheets of primary writing/drawing paper or journals are needed for writing and drawing. Number each page in the book. Page number one contains the words, "I am Jazz!" There are 23 pages in total. It is important to number the pages so you know where to stop and complete the prescribed activities.

Layout- Write the headings and add small picture identifiers next to the headings(these should be prepared ahead of time)

Appearance (include a pair of eyes)

Jazz Character Splash (nothing should be drawn here ahead of time as you will draw a picture of Jazz below WITH your students. You do not have to be an artist. The process, not beautiful artwork, is the goal.)

Feelings (include a heart)

Interests (include a paintbrush and palate)

Character Traits (include an outline of a person)

Actions (include a simple picture of a person running)

Chart 4.1 Character splash for *I Am Jazz* (sample layout)

1. Introduction (3 Minutes)

Introduce the book to the students. Explain that it is an autobiography about an actual gender creative little girl named Jazz. Autobiographies are books that are written by people about their lives. These books are nonfiction or true stories. To the tune of *London Bridge is Falling Down*, sing the Nonfiction Song—"Nonfiction books are real, books are real, books are real. Nonfiction books are real, they *really* happened." Then identify Jazz Jennings and Jessica Herthel as the authors. State that Jessica Herthel helped Jazz, who was thirteen years old at the time the book was written, put her words into this book. Lastly, identify the Illustrator—Shelagh McNicholas.

2. Main Character (3 Minutes)

Explain to the students that the illustrator draws pictures to help readers understand the author's words. Ask the students what they can predict about the book based on title and the illustrations on the front cover. Give them an opportunity to make predictions. Guide them toward discovering that the book is about a little girl named Jazz. Hypothesize that she is the main character as her picture and her name are on the front cover. Explain that as the book is an autobiography, the people on the front cover are probably important people to her. Read the first three pages of the book. Stop to confirm predictions about how she was identified as the main character. Ask the students for evidence that this is true.

3. Read/Identify Vocabulary (9 Minutes)

Continue reading pages 4–8 until the words, "born this way" appear. Say, "Let's read this part again and look at the illustrations to help us understand what the author is telling us." Look at the illustration on page 7 where Jazz is dressed as a boy and she is depicted as crying. Then look at page 8 where Jazz is painting herself and she is dressed as a girl and is very happy. Call attention to the word transgender in the display. Explain that transgender means that a person with a girl body can have a boy brain or a person with a boy body can have a girl brain. State that people are born this way and there is nothing wrong with them, and that these individuals can be friends with anyone just like any other people with friends (QLF Principle 9). Explain that having a girl brain may mean (but not always) that a person may like certain things that some people think are only for girls—such as the color pink, ballet, long hair, and dresses. If someone has a boy brain, it may mean (but not always) that the person likes things that some people think are just for boys—such as the color blue, football, short hair, and trucks. Stop and make sure to answer any questions that the students may have. Draw attention to the words "girl body" and "boy brain" on the display.

Call attention to the term *gender creative*. Pull from what the students know about the word creative, to help them understand the term gender creative. Explain that Jazz is gender creative because she dresses and acts in a way that best fits who she is and not how other people think she should be.

4. Character Splash (15 Minutes)

With the help of the students, begin to complete the character splash. Ensure that they can see the cover and ask them to point out how Jazz looks. As a student identifies a physical trait, add it to the list on the character splash (Chart 4.1) (The character splash should include what is important for understanding Jazz's uniqueness. Children will notice many things. Record all of the traits, but especially the physical traits that depict her femininity) (QLF Principle 3). Begin to draw the character until you have completed the illustration.

Show the students the pictures of Jazz completing the activities that she enjoys on pages 2–5. Ask the children to then identify her interests and add them to the character splash (Chart 4.1). These are important to note as they help us to understand Jazz as a character. Chart 4.2 is a sample of a completed chart though the actual character splash should reflect the words provided by the children.

Jazz Character Splash

Appearance		Feelings
Shoulder length, brown hair		
Bangs		
Brown Eyes		
White headband with yellow	(Picture of Jazz)	
sunflowers		
Pink and white striped shirt with		
squiggly stripes		

Interests

Pink, silver, green
Singing
Sports
Make-up and dress-up
Mermaids

Character Traits		Actions

Chart 4.2   Character chart for *I Am Jazz*

5. Follow-Up (15 Minutes)
Students can complete the follow-up activity at their seats. In their journals or on a sheet of paper, ask students to write and draw their opinions
regarding what it might be like to have a boy body and a girl brain. If
needed, write this sentence starter on the board for the students to reference, "Having a boy body and a girl brain would be…" Depending on the
level of the students, it may be beneficial to brainstorm a list of possible
answers before sending the kindergartners back to their seats. It would
also be helpful to walk around and conference with the students about
their writing.

Session 2

Prepare Character splash materials as described in previous lesson, multiple hearts (foam or stiff paper), a ball made of soft material, and primary writing/drawing paper or journals with a space for writing and
drawing.

1. Reintroduction of Character (2 Minutes)

Flip through the pages read during the last session. Remind students that the story is about a gender creative little girl named Jazz who loves to pretend and have fun with her friends. She is a transgender girl; she has a girl brain and a boy body.

2. Read/Identify Vocabulary and Feelings (15 Minutes)

Read pages 9–10. Discuss page 9 where Jazz is with her mom and she explains that she is not a good boy, she is a good girl. Dialog about how Jazz feels different from how she looks. This demonstrates her gender creativity. Lead students to examine what the text says and then ask, "What does this help us understand? What does it mean to have a boy brain and a girl body?"

Explain to the students that Jazz's family thought that she was a boy because she had a "boy body." Call attention to the picture of Jazz holding the mermaid and the crystal ball on page 9. State that she is probably two or three years old in the picture. Ask the students if they remember who picked out their clothes when they were two or three years old. Explain that just like the students' parents likely picked out their clothes, Jazz's parents likely picked out her clothes. The clothes they chose for her were traditionally considered clothes intended for boys (QLF Principle 3). Call attention to her short haircut. Explain that the parents likely gave her a short haircut for the same reason they gave her clothes that were intended for boys. State that Jazz previously told us that she had a "girl brain." This means that the short haircut and the clothes for boys probably make her feel *uncomfortable*. Write the word uncomfortable on a heart and paste it on the character splash. Discuss what the word uncomfortable means, like a scratchy sweater, a hard pillow, or being forced to do something that is not welcomed. Ask a few students to share out a time that they felt uncomfortable. Then show the students the picture of Jazz wearing the beads and the crown and explain that these items made Jazz feel more comfortable on page 10.

Call attention to the word confused on any vocabulary display. Explain that confused means when something does not make much sense. Ask the students why Jazz's family felt confused. Read through the sentence, "this made me mad!" on page 13. Discuss the look on Jazz's face. Explain that she felt mad, but also *devastated* when she was forced to wear clothes intended for boys (QLF Principle 3). Have the students explore the illustration aloud to try to figure out what devastated means. Then, add the word devastated to the character splash.

Read page 14 that begins with "Still" and ends with "telling a lie." Point to the word convince on the vocabulary display. State that convince

Jazz Character Splash

Appearance		Feelings
Shoulder length, brown hair		Uncomfortable
Bangs		Devastated
Brown Eyes		
White headband with yellow	(Picture of Jazz)	
sunflowers		
Pink and white striped shirt with		
squiggly stripes		

Interests

Pink, silver, green
Singing
Sports
Make-up and dress-up
Mermaids

Character Traits		Actions

Chart 4.3   Character splash for *I Am Jazz* (sample of what you would expect to have completed at this point in the lesson)

means trying to get someone to believe something. Call three students up to the front of the room. Have one pretend to be Jazz and the other two to be Jazz's parents. Have the student playing Jazz try to convince the students playing her parents that she is really a girl. At this point, the Chart should look like the one below (see Chart 4.3)

3. Questioning Game (8 Minutes)
Have students stand up in a circle. Tell them that they are about to play the question game! Explain that a ball will be tossed and they will be asked questions about the story. When they get the ball, they will answer the question and then throw the ball back to the teacher. Ask them the questions below (add additional questions so everyone gets to have a turn).

1. Who is the main character in the story?
2. What is the story about?
3. Why does Jazz feel uncomfortable? (QLF Principle 3)
4. In which places does Jazz feel mad and devastated when she has to wear clothes intended for boys? (QLF Principle 3)
5. How do we know that Jazz is a gender creative child?

6. When did Jazz first tell her family that she was a girl?
7. Who giggled at Jazz and called her a funny kid?
8. What are some things that Jazz likes to do?
9. Why is Jazz different from her friends?
10. When Jazz got older, what did she like to play?
11. How would you help a friend who was transgender? (QLF Principles 9 and 10)
12. How do you think Jazz would feel if she could wear clothes meant for girls when she left the house? (QLF Principle 3)
13. Why did the authors write this book? What did they want you to know?
14. What do most of our books and television shows teach us about girls and boys? (QLF Principle 6)

4. Describe How Pictures Match Words/Vocabulary (5 Minutes)
Show students the picture with Jazz and the ballerinas on page 14. Explain that the authors revealed how pretending to be a boy made her feel like she was lying. State that people sometimes feel upset and disappointed in themselves when they lie. Focus on the look on Jazz's face and Jazz's body language. She is twisting her feet and pulling on her shorts. Discuss that the illustrator drew a picture of Jazz looking sad because she was not being her true self on page 14. Illustrators help us understand the story by creating pictures that match or explain the author's words. Ask the students to stand up and pretend that they are forced to behave in a way that does not fit who they are and they feel like they are lying. Have them mimic some of the things that Jazz is doing in the picture on page 14.

5. Follow-Up (15 Minutes)
Write the following question on the board: "How could Jazz's parents make her feel more comfortable?" Students then should be sent back to their seats to answer the following question. In their journals or on a sheet of paper, ask the students to write and draw their opinions. Walk around and conference with the students while they are writing.

Session 3

Prepare Students will need to bring their writings from the previous session to this session, and their character splashes. Other materials include, cutout feeling hearts, primary writing/drawing paper or journals with a space for writing and drawing and plenty of markers/crayons.

1. Gallery Presentation (10 Minutes)
Have the students sit in a circle with their writings/drawings from the previous session. Give each student a turn to read their work and share their opinions.

2. Read/Identify Vocabulary and Feelings (10 Minutes)
Start reading on page 15 where it says, "Then one amazing day...," and conclude with the page 17 where it ends with the words, "like being ME!" Ask the students how they think Jazz felt when the doctor explained to her parents that she should be allowed to be herself. Introduce the word relieved and state that it means that something you were worried about did not happen or got better. Have the children take deep sighs to act out feeling relieved. Add this word to a heart on the character splash.

Explain how the authors said that Jazz was able to wear girl clothes and grow her hair out long. Show the students how the illustrator drew a picture of this to help us to see how Jazz was changing, on page 17. Ask them to pay particular attention to Jazz's face. Explain that Jazz felt *thrilled* when she was able to be herself (QLF Principle 3). Strive to explain that thrilled means really, really, really happy—like how we might feel if we were told that we could take all of the toys home from the toy store. Put thrilled on a heart on the character splash. Have several students share out times that they felt thrilled. Encourage them to use the sentence starter, "I felt thrilled when..."

Continue to read page 18. Stop with the words, "happy with who I am." Call attention to the words different and important on the vocabulary display. Explain that different means when something is not the same as something else. State that Jazz feels different from the other kids at school because the other children with boy bodies have boy brains. Discuss the meaning of the word important. Explain that something that is important is something that matters very much or matters the most. For example, it is not important if our friends are tall or short, it is only important if they are kind. It is also not important if Jazz is transgender or not, it is only important that she is happy and with whom she is most happy (QLF Principle 9). Explain that Jazz felt *supported* because her mother said being different was okay. This made her feel like her mother would support her as a girl. Add the word *supported* to a feeling heart on the character splash.

Read page 19 that begins with "Being Jazz" and ends with "teachers at school." Revisit the word confused. Discuss what clues in the illustration show that other students and the teacher were confused.

3. Character Splash (10 Minutes)

Explain to the students that together they will fill out the character traits section of the character splash (see Chart 4.4 below). Explain that character traits are ways to describe people based on their words and their actions. Use examples of several students from class. For instance, _____ is friendly because he always smiles at other people. _____ is helpful because she likes to help her friends clean up their toys. _____ is trustworthy because he always tells the truth. Explain that characters in books have character traits just like people do. Tell the students that they are going to be detectives and try to find character traits about Jazz. Students should use the words that the authors have given in addition to the pictures that the illustrator has drawn to help figure out her character traits. Then, flip through the book and as the class discovers them together, list the terms on the character splash. Provide justification for the character traits listed under the actions section of the character splash. Next, use the character traits/actions listed below but feel free to personalize it for each group of students.

4. Follow-Up

Scribe the following question on the board, "Why were Jazz's teachers confused?" Remind the students that when Jazz grew out her hair and started growing it long, some people were confused (QLF Principle 3). Ask the students to share out several of their answers and scaffold where necessary. Send the students back to their seats to answer this question and draw a corresponding picture in their journals. It may help to leave the corresponding page in the book on display for the children to reference while they are writing.

Session 4

Prepare Character splash materials such as markers/crayons, cutout feeling hearts, primary writing/drawing paper, or journals with a space for writing and drawing.

1. Finish Book/Vocabulary (17 Minutes)

Read from page 20 where it begins with, "At the beginning of...." Stop to discuss the word normal (call attention to vocabulary display). Explain that feeling normal means feeling things that create comfort or safety.

However, forcing Jazz to use the boys' bathroom or play on the boys' team would not be normal to her because she truly is a girl (QLF Principle 3). Draw the students' attention to the feeling words on the character splash (Chart 4.4). Ask them which one they think applies to how she might be feeling (they might say uncomfortable or devastated). Have them focus on the picture for clues. Point out her body language, the look on her face, and the fact that she is alone. Finish the remainder of the book calling attention to/explaining the vocabulary words tease, ignore, as well as crummy.

2. Character Splash: Character Traits and Actions (5 Minutes)
In the same method as in the previous session, complete the character splash using information about character traits and actions (see Chart 4.5 below).

Jazz Character Splash

Appearance		Feelings
Shoulder length, brown hair		Uncomfortable
Bangs		Devastated
Brown Eyes		Relieved
White headband with yellow	(Picture of Jazz)	Supported
sunflowers		Thrilled
Pink and white striped shirt with		
squiggly stripes		

Interests
Pink, silver, green
Singing
Sports
Make-up and dress-up
Mermaids

Character Traits	Actions
Imaginative	Pretends she is a mermaid
Playful	Has fun with friends
	(dressing up and doing gymnastics)
Artistic	Likes to draw
Authentic	Is herself no matter what

Chart 4.4   Character splash for *I Am Jazz* (sample of what you would expect to have completed at this point in the lesson)

Jazz Character Splash

Appearance		Feelings
Shoulder length, brown hair		Uncomfortable
Bangs		Devastated
Brown Eyes		Relieved
White headband with yellow	(Picture of Jazz)	Supported
sunflowers		Thrilled
Pink and white striped shirt with		
squiggly stripes		

Interests

Pink, silver, green
Singing
Sports
Make-up and dress-up
Mermaids

Character Traits	Actions
Imaginative	Pretends she is a mermaid
Playful	Has fun with friends
Artistic	Likes to draw
Authentic	Is herself no matter what
Brave	Ignores bullies

Chart 4.5   Character splash for *I Am Jazz* (sample of what you would expect to have completed at this point in the lesson)

3. Reread Entire Book (7 Minutes)

It is important to reread the entire book so that the students have the opportunity to hear it in its entirety. After the completion of this lesson, add the book to the classroom library so that students can practice "reading" it on their own.

4. Follow-Up

Ask the students the following question, "How can we be friends with all people, including people who are transgender?" (QLF Principles 9 and 10). Discuss answers to this question with the students. Write some of their suggestions on the board. Ask them to pick one idea and finish the following sentence in their journals/on a piece of paper. They should include an accompanying picture. "I can be friends with transgender people by…" Depending on the level of the class, it may be helpful to write the sentence starter on the board.

THE ROLE OF RECOGNITION IN *I AM JAZZ*

Although the QLF principles can be applied to any text, *I Am Jazz* was deliberately selected for its powerful portrayal of how the recognition gap can impact young trans* children. The title in and of itself offers a poignant reminder to listen to and trust children, however they self-identify. As Miller stressed in the introduction to this book, recognition is essential for those whose gender identity does not conform to the binary. The misrecognition that Jazz suffered in the early years of her life caused her to experience a distress that we as early childhood educators would never wish on our littlest learners. Kindergarten students particularly will resonate with this concept and yearn for acknowledgement and recognition.

These lessons, and others like them, are critical in early childhood education. When children learn at an early age to respect, appreciate, include, support, and celebrate people among the entire gender identity spectrum, incidences of gender policing and bullying in schools can be greatly reduced. However, in these lessons, the *unlearning* of gender norms is even more critical than the *learning* of anti-bias concepts. The disruption of the mundane, the identification of microaggressions, and the sanctioned freedom of gender expression can set gender creative children on a radically different path than the one that has been offered to them in the recent past. The new educational atmosphere born from literacy environments steeped in the QLF will support students toward positive identity development. As educators, that is something we desire for *all* of our children.

NOTES

1. This study was approved by the IRB of Arizona State University.

REFERENCES

Baker, J. M. (2002). *How homophobia hurts children: Nurturing diversity at home, at school, and in the community.* New York: Harrington Park Press.
Butler, J. (2004). *Undoing gender.* New York/London: Routledge.

Butler, J. (2006). *Gender trouble*. New York: Routledge.

Cannella, G., & Viruru, R. (2004). *Childhood and postcolonization*. New York: Routledge.

DePalma, R., & Atkinson, E. (2009). 'No outsiders': Moving beyond a discourse of tolerance to challenge heteronormativity in primary schools. *British Educational Research Journal, 35*(6), 837–855. doi:10.1080/01411920802688705.

Ehrensaft, D. (2012). From gender identity disorder to gender identity creativity. *Presented at the National Workshop on Gender Creative Kids.* Concordia University, Canada. Retrieved from https://www.youtube.com/watch?v=pVt TRDvTYgs&feature=youtu.b

Foucault, M. (1995 [1975]). *Discipline and punish: The birth of the prison* (trans: Alan Sheridan). New York: Vintage Books.

Kitchin, R., & Lysaght, K. (2003). Heterosexism and the geographies of everyday life in Belfast, Northern Ireland. *Environment and Planning, 35*(3), 489–510.

Morrow, D. (2004). Social work practice with gay, lesbian, bisexual, and transgender adolescents. *Families in Society, 85*(1), 91–99.

Norton, J. (1997). "Brain says you're a girl, but I think you're a sissy boy": Cultural origins of transphobia. *Journal of Gay, Lesbian Bisexual Identity, 2*(2), 139–164.

Rowell, E. H. (2007). Missing! picture books reflecting gay and lesbian families. *YC Young Children, 62*(3), 24.

Sullivan, A. L. (2009). *Hiding in the open: Navigating education at the gender poles: A study of transgender children in early childhood* (Order No. 3361853). Available from ProQuest Dissertations & Theses A&I: Social Sciences; ProQuest Education Journals.

CHAPTER 5

Beyond This or That: Challenging the Limits of Binary Language in Elementary Education Through Poetry, Word Art, and Creative Bookmaking

benjamin lee hicks

Queer Literacy Framework Principles:

2. Understanding gender as a construct which has and continues to be impacted by intersecting factors (e.g., social, historical, material, cultural, economic, religious);
5. Opening up spaces for students to self-define with chosen (a)genders, (a)pronouns, or names; and,
8. Understanding that (a)gender intersects with other identities (e.g., sexual orientation, culture, language, age, religion, social class, body type, accent, height, ability, disability, and national origin) that inform students' beliefs and thereby, actions.

b.l. hicks (✉)
Ontario Institute for Studies in Education (OISE), University of Toronto, Toronto, Canada

© The Editor(s) (if applicable) and The Author(s) 2016   81
sj Miller (ed.), *Teaching, Affirming, and Recognizing Trans and Gender Creative Youth*, DOI 10.1057/978-1-137-56766-6_5

What the Body Comes to Believe About Speaking

My own trans* body remembers the depth of tiredness that comes from not understanding how to speak. I remember the futility of trying to splice together fragments of a language that was too limited to tell the story of myself to anyone, including myself. As a child, this took up so much of my own substance that wanting to disappear felt not only natural but also easy, expected, and "right." It has taken a long time to learn that the standards of language were not constructed to include those of us who exist in the in-be-tween, and even longer to understand that this is not something we need to be ashamed of.[1]

We all learn the words that we are to use and the way that we are to use them—*including how loud, how often, and with how much conviction*—in the same way that we learn whether or not we should consider ourselves worthy and deserving of love. As adults who work with children, we have an enormous impact on the shape of that self-belief in every child with whom we are in relationship. We covertly inform them of how they are to identify in relation to the words that we teach with the same intensity that we instruct the more obvious elements of reading, writing and speaking. When the things that we say and do in our classrooms depend entirely on binaries and absolutes, we are actively supporting the privilege of some students at the expense of the life force of others.

The idea that rigid standards and rules of language can provide a viable way for every person to share their story accurately is a myth. In the education system, this fallacy supports the notion that one can teach about storytelling without actually wanting to acknowledge the *whole* truth of our students' experiences.

Teaching the History of "How"

we are taught to disremember these things
that evade collective memory like the origins of the alphabet:
these twenty-six letters that spell
"i forget"

A system of communication is not only a means of relating to others; it is the subconscious crux of everything that our bodies come to believe about speaking and being heard (Hicks 2007). If we are first taught that this system is all hard edges, sharp corners and absolute rules, we are simultaneously ingesting a message that there are distinct limits around what the mind is capable of conceiving and creating; *around what an individual can possibly do and be and become.*

Skipping over the contextual genesis of how the opinions of individuals shift into societal norms is a significant determinant in how human beings learn to shun people and ideas perceived as deviant from these norms. This chronic omission of context is of great relevance for how educators are taught to instruct young children in language development. For example, the current version of the English alphabet is just that; *a version.* These letters look, sound, and stay in the order that they are currently found due to a multitude of factors including politics, religion, art, science, economics, war, genocide, and colonialism. The alphabet that is often taken for granted is a combined product of all that has been documented and/or omitted from the history of the western world (Sacks 2003). We teach very young children a simple rhyming song to learn the letters of the alphabet because that is an easy and adaptive way to retain important information. While there is nothing wrong with the reproduction of this philosophically based pedagogy, it can neglect the impact of how historical context informs what students think and how they learn and communicate. In so doing, teachers become complicit in raising generations of humans who may resist flexible thinking. This example is not so much about teaching the history of the alphabet as it is about considering whether the way that we teach our students to read, write, and speak effectively is working in opposition to our hopes about how they will see, hear, consider, change, respect, include, feel, love, and be recognized more deeply *in* that communication.

Co-constructing a Community Worth Keeping

Sustainable faith in the possibility of community—in an uncompromising foundation of equity that challenges institutionalized oppression in walk as well as talk—must be fueled by love. This is the kind of love that knows you can't really love any other thing or person very deeply unless you practice loving yourself. This is the love that makes kindness and compassion non-negotiable in every relationship, both interpersonal and systemic. I will gift all my professional energies to a love-fueled, in-motion, potentially messy model of change if it can help to unbind generations of polite and static intent.

Any relationship has an effect on the trajectory of its participants. In the case of human beings and their relationship to the system by which they communicate with other humans, this spin-off is exponential (Abley 2003). When we are not taught early on that concepts like "language rules" are in fact the constructs of another fallible human, it becomes increasingly difficult for us to consider that other "absolutes" such as gender, sexuality, race, religion, and ideas about "ability" are far more multifaceted than a binary perspective allows us to see them. Growing up in a system where we are taught to remember rules and recite facts makes it entirely more likely that we will forget how to truly speak authentically. For those who have also been told repeatedly through the violence of words and actions that their skin color, religious beliefs, socio-economic status, differing abilities and/or un-typical gender expression are unwelcome, to speak at all requires more courage and energy than anyone should be expected to muster.

As elementary school educators we can and *should* talk very clearly and directly about all the ways that people are labeled with words that they did not choose for themselves. We should have deep and honest discussions with students of all ages about what it means to identify as *both/and/either/ or/neither/beyond/between* in any number of contexts. Simultaneously, we need to actively model how one might curiously, kindly, and respectfully question the labels that they are given which are not expansive enough to support their whole selves. What better way to show trans* and gender creative kids who will spend their whole lives working to find stability in change that *we believe in their magic?*

This belief is the space where poetry, word art, and creative bookmaking can facilitate dynamic growth in elementary school classrooms. When this content is taught in the context of the QLF (Miller 2015) the stories of trans* and gender creative kids will finally have the opportunity to rise up with them.

THE PLACE OF POETRY AND WORD ART IN A QUEER LITERACY FRAMEWORK

i imagine that there is a place just behind my eyes where poetry occurs.
that there is no need for forgiveness here,
because there has been no such thing as harm.
there is no mis-directed, re-enacting, side-ways-shooting energy that

was–is–will–be shame or hate or blame and as such;
there is still all the time and space in the universe for story-telling that is
the coming together of beginnings, endings and in-be-tweens.

Poetry and word art are variations of storytelling to which I owe my life many times over because they have gifted me with possibility. As a child, it was inside of these continuums that I first found evidence of fluidity. No one taught me when I was young that I could be anything other than what their words said I was, but the secrets I intuited through language-that-was-also-art gifted me with enough connection to trans*formation that even when I couldn't feel why, I still knew that there was reason enough to stay. Adding, subtracting, and recombining fragments of words through poetry felt like a second chance... *felt like transition*. Just as the physical bits of my body did not match the way that my spirit functions in relation to other people's constructs of gender, the standards of language that I was born into did not match the way that my story can be told. Poetry is the closest that I have come to remembering—*honoring*—with every last word-and-breath that much more than one thing can be "true" at the same time.

we do not have many words in this english language for the in-be-tween.
we have a lot for 'this' and for 'that'
and for 'either' and 'other' and 'or'
but when it comes to trying to tell the story of an experience which exists in
several places and spaces of the spiral consciousness at the same time;
*which is not only **both** but also **and***
it is what we name "poetry" that comes closest for me.

Creative Bookmaking as Transformative Act

Words are inherently dynamic entities whose contexts can be reclaimed creatively, progressively, and politically in order to tell our stories in ways that are more relevant to the diversity of our experiences.

Take the word "*book*" for example: ***Book*** is a word that we automatically implicate as something that is fixed and stationary by putting it in the category of "noun." We are given innumerable books to read throughout our lives and, because we are rarely told otherwise, we come to believe that the object itself is as indisputable as the stories, facts, and ideas contained within. If the seemingly innocuous word "book" can contain so much of someone else's agenda for how individuals should think, learn, and behave, imagine for a moment how heavily words like *girl* or *boy* weigh on a young person whose truest knowledge of themselves includes bits of "girl" and "boy" and "both" and "neither" and more things existing between...

Now, imagine what might happen if we were to teach our students about the innumerable creative ways that books can be constructed and deconstructed to form stages for our stories; and, about what it would mean if a "book" were also a verb and an active and dynamic partner in the process of language learning. It is from within these convergences that the potential of bookmaking as a creative practice meets poetry and word art, and intersects most potently with social justice education. This intersection is a method that can both support and celebrate messages of resistance, creative reformation, and above all—*hope*.

To give our students and ourselves permission to consider the beautiful complexities of our lives through creative language learning is also about teaching the importance of expending energy in the direction of things that are hope-*full*. *Things like change.* To change the place that words like "inclusivity" and "acceptance" hold in the education system from abstract concepts to non-negotiable actions, we must also reimagine the ways that we will care for one another and ourselves sustainably in this process.

PREPARATION: INTENTIONAL COMMUNITY BUILDING

> *i remember what it feels like to be left alone in body-memories of non-existence.*
> *i remember and so, i have learned to carry the words of my story just as close*
> *as words like sustainable, like community,*
> **like love.**
> *sometimes too close, and sometimes just close enough, but in truth*
> *i am tired of deciding which is what.*
> **this** *is why i write poetry.*

I have found it helpful to redefine "sustainability" as something that is continuously self-reflective, changing, learning, and growing. Growth need not be seen as only a forward or upward movement, but rather as the combined time and space where learning emerges from the experience of making mistakes. Such possibilities present critical developmental possibilities to inform both personal and systemic integrity. In a classroom community context then, all members should be taught and encouraged to support one another in this process—and ultimately to recognize and be recognized by the other (Miller, this volume, Chap. 1).

The Explicit Teaching of Love

A priori, every living being is entitled to respect. Trust, on the other hand, can and should be earned through time, attention, and effort. If educators are truly invested in building an authentic, sustainable, and loving community with their students, the two must go hand in hand. When I speak of "loving community" in the classroom, I am thinking about the kind of explicit teaching of love that bell Hooks (2000) calls for when she writes, "Had I been given a clear definition of love earlier in my life, it would not have taken me so long to become a more loving person. Had I shared with others a common understanding of what it means to love it would have been easier to create love" (p. 11).

I am writing about trust and love in the "preparation" section of this curriculum because the way that this material works in classrooms can impact students' feelings of safety and as a result, their willingness to share their most genuine selves with one another and with the teacher. In any classroom that I teach, ranging in grade level from kindergarten to grade six, I spend at least two weeks at the beginning of the new school year working through intentional community building activities with my students. However one chooses to go about community building, the intentional and collaborative construction of a loving, supportive classroom community (Palmer 2007) will save immeasurable time and energy when you begin to work more continuously with the Queer Literacy Framework (Miller 2015). Taking care to consider the interior lives, social realities, and feelings of all students is not something to find time for in addition to the "regular" curriculum. These, I proffer are inseparable.

The Lesson Plan: Challenging the Limits of Binary Language Through Poetry, Word Art, and Creative Bookmaking—A Lesson in Four Parts

society likes its certainty;
its binaries and boxes and exactitudes.
but when society gets that certainty, we lose our revolutionaries.
*when society gets its proof for all of the **how** and **why** and **what** are you?*
we lose our light,
our capacity to love more deeply, and
our actually different ways of seeing, of doing, and of be-ing in the world.

General Introduction

These lesson plans are very much a beginning. They are the first few sentences of a dialog that I hope will be taken up by teachers and then evolve organically through careful listening, observation, and direct responsive action to student needs. The activities presented here are an invitation to continue to empirically observe the immense potential that bookmaking as a creative practice has for increasing student engagement and inclusivity in any subject taught.

The processes of free-form poetry, word art, and creative book construction are forms of language learning which are open ended enough that when teachers employ them in the context of the QLF, they can facilitate the empowerment of student thinking and foster radical self-acceptance and self-definition as well as the unconditional support of this right for others (Principle 5). The group discussions and collaborative work described in lessons one and two resist the tendency of the education system to "essentialize student identities, (and recognizes instead) how intersections of sexual orientation, culture, language, age, religion, social class, body type, accent, height, ability, disability, and national origin, inform students' beliefs and thereby, actions" (Miller 2015) (Principle 8). As the students progress toward more independent work in lessons three and four, the decisions that they make for how their own self-identity will be communicated visually in words, shapes, colors, and page-construction become opportunities to explore, question, and understand more about the ways that many intersecting factors of their identity, including gender, are constructed (Miller 2015) (Principle 2).

The plan is organized into four parts for ease of explanation, but those parts could be further divided or more compactly combined to suit each class's needs. I have written about these lessons with my most recent grade three/four class in mind, but that group of students also included literacy levels ranging from prekindergarten to grade five. As such, I have included a few notes on differentiated instruction to explain what worked well for those who struggle with reading and writing as well as those on the very advanced end of the spectrum.

Assessment

Please consider using these lessons as a continuous process rather than as a series of instructions for assessment. At the onset of this work, there is great value in stepping back from the direct assessment of individual literacy skills and instead focusing attention on each child's comfort level about sharing more of their true selves with others. Some possible considerations for authentic and liberatory (Miller 2008) assessment include:

- Whose voices dominate the discussions and whose are missing?
- What do these observations suggest about the culture of the classroom community?
- What would it be like to work **with** your own students to co-create an assessment process for the dynamics of the classroom community while simultaneously undertaking these activities?

However the teacher proceeds, I encourage you to also reflexively consider answers to these questions.

Part One: "Most-Me" Show and Share

a letter is a situation,
its shape, the sound of centuries shifting.
a letter is more than the words that we name,
as all things are more than the names we call words.

Preparation

In advance of this first lesson, discuss the idea of "most-me" with your students.

Most-me is an idea that I first introduced in a set of LGBTQI-inclusive Physical Health Education lesson plans that I developed for my grade six class in 2011. The term refers to the truest-feeling way that we can find to describe ourselves. It is permission to give back all of the labels that are put on us by others and to recognize and celebrate our own uniqueness. A *most-me object* is a personal item of any description that can be used to help describe how one identifies oneself most accurately. A couple of days in advance of the lesson start date, send home a note to families explaining the idea of the *most-me object* and ask that all students choose something that they would like to bring in and share on the day that you expect to begin.

Materials
 - 8.5″ × 11″ paper (or similar) in a variety of colors
 - markers
 - a class set of scissors
 - *most-me* objects brought to school by class members

Suggested Timing

Timing for this section will depend on the size of a class. As a general guideline, allow 5 minutes per student as well as an extra 15 minutes for the introductory process and 15 minutes for conclusions. For larger classes, this may be an activity that can be spread over subsequent days.

Activity Description

This lesson begins with a discussion about the idea of *most-me*. For instance, I first ask the students what they think these words mean and from there the conversation develops based on their responses. Some additional questions that can be useful are:

- Who do you think gets to decide what is "most-you"? Why do you think this?
- Have you ever had someone else try to tell you who you are and what you should like? If so, what did that feel like? Is it always a negative feeling?
- What factors might change what a person chooses to share about themselves?

To continue, I model the process of a show and share by talking about my own *most-me* object first. I describe what it is, how it looks to me, and why I chose to bring it to represent who I believe I am. This sharing helps to break the ice and provides a concrete example for students to follow. While I am sharing, I write down key words from my description on a piece of 8.5″ × 11″ colored paper (see Fig. 5.1).

Each student, in succession, has the opportunity to share a *most-me* object with the class and I continue in the role of recording key words from their descriptions on colored paper. Once all the objects have been shared and these initial words have been recorded, I ask a couple more questions of the whole group;

- Was it easy or hard for you to share what you like about this object? If so, explain? (*the general consensus is usually "easy" which leads into the next question);
- Is it easier or harder for you to say kind/complimentary things about yourself?

Fig. 5.1 Documenting key words from student descriptions of "most-me" objects (Photo credit: Grace Yogaretnam)

- Why do you think this is? (again—general consensus is usually "harder")

At this point, I will often mention that these objects they have been describing as "beautiful" or "shiny" or "amazing" are also the things that they chose to represent themselves, *even if these words are much easier to give to an object than to themselves.* The conversation may then turn to how it can be easier to say honest and kind words about our friends than ourselves. To finish off this portion of the lesson, I invite the students to gift one another with words that speak of the positive things others see in them. I add these words to each child's paper as they are gifted and when the whole class is finished with their offerings, students help to prepare for the next part of the lesson by cutting apart their paper into individual word strips that can then be repurposed and shared among the group.

Differentiation for This Lesson
I have invited students who benefit from further enrichment to support their classmates with this activity in a number of ways, including:

- Working alongside me to document the "most-me" keywords that are shared by other students
- Meeting one-on-one with a student who has high anxiety with group work prior to the class discussion to assist them in articulating their thoughts

These pairings may result in various levels of support ranging from "practice" speaking their ideas out loud, to writing out a complete list of ideas that is shared with the class on their behalf.

Part Two: Collaborative Poetry: Who Are WE?

*a word is a modular unit, a tree
and each letter should breathe
like the universe expanding.*

Preparation
For the second lesson, a large floor or table space is needed for the entire class to be able to comfortably sit around. This is where the cut up word papers can be spread out for easy access and use by everyone during the composition process.

Materials
- all of the words precut from colored paper during part one of this lesson
- more blank paper strips and markers

Suggested Timing
60–90 minutes

Activity Description
Students will now be working together to co-create a free-form poem about the identity of your classroom community. The poem will be composed mainly of the words generated during the *most-me* show and share process, but it is also a good idea to have some blank paper strips on hand for any additional words that the students want to add in. There is no real recipe to ensure that this process works perfectly. However it plays out, collaborative poetry is a great opportunity to practice active listening, turn taking, and compromising skills as students work together to suggest lines and try out variations until something that everyone feels good being a part of begins to develop (see Fig. 5.2).

Differentiation
I will often ask students on an enriched learning plan to help my non-readers identify the words and ideas that are important to them. If students work better in smaller groups, it is also possible to do this part of the lesson with the class split into several mixed-ability groups. The teacher's role is then to rotate between each group and offer support if needed. Once all the collective poems are complete, come back together as a class and have each group share and discuss what they have composed. Full classes may then wish to work together to combine portions of each of these small group poems into one big collaborative piece.

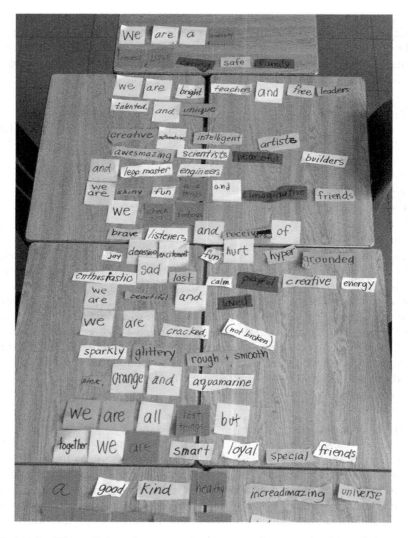

Fig. 5.2 The collaborative poem in process of my grade three/four class (2015)

Part Three: Individual Poetry: Who Am I?

a tree grows in more than one way,
like a word
when the cells shift or parts
break through layers to re-form.

Preparation

I generally do this portion of the lesson on a new day because the preparations are a bit more labor intensive. First, to create a template that contains all of the words generated in part one of this lesson, I write these out very neatly on a white sheet of copier paper in the equivalent of about 24 font size, but typing is of course an option. For my younger groups, I also draw lines between all of the words so that even if they are struggling with reading they still know where to cut (see Fig. 5.3).

Materials

   – one sheet of 8.5″ × 14″ paper per class member
   – one photocopy of the word list template per student
   – pencils, erasers, coloring mediums, scissors, and glue sticks

Suggested Timing
90–120 minutes

Activity Description

Begin by showing students how to fold their sheet of 8.5″ × 14″ paper into three equal sections (8.5″ × 5.3″ each). This little fold-out book will be their word-canvas for this composition.

Students now have the opportunity to work on their own, using only the words that they personally choose, to compose a story of "self." Each student will receive a photocopied list of the same words that were used in the group process to get them started and are then free to add or omit any that they choose (see Fig. 5.4).

The goal at this stage is for each student to compose a self-identity poem on the threefold paper and to title and illustrate the finished product as time permits (see Fig. 5.5).

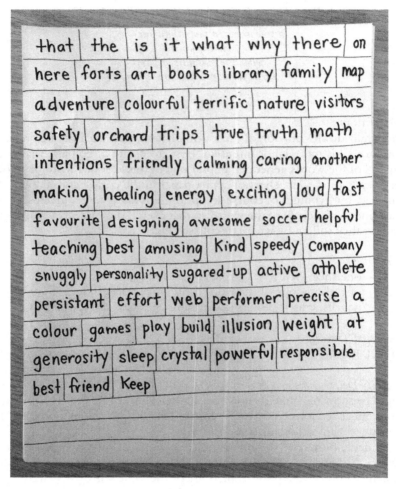

Fig. 5.3   One page of the template containing all the words that were generated in part one of this lesson

Differentiation

Many students who have difficulty writing really enjoy this activity because it relieves the pressure of getting ideas out of their heads and onto paper in decipherable spelling. Instead, they are invited to just "play" with the mountain of cut up words before them. As one such grade four student reported, *"This big*

Fig. 5.4 Sebastian (grade four) choosing the words that he will use to compose his self-identity poem (Photo credit: Grace Yogaretnam)

pile of words is both scary and exciting!" On the same day, a gifted grade three student remarked, *"I like taking these ideas and then free-handing the poems best. It is like free-handing drawings. It is more creative."* If they don't end up using a single one of the cut-up words in their final poem but still manage to write something genuine and original, that is completely fine.[2]

Part Four: Word-Art Mini-Books

> *i want for words that are more like their letters,*
> *and less like a system of trying to define.*

Preparation
For younger children and/or those with fine motor delays, I would suggest premaking some blank mini-books in advance of this lesson. Please see Fig. 5.6 for instructions on folding these simple books and/or refer to

Fig. 5.5 Jade's completed self-identity poem booklet: interior view (grade three)

the link provided in the references section of this chapter (Snyder 2005). Teachers may also wish to make an example book to demonstrate ways that a student could use extra bits of paper and cardboard to alter the form and shape of their book if they choose.

Materials
- one prefolded mini-book per class member
- pencils, erasers, coloring mediums, scissors, and glue sticks
- scraps of paper in various colors, textures, and weights

Suggested Timing
The activity can span from a couple of hours to a couple of days on this section of the project. As always; *adapt as needed and wanted to your particular situation.*

Activity Description
For this mini-book, students will use the self-identity poem that they composed in part three as their base text and then continue to expand

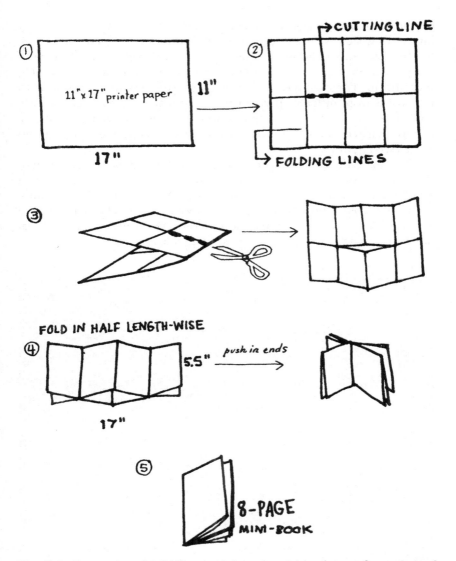

Fig. 5.6 Instructions for folding an eight-page mini-book out of one piece of 11″×17″ paper (Graphic: benjamin lee hicks)

on the space that they have opened for themselves here to explore many intersecting factors and aspects of their identities (QLF, Principles 2 & 8). Teachers might choose to give little to no instruction at this stage of the project, or they can offer a few instructions and parameters to help them begin. For example, I recently asked students to choose four to five words from different parts of their poem that they felt particularly connected to. I then demonstrated how one might turn a word into a picture that tells more of its personal meaning than the letters could do alone (see Fig. 5.7).

The suggestion was to then spread these word drawings through the pages of the blank mini-book and to write the rest of the poem in around them. This creative variation also led to lots of other exciting departures from a more traditional book format, such as flip-out pages to accommodate extra-long words, and windows cut through pages to reveal double meanings and hidden gems (see Fig. 5.8).

Fig. 5.7 Ji-Hoo's word-art version of "BRIGHT ENERGY" integrated into the first page of her identity-poem mini-book (grade three)

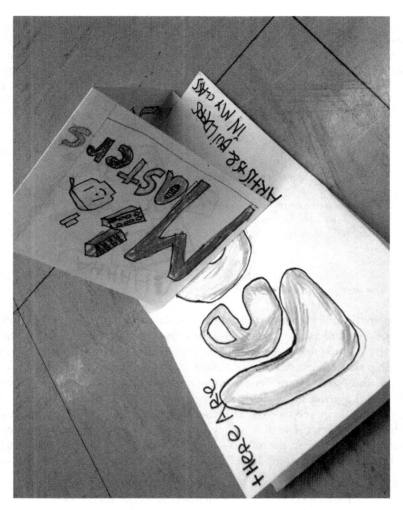

Fig. 5.8 Sebastian's mini-book with the line "there are Lego masters, artists and builders in my class," enhanced by a fold-out section of word art that itself becomes a structure (grade four)

Differentiation
These mini-books are a great opportunity for students who are not reading and/or writing independently to have more creative independence.

They can forgo the rewrite of their entire poem text in favor of creating a visual and tactile book composed only of the words that hold the greatest personal importance to them. For students who appreciate an additional challenge, try introducing them to more advanced book construction techniques (Laplantz 2001) and later create opportunities for them to share their learnings with the class.

Sustainable Change Is Slow...

the words to tell our stories have been so scarce;
so scarce and so, so sacred,
that we have planted and tended to every single one of them ourselves.
we have cultivated every tiny, precious piece of knowing
so that every single one of us can really know what it tastes, sounds, looks, feels
like
to build something real.
because you know; that is how we are still here at all,
and here is a gift that we have fought forever to learn how to give ourselves.

The North American education system is built upon binaries (Jung 1969). It does not fully serve anyone who is not exclusively "this *or* that," which negates a whole lot of people when we include how race, ethnicity, citizenship status, socioeconomics, sexuality, and ability intersect with gender in this discussion about better supporting and celebrating continuums of identity. Layering ideas about *un*gendering on top of these divisive constructs can help keep kids safer in the short run, but should not be considered synonymous with actual systemic reformation. To make positive, sustainable change in our schools means letting go of our own guilt and/or fears about "not doing it well," or "not knowing how to begin."

Transformative Learning Begins with You

remember that people are beauty-full creatures,
both needing/not-wanting to be seen.

Allowing ourselves as educators to celebrate that we are still and always learning (and that there is actually something essential and beautiful about this) is an act of integrity that helps make transformative education possible. In theory, this shift is about recognizing that the individual is the only person who truly has the power to determine what kind of force one wants to be and enact in the world. In more practical terms, it is about taking the time to get to know and then to challenge one's own strengths, fears, and gaps in understanding. As we both individually and collectively allow ourselves this level of emotional honesty, we can shift our perception of the things that we do not know from "weaknesses" into dynamic opportunities that deepen our professional practice.

Practical Strategies for a Self-Reflective Teaching Practice

Integrating reflexive practice into each teaching day *is* an excellent way to maintain this awareness. While it helps to be familiar with the material that we are teaching, one needn't be an expert other than to be present and conscious while preparing and presenting a lesson. The form that this process takes is much less important than whether the reflection is occurring intentionally, consistently, and in a format that feels helpful to self and other.

In my own practice, I have developed a daily photographic and written reflection process that is derivative of Emergent Curriculum and the Reggio Emilia approach to early childhood education (Gandini et al. 2005; Wein 2008). I have maintained this practice in a variety of forms over the past eight years and it is a continuous and invaluable reminder that I cannot teach anything effectively without responding directly to the needs, interests, and experiences of the specific children in front of me.

THOUGHTS FOR BEGINNING AGAIN

What would it be like to pay more direct attention to the education of hearts in elementary education?...

In order to help sustain the work of intentional community building that we have been contemplating throughout this chapter, we also need to commit to a recognizable, visible, and uncompromising process of reconnection with our students, our colleagues, our broader school communities, and ourselves.

The direct anti-transphobia, anti-homophobia, and bullying prevention work that is starting to happen in public education desperately needs to be done more consistently and overtly in order to help affirm and support queer, trans*, and gender creative kids who are being hurt by the system as it is right now (Kosciw et al. 2014; Meyer in press; Miller et al. 2013; Blackburn et al. 2010). In the primary grades particularly, where the majority of our direct teaching time is dedicated to language acquisition and application, use of the Queer Literacy Framework (Miller 2015) must subvert form as well as content. It is our responsibility to craft messages of fluidity and personal choice as we teach our students how to think critically about the world so that they can begin to *"imagine a world where anyone can safely, and even joyfully, express themselves in the way they have always wanted to"* (Bornstein 2006)

Let us also acknowledge that the act of *"imagining a world"* where daily hurt and alienation does not exist can be a lonely and vulnerable task for someone who has never experienced a safe, consistent, and supportive community. This is another important reason why this lesson plan is merely a beginning and should always be paired with genuine community-building work. We must be tireless in our optimism, but also in our practical efforts, our self-care, and our support of one another as allies in this work.

Earlier in my own process of gender transition, I wrote a poem that concluded with the words, *"every living thing, at every living moment, is ALL-ways in transition."* I bring myself back to this combination of words frequently because they are a sweet reminder that change is both inevitable and beauty-full. If we can do nothing more specific in our own teaching practice than to share that simple truth with our students every day through all that we say and do, we are already helping to grow a generation of young people who will be better able to recognize, accept, affirm, and celebrate their own lives as well as those of trans*, (a)gender, and gender independent people.

NOTES

1. My poetry has been woven throughout this chapter to braid these ideas together and to model how words-as-poetry become more than the sum of their standard definitions. Poems are word paintings that can help to describe our experiences as feelings and connections as opposed to chronologies alone.

2. * Special Thanks: A very big thanks goes to Toronto artist, writer, and activist Anna Camilleri for generously sharing her introductory activities for teaching free-form poetry, which inspired parts 2 and 3 of this lesson plan.

To learn more about the work that Anna has done with *The Triangle Program*—an alternative high school program for LGBTQ youth (Camilleri 2013)—as well as with my own class of grade 2–3 students (Camilleri 2014), please see the references section of this chapter.

REFERENCES

Abley, M. (2003). *Spoken here: Travels among threatened languages*. Toronto: Random House Canada.

Blackburn, M. V., Clark, C. T., Kenney, L. M., & Smith, J. M. (2010). *Acting out: Combating homophobia through teacher activism*. New York: Teacher's College Press.

Bornstein, K. (2006). *101 alternatives to suicide for teens, freaks and other outlaws*. New York: 7 Stories Press.

Camilleri, A. (2013). *Triangle Program Zine Projects: 2011*, www.youtube.com/watch?v=rMFrNjH1SSQ

Camilleri, A. (2014, April 14). *Winchester Park Public Art Project: Dispatch #4*, www.reddressproductions.blogspot.ca/2014/04/the-winchester-park-public-art-project_21.html

Gandini, L., Hill, L., Cadwell, L., & Schwall, C. (2005). *In the spirit of the studio: Learning from the atelier of Reggio Emilia*. New York: Teacher's College Press.

Hicks, H. (2007). You are a girl: An installation of mixed-media print, drawing and painting. *International Feminist Journal of Politics, 9*(3), 410–420.

Hooks, B. (2000). *All about love: New visions*. New York: Harper Perennial.

Jung, C. (1969). *Archetypes and the collective unconscious: Collected works of C.G. Jung, Volume 9 (Part 1)*. Princeton: Princeton University Press.

Kosciw, J. G., Greytak, E. A., Palmer, N. A., & Boesen, M. J. (2014). *The 2013 National School Climate Survey: The experiences of lesbian, gay, bisexual and transgender youth in our nation's schools*. New York: GLSEN.

Laplantz, S. (2001). *The art and craft of handmade books*. New York: Lark Books.

Meyer, E. J., Tilland-Stafford, A., & Airton, L. (in press). Supporting transgender and gender-creative youth: What we can learn from their teachers. *Teachers College Record*.

Miller, S. (2008). Liberating grades/liberatory assessment. *International Journal of Critical Pedagogy, 1*(2), 160–171.

Miller, S. (2015). A queer literacy framework promoting (a)gender and (a)sexuality self-determination and justice. *English Journal, 104*(5), 37–44.

Miller, S., Burns, L., & Johnson, T. S. (2013). *Generation BULLIED 2.0: Prevention and intervention strategies for our most vulnerable students*. New York: Peter Lang.

Palmer, P. (2007). *The courage to teach: Exploring the inner landscape of a teacher's life*. SanFrancisco: Jossey Bass.

Sacks, D. (2003). *Language visible: Unraveling the history of the alphabet from A to Z*. New York: Broadway Books.

Snyder, M. (2005). *Fiji Island Mermaid Press: How to make an 8-page book out of a single sheet of paper*. http://www.fimp.net/makeabook.html

Wein, C. (2008). *Emergent curriculum in the primary classroom: Interpreting the Reggio Emilia approach in schools*. New York: Teacher's College Press.

CHAPTER 6

The Teacher as a Text: Un-centering Normative Gender Identities in the Secondary English Language Arts Classroom

Kate E. Kedley

Queer Literacy Framework Principles:

2. Understands gender as a construct that has and continues to be affected by intersecting factors (e.g., social, historical, materials, cultural, economic, religious);
3. Recognizes that masculinity and femininity constructs are assigned to gender norms and are situationally performed; and,
4. Understands gender and sexuality as flexible.

INTRODUCTION: QLF AND TEACHER AS TEXT

Teachers at the front of classrooms are "read" and "made legible" by students as they teach and interact with them formally and informally. Through these interactions, students tend to make assumptions about

K.E. Kedley
University of Iowa, Iowa City

© The Editor(s) (if applicable) and The Author(s) 2016   107
sj Miller (ed.), *Teaching, Affirming, and Recognizing Trans and Gender Creative Youth*, DOI 10.1057/978-1-137-56766-6_6

their teacher's gender and sexuality. Through readings of the teachers' clothing, hair styles, mannerisms, and actions, students gauge their teachers' levels of femininity, masculinity, and their sexuality (or the gender to which they assume the teacher is attracted to). They learn what gender is not through textbooks or class discussion but from interactions with other gendered beings, including teachers. If someone's gender or sexuality is not immediately "readable," students often go to great lengths to "discover" it. They ask others if the person in question is gay; they whisper in hushed tones to each other about seeing them in public with another man or with another woman. They continue this line of inquiry until the person's gender and sexuality are clearly resolved and readable. What is so compelling about reading and reconciling (and resolving) the gender and sexuality of others? What is it about unreadable teachers and students that prompts these inquiries?

Building from these *a priori* inquiries, the objective of this chapter is to prompt discussion about ways to push back on socially defined limits of (a)gender in Secondary English Language Arts (SELA) classrooms by seeing the teacher as a text (Clark 2010). Our current conceptions of gender are limiting for both teachers and students, and as possible sites for disruption, the SELA classroom can either perpetuate or challenge normative gender categories. Such classrooms contribute to a narrowing of the gender binary when they do not include a space to discuss multiplicities of (a)gender options, and when literacy teachers inadvertently endorse these strict limits by ignoring the presence of alternative (a)gender configurations. This begets the following questions: Do literacy teachers discuss (a)gender diversity and recognition within reading, writing, and speaking activities? In what ways do teachers position themselves and each other within the limits of the gender binary? SELA classrooms need to facilitate critical discussions of (a)gender using the texts already inherent in the space, including recognizing the teacher as a text that is read by students.

In an effort then to actively challenge this normative category, I draw on the intersection of QLF (Miller 2015) and teacher as text (Clark 2010). The rationale for this work builds from my own personal teaching experience as a SELA teacher, my educational history, and on my prior inability to take risks and engage with the topic of (a)gender diversity.

UNDERSTANDING OF GENDER INDOCTRINATION

(A)gender self-determination and social recognition of others' (a)gender put us in a bit of a paradox. Our self-determination is partially dependent on social norms and socially constructed configurations of (a)gender and (a)sexuality (Butler 2004; Miller, this volume, Chap. 2). From within this paradox, I offer the suggestion to read the teacher as a text. These ideas are based on the fact that, currently, there are few gender configurations that allow us to be recognized as "readable" and "legible" to others. We are taught to read others as either male or female, and we are told there is no possibility that a person could be both or neither, or some combination of the two. If someone is not "readable," we work to "discover" their gender within that binary.

In order to allow more space for students to self-determine their (a)gender and to be recognized as such by teachers and classrooms, I offer suggestions about how to enlarge the classroom space for what is "readable" and what is considered "legible" in terms of (a)gender. As a result, students will learn that there are options beyond the male and female binary and that they need not be relegated to one or the other.

While we have a deeply rooted history of gender based on two configurations—man and woman—our options for how we can understand (a)gender is shifting. As groups within society actively resist social hierarchies and create visibility and space for themselves and others, teachers need to be open to such shifts that account for the larger choice in (a)gender self-determination and recognition.

For students, current gender configurations can be oppressive. To free all students and teachers from oppressive gender norms, schools and society need to make space for (a)gender self-determination to be actualized (Miller, this volume, Chap. 2). These shifts must expand what is currently understood as gender "normative" and move from margin to center in genuine and authentic ways. This provokes the following questions: How do we, as teachers, react when a student has an "unreadable" gender in our classroom? How do we provide students and classrooms with more (a)gender options, outside of male and female? Taken together, the QLF and teacher as text present tools for gender flexibility and for a constant reconfiguration and reimagination of (a)genders.

MOVING GENDER FLEXIBILITY INTO THE ELA CLASSROOMS

I primarily draw on three principles of the QLF: 2, 3, and 4 (Miller 2015). Principle 2 suggests we understand that gender is a construct that forever has been and continues to be impacted by other cultural factors. "Woman," for example, has been defined differently across time and space. Woman does not mean the same thing today as it did centuries ago, and the role and position of "woman" in society has changed as well (and varies even in the same region depending on culture, race, religion, class, etc.). With the recent media presence of transwomen such as Laverne Cox, Janet Mock, and Caitlin Jenner, our limits for understanding gender are shifting, even as historically we were reluctant to believe that gender is flexible. Even so, there are still questions and limitations about what makes a "real" man or a "real" woman, what it means when someone is a combination of both or neither, or what gender is in the first place. Therefore, Principle 2 is used in this chapter to push back on current definitions of man and woman, expand who can be readable in those positions, and develop conceptions that reject a simple binary and are more inclusive of multiple, or even an infinite amount of, (a)genders.

Principle 3 recognizes that even though society has been primarily conditioned to see gender and gender expressions as binary (as either male/masculine or female/feminine, but never both nor neither, and certainly without overlap), in reality, these norms are situationally performed by everyone, including non-trans* identified people. Principle 3 reminds us to point out those places in which gender is not performed normatively (and when it is) and ask each other what should be done with that information: How do people make themselves readable or not? How do teachers subconsciously police students who try to subvert the traditional gender binary by coercing them to return to the binary with comments, jokes, suggestions, and praise? How do readings of students—as either male or female—remove students' opportunities for (a)gender determination? Principle 3 reminds teachers to recognize that students situationally perform gender. Students and teachers alike may perform femininity and masculinity differently in the classroom than when they are at home or with groups of friends, for example. Recognition of those shifts in gender is paramount to recognizing that the binary doesn't exist in the way we endorse it.

Principle 4 understands that gender is flexible. Gender is flexible in individuals and is flexible across regions and cultures. This principle prompts teachers to acknowledge that the categories described as "normal" for feminine and masculine are very rarely met by anyone, at every point of their life. If gender is not regarded as flexible, social norms tend toward the binary. For instance, if someone presents as outside the binary and challenges dominant perceptions, macroaggressions (such as laws, rules, and cultural norms) and microaggressions (such as teasing, comments on gender, and assumptions) and biased beliefs tend to police a person into gender "normalcy."

Combined, these three principles inform my understanding of how a QLF can be used to view the teacher as a text in a literacy classroom in order to challenge normative gender categories.

Queer Theory in the English Language Arts Classroom

Queer theory is not one unified field of study (Britzman 1995; Butler 1990, 1993, 2004; Sedgwick 1990; Sykes 2011). There are, a number of components I borrow from different interpretations of queer theory of and I will briefly touch on for the sake of clarification. These components are parallel to Principles 2, 3, and 4 of the QLF and influence my understanding of the social and political categories of (a)gender in the SELA.

Queer theory allows teachers and students to shift the focus from trans* and gender creatively identified students (or LGBT-identified, more generally) to all students. Queer theory suggests that gender (and sex and sexuality) categories are "messy, slippery and always in flux" (Ryan and Hermann-Wilmarth 2013, p. 145). Queer theory asserts that there is no natural linkage between sex, gender, and sexuality (Butler 1990, 1993, 2004), even though there is often assumed to be. A person assigned female at birth is no more inclined to be feminine than they would be inclined to be masculine, (a)gender, gender creative, gender flexible, genderqueer, or a plethora of other options (or heterosexual, homosexual, bisexual, etc.). A person who is masculine is not more suited to heterosexuality than homosexuality, and masculinity is not related to assignment at birth of male or female. The presumed "normative" link is influenced by social constructions of feminine and masculine. Even as our culture is becoming increasingly more accepting of different (a)gender and (a)sexual identities, they are rarely accepted as "normal." When they are accepted, they are still seen as a secondary alternative rather than something that naturally occurs.

Students typically arrive in school with a limited experience of teachers as active participants in gender deconstruction. In fact, as teachers reinforce these seemingly permanent and naturally existing binaries, students begin to experience a psychic split between what they have come to know about their (a)gender from social media, peer groups, and parents. Teachers can disrupt and show the gender binary as temporal (Butler 1990) and highlight that female masculinity, male femininity, or other gender configurations are accepted culturally. This deepens the recognition and affirmation of the (a)gender realities of all students. In so doing, they generate a recognition that not all students live according to "normative" conceptions of gender identifiers.

Rationale: The QLF and Teachers as a Text in the English Language Arts Classroom

I have been a SELA and college-level English instructor for nearly 15 years. As I look back on my first years of teaching, it is hard to immediately recall instances of when gender and sexual diversity issues came up in my classroom. I didn't assign books or introduce topics that would have created a space for discussion about gender and sexual diversity. I was never quite comfortable when students brought up questions in front of the class or when they asked my opinion about gay marriage, transgender issues, or the pending formation of a Gay-Straight Alliance. In terms of my own sexuality, I've neither been out nor closeted, but my gender has always been presented in a way that students "read" as non-normative. I generally don't "out" myself or directly say I identify as queer or trans*, but I don't hide parts of my life that would make that otherwise known.

Teacher Reticence and Teacher as Text

That being said, I thought a "neutral" stance was appropriate. Had I had a more critical educational foundation about issues related to gender and sexuality, I would have realized how problematic such perspectives were. In retrospect, I was uncomfortable with these topics when I taught because I didn't think I knew enough to support students in their desires to talk openly. I was concerned that some students might tell their parents what we were talking about. I feared someone might use a slur, and I wasn't equipped to handle that effectively. I was concerned that conversations might even move out of my own comfort zone as a teacher. Regardless of the teacher's (a)gender identity, these are discussions and negotiations that come up in every literacy classroom.

Even with all of that going on, my initial perception was that these discussions weren't happening in my classroom or even in the school, or, if they were, they were mostly under the radar. My instinct at the time was to contain these discussions in a space where I was comfortable, which was (a)gender topic avoidance. Over time, I began thinking of ways I could be a more effective teacher regarding the topic of (a)gender diversity. Rather than avoiding it, I wondered, how could I support my students in understanding gender norms and the multiple pathways to their deconstruction? I wondered, how I could allow students to read me as a text, one that upended rather than supported the gender binary? The strategies I suggest come from these reflections.

As I continue to reflect on my past teaching, topics related to gender were ever present in my classroom, even as I tried to temper their entry. With the benefit of time and experience, I realized that there was a contradiction between a teacher who wanted to avoid the topic of gender and the students who continually attempted to bring this topic into the center of classroom.

To try to handle the internal cleft I felt, I distanced myself from students' queries. For instance, when I asked students to write persuasive essays defending "traditional" marriage, I didn't offer constructive criticism the way I would have with other topics. Beyond my classroom, students asked me in front of the class if I thought some teachers in the school were gay. Out of respect to my colleagues' privacy, I ignored those queries, neither confirming nor rejecting their suspicions. Even when students pushed me more on this topic and inquired about teacher's "roommates"—when I actually *knew* their gender identity or sexual orientation but kept quiet—I diverted inquires back to themselves by asking them how they might feel if someone asked about their gender or sexual orientation identities. Because of my trepidations in dealing with gender and sexuality, coupled with how often it came up in my classes, I began thinking about ways to allow more flexibility and space for (a)gender recognition and self-determination.

As a teacher, I know we struggle with comfort zones, our own histories, insecurities, and strengths. We deal with parents, with students, with administration, with available materials, and with the complexities and intersections of race, gender, sexuality, religion, citizenship status, national origin, ability, geography, and language, both in and out of our classrooms. In an effort to actively engage with (a)gender recognition and diversity in SELA classrooms, I suggest teachers focus on disrupting gender norms by strategically using a trans* pedagogy (Miller, this volume, Chap. 1) in one primary area: the teacher as a text, read by students.

Within the QLF, trans*ing identities is prevalent. Teachers are open to students' recognizing their own flexible and situated (a)gender identity and creating spaces that allow for that within the classroom. In fact, in the QLF, gender is addressed within all contexts as flexible, open to change, and as something worth exploring. Evidenced in Principle 2, Miller encourages teachers to "actively push back against gender constructs" and provide spaces to explore gender construction; in Principle 3 to support "various and multiple performances of gender"; and in Principle 4 asks both teachers *and* students "to examine the flexibility of gender across time and space, and in different contexts." Miller concludes that as teachers draw upon a trans*ing of language to help inform our practice, these challenges can foreclose the gender binary and dissolve the *recognition gap* (Miller, this volume, Chap. 1). Within this line of thinking, those who sit outside the traditional gender binary no longer need to be thought of as outliers, as undesirable, as unrecognizable, or as something to be fixed or coerced back into the binary. Instead, they are recognized as a person whose (a)gender is recognized and validated within the classroom. Teachers provide a readied example of what it means to be a gendered and readable professional. Teachers *are* texts (Clark 2010) that are "read" by students in the classroom. Through casual and formal conversations, salutations, and greetings, and by their simple presence at school activities, teachers provide a legible and recognizable text that is readable (or not readable) daily. Before students read novels and short stories in SELA classrooms, they read the teacher. They read the teacher's clothing and hairstyles and understand if they appropriately match the teacher's gender. The teacher as a text provides rich opportunities for teachers to examine the ways in which they draw upon and challenge (a)gender constructions and how they recognize and represent their gender ascriptions. I encourage teachers to consider the ways in which they themselves reenforce gender norms and look for ways to actively stop reenforcing those norms. By strategically using a trans* pedagogy, teachers can involve all students in a quest to think about how gender, gender diversity, and gender policing affect their lives and the ways they occupy those spaces.

Practicing These Principles in the SELA

Our social and cultural lives, which have informed us from birth, in and out of literacy classrooms, have typically inured us to see the gender binary in readable and legible ways. While classrooms don't always lead students into the gender binary, students often align themselves with the sex they were assigned at birth. This process is subtle enough that it is hardly recognizable. This inurement to the gender binary is so ingrained that when interacting with someone's (a)gender that seems illegible, confusing, or ambiguous, people may be "incapable of interacting and at a loss as to how to communicate" (Gilbert 2009, p. 93). This chapter asks how teachers as texts can be sites of disruption to the gender binary.

Classrooms, as we know, reinscribe gender norms (Apple 2002; Arnot 2002). Conversely, they can also be sites for disruption and contestation. I suggest that some of the most difficult barriers to achieving recognition for (a)gender diversity are in the unseen, unexamined, and genuine relations within classrooms. These interactions are created outside of formal lesson planning, materials, activities, and classwork. Since gender norms are reinforced through our subconscious and even purposeful interactions and actions, in order to contest gender norms, teachers must be open to discovering how they reinforce these norms with their students. Recognizing the teacher as a text is one such possibility.

Scholars have suggested that texts are a useful and generative way to introduce gender diversity in ELA and SELA classrooms and a way to ensure all students have access to books representative of themselves and their lives (Smolkin and Young 2011). However, adding these texts "to combat homophobia without addressing the ways in which heterosexuality is constructed as normal, does little to redress unequal power relations and privilege associated with sexual orientation and gender identity" (Schieble 2012, p. 207). Hermann-Wilmarth 2010 "trusts in the power of literature to stimulate" conversation that can address alternative family structures (p. 188), but recognizes that when taught alone and without other resources, it "might not alter systems of belief" (p. 189).

For this reason, this chapter suggests that along with critical lesson planning, the QLF is a site for examining the invisible interactions in classrooms that reinforce gender norms and prevent (a)gender self-determination. To this aim, the single most important strategy for such disruption of a reindoctrination of the gender binary is the identity and daily readability of the SELA teacher as text (Clark 2010). By thinking of the self as text, teachers can use their presence to actively try to shift the restrictions of the gender binary that is within their classroom and beyond. Teachers can prompt themselves and their students to explore, engage, and understand how gender is constructed in their own presence in the classroom.

The reinscription of gender norms and behaviors is often unintended, but when teachers unconsciously communicate to students the gender binary as normal, they assert a dominant narrative that informs and positions students within gender-typical identities. As an exercise to move beyond this dangerous possibility, LGBT and non-LGBT SELA teachers can look for ways they assert their masculinity and femininity in normed ways. The ensuing question is how can teachers who identify within normative gender categories support (a)gender diversity in students and be a supportive and strong ally for all students in their varied (a)gender expressions?

As an exercise for possible self-awareness about gender norms and (a)gender self-determination and recognition, SELA teachers can think about how they are policed into binary gender categories and how they reject binary gender categories. Below, I offer a series of questions for SELA teachers to consider about their own (a)gender in the classroom. These questions position the teacher as a text whom students read on a daily basis, and the questions are written with the assumption that students learn what gender is by reading their teachers. In reading and thinking about these questions, SELA teachers will see how their (a)gender is read by students.

The TEACHER as the TEXT and the QLF: Questions for Secondary English Language Arts Teachers
Primary questions:

What are students learning about gender from my presence in the classroom? In what ways will students read me (as a text) that supports gender norms? In what ways will students read me (as a text) that challenges gender norms?

For example: How well do I "fit" within the traditional gender roles? Will students read me as a challenge to their understandings of (a)gender? Will students read me as supporting normative gender roles? Why is it important to think about when aiming for (a)gender diversity and recognition?

How can I discuss the topic of my own (a)gender determination honestly and openly with students?

For example: How can I talk about the ways I consciously and unconsciously support the gender binary by my presence in the classroom? How can I talk about the ways I consciously and unconsciously disrupt the gender binary by my presence in classrooms?

QLF-specific questions: (QLF Principle 2)	QLF personal reflection and exemplars:

QLF-specific questions: (QLF Principle 2)

How will my students read me as an (a)gender text in the classroom?

How does my presence in the classroom push back on traditional definitions of woman and man, and how does it support the traditional definitions?

How can I use my presence in the classroom to reject the gender binary?

(QLF Principle 3)

How can I allow students to read the instability of my own gender?

How can I allow students to see that (a)gender readings of me are situationally preformed?

(QLF Principle 4)

How do I position students as (a)gender texts in my classroom, and does it allow for flexibility?

What are other students learning from how I position them and each other?

QLF personal reflection and exemplars:

Some elementary students innocently called me "Mr. Kate" while others called me "Ms. Kate"—this was a clear example of gender incongruity (the masculine "Mr." coupled with the feminine "Kate"), in addition to the students diverging in how they identified me (some with the feminine "Ms." and others with the masculine "Mr."), often in the same space. This made other teachers and parents uncomfortable. I didn't "correct" students and instead allowed them to identify me as both male and female, sometimes simultaneously

When students asked if I was a boy or a girl, rather than answering directly, I would ask them why they were asking. They often could not pinpoint an answer, and instead began to accept that I didn't fit their already existing definitions of female or male. This prevented me from being "read" by students within the traditional gender binary

In the classroom, I attempted to purposefully use and normalize examples of people who sat outside the gender binary, including cisgendered examples. Female athletes, stay-at-home fathers, and other examples, including in our own lives as teacher texts, are examples that show the binary is much more flexible than we generally admit. Additionally, I looked for examples where my own gender was flexible. Do I embrace my femininity in the workspace but on weekends with friends I take on a more masculine identity? Do I hide some parts of my identity to be more readable and avoid shame?

As a SELA teacher, this series of questions and the QLF Principle 4 are the hardest to embrace and the ones I continue to work the hardest on. I often gender students without allowing them to self-determine their (a)gender. Instead I use an official school record or gendered name to make them readable. Why do I do this? Why is it important to me? Do I treat students differently based on the assumptions I make? How often do I treat the girls and boys as naturally different groups of students?

When teachers take the time to truly self-reflect on this series of questions, they can then take the step to make space for gender norm disruptions in their classroom. Teachers can look for ways they can validate conventional gender expressions *and* think about ways to support the emergence of (a)gender and (a)gender creative configurations. By refusing to position students within the binary, teachers "actively support students' various and multiple performance of gender" (Principle 3). Therefore, trans* as a critical pedagogical tool can push against gender normativity, and thinking of the teacher as a text, read by students, allows for a more flexible recognition of (a)gender diversity.

CENTERING (A)GENDER IN THE SELA CLASSROOM

While we know that not all teachers identify as gay, lesbian, bisexual, trans*, or queer, *all* SELA teachers can look for powerful and critical ways to normalize discussions about (a)gender. Along with purposeful lesson planning and use of materials that can move students toward (a)gender self-determination, teachers must explore their subtle and subconscious ways of upholding gender norms. For true change to occur about the normalization for (a)gender expression in schools to be sustained, teachers must expand their own understandings of what gender is and disrupt where, how, and in what ways gender norms are reinforced.

WORKS CITED

Apple, M. (2002). *Official knowledge*. New York: Routledge.

Arnot, M. (2002). Cultural reproduction: The pedagogy of sexuality. In *Reproducing gender? Essays on educational theory and feminist politics* (pp. 41–53). London: Routledge-Falmer.

Britzman, D. (1995). Is there a queer pedagogy? Or, stop reading straight. *Educational Theory, 45*(2), 151–165.

Butler, J. (1990). *Gender trouble: Feminism and the subversion of identity*. London: Routledge.

Butler, J. (1993). *Bodies that matter: On the discursive limits of sex*. London: Routledge.

Butler, J. (2004). *Undoing gender*. London: Routledge.

Clark, C. (2010). Preparing LGBTQ-allies and combating homophobia in a U.S. teacher education program. *Teaching and Teacher Education, 26*(3), 704–713.

Foucault, M. (1980). *Introduction to Herculine Barbin: Being the recently discovered memoirs of a nineteenth-century French hermaphrodite*. New York: Pantheon Books.

Gilbert, M. (2009). Defeating bigenderism: Changing gender assumptions in the twenty-first century. *Hypathia, 24*(3), 93–112.

Hermann-Wilmarth, J. (2010). More than book talks: Preservice teacher dialogue after reading gay and lesbian children's literature. *Language Arts 87*(3), 188–198.

Krywanczyk, L. (2007). Queering public school pedagogy as a first-year teacher. *Radical Teacher, 79,* 27–34.

Lewis, C. (1999). *Literacy practices as social acts: Power, status and cultural norms in the classroom.* Mahwah: Lawrence Erlbaum Associates.

Miller, s. (2015). A queer literacy framework promoting (a)gender and (a)sexuality self-determination and justice. *English Journal, 104*(5), 37–44.

Miller, s., Burns, L., & Johnson, T. S. (2013). *Generation BULLIED 2.0: Prevention and intervention strategies for our most vulnerable students.* New York: Peter Lang.

Ryan, C. L., & Hermann-Wilmarth, J. M. (2013). Already on the shelf: Queer readings of award-winning children's literature. *Journal of Literacy Research, 45*(2), 142–172.

Schieble, M. (2012). A critical discourse analysis of teachers' views on LGBT literature. *Discourse: Studies in the Cultural Politics of Education, 33*(2), 207–222.

Sedgwick, E. K. (1990). *Epistemology of the closet.* Oakland: University of California Press.

Smolkin, L. B., & Young, C. A. (2011). Missing mirrors, missing window: Children's literature textbooks and LGBT topics. *Language Arts, 88*(3), 217–235.

Sykes, H. (2011). Hetero- and homo-normativity: Critical literacy, citizenship education and queer theory. *Curriculum Inquiry, 41*(4), 419–432.

Vavrus, M. (2009). Sexuality, schooling, and teacher identity formation: A critical pedagogy for teacher education. *Teaching and Teacher Education, 25*(3), 383–390.

CHAPTER 7

The T* in LGBT*: Disrupting Gender Normative School Culture Through Young Adult Literature

Katherine Mason Cramer and Jill Adams

Queer Literacy Framework Principles:

6. Engage in ongoing critique of how gender norms are reinforced in literature, media, technology, art, history, science, math, and so on.

While popular TV shows such as *Glee*, *Orange Is the New Black*, and *Transparent* introduce audiences to "unique issues faced by trans people—like safe access to bathrooms and hormone therapy" (Morris 2015), most of our schools are not safe spaces for trans*[1] and gender creative teens to come out (Kosciw et al. 2014). In *The Right to Be Out: Sexual Orientation and Gender Identity in America's Public Schools*, Stuart Biegel (2010) explains that teachers and students must realize that unlike gays and lesbians, who may opt to come out over time and in different contexts of their lives, "transgender persons cannot come out gradually unless

K.M. Cramer (✉)
Wichita State University in Kansas, Wichita, USA

J. Adams
Metropolitan State University of Denver, Denver, USA

121
sj Miller (ed.), *Teaching, Affirming, and Recognizing Trans and Gender Creative Youth*, DOI 10.1057/978-1-137-56766-6_7

they change environments. Once they begin presenting differently as part of their transition process, they are immediately and abruptly out to those who knew them previously" (pp. 178–9). In addition, "as the most misunderstood of any identifiable group in existence today," transgender people often cannot expect support from all members of their family, friends, and community (Biegel 2010, p. 180). When discussing transgender youth in K-12 public schools, Biegel also notes that "the great majority of Americans have never interacted knowingly with a transgender person, and even fewer have developed any sort of close personal relationship with one. Thus, educators seeking to move forward in this area would do well to identify memoirs, films, novels, poetry, and other works of art that document the experiences of those who identify under the transgender umbrella" (p. 185). In the English language arts classroom, the field of young adult literature (YAL) offers critical opportunities across a variety of subgenres for teens and teachers alike to learn more about trans* and gender creative identities and/or to have their own experiences mirrored back to them. Drawing upon such recognizability within YAL that features trans* and gender creative characters, teachers can help secondary students identify and critique gender normative practices in their school and home communities (Miller 2015), while helping them not only recognize the lived realities of all gender identities but become more knowledgeable about, welcoming toward, and appreciative of them as well.

A Brief History of the Portrayal of Trans* Youth in Selected YAL

Children's and young adult literature has seen a rapid increase in both the number and diversity of titles that feature trans* and gender creative characters, with more than 50 published in the past decade and another half a dozen published in 2015 (Alter 2015). As Talya Sokoll (2013) notes, however, some of these titles "remain largely unknown … due to the relatively small reach of the publishing houses making them available" (p. 24). Sokoll further recommends that readers in search of YAL with trans* content consult reading lists on Goodreads.com as well as blogs like Lee Wind's *I'm Here, I'm Queer, What the Hell Do I Read?* (pp. 25–26). In our own readings of such texts, we noted that some authors choose to write in third person or from the perspective of cisgender allies while others opt to allow trans* characters to narrate the story, giving readers a range of perspectives from which to enter the text.

While Julie Anne Peters' 2004 novel *Luna* is usually considered to be the first young adult novel to feature a transgender character (Cart and Jenkins 2006, p. 138), we argue that Carol Plum-Ucci's 2002 novel *What Happened to Lani Garver* actually earns that distinction, with its thoughtful portrayal of Lani, who refuses to conform to gender expectations and doesn't want to be put in a box. While the narrator Claire accepts this ambiguity, the rest of the small New England island community does not, and Lani pays the ultimate price. This text raises questions about how we perceive, construct, and police gender expression. In Peters' *Luna* (2004), we meet Luna through her sister Regan's eyes, learning that while Luna's assigned sex is male (her birth name is Liam), she is confident in her female identity and anticipates the day when she can embody that identity. Peters' use of Regan to tell this story allows cisgender readers a way to empathize both with Regan and with Luna. This is also the case in the novel *I Am J* (2011) by Cris Beam, set in New York. This third-person narrative depicts J's struggles as he waits to wake up and become a "real boy." Initially, as his body betrays him, J strives to keep himself invisible, but later decides to embody his true identity, going stealth so that even his love interest Blue doesn't realize he is transgender. This text takes self-determination a step further than *Luna*, as Beam consistently refers to J with masculine pronouns, and J truly lives as a male.

More recently, authors have depicted allies' romantic attractions to transgender characters, perhaps to allow cisgender readers a point of entry into the story. In Catherine Ryan Hyde's 2010 novel *Jumpstart the World*, 15-year-old Elle lives in New York City and is attracted to her neighbor Frank but initially rejects his friendship upon learning he is transgender. Honest and awkward, Elle sometimes regrets her words and actions, but as she learns to appreciate Frank for who he is, she also acknowledges the beauty in difference and practices capturing that beauty on film. While Elle and Frank's relationship never progresses beyond friendship, Brian Katcher's 2009 novel *Almost Perfect*, set in Missouri, depicts a romantic relationship. After breaking up with his girlfriend, high school senior Logan develops a friendship with quirky, beautiful Sage, who is new to the school. Although he initially rejects Sage when she reveals her assigned sex (male), their friendship survives and Logan confronts his own romantic attraction to Sage. Logan's choice to establish both a friendship and a romantic relationship with Sage allows the reader to envision the challenges faced by transgender people, as well as their allies and lovers, within the novel's particular time and space. It also forces the reader to question how much our assigned gender truly matters when it comes to love and friendship.

While most of the previous novels are narrated by cisgender characters/allies, the following texts provide greater insight into trans* experiences by allowing trans* and gender creative characters to narrate the tale themselves. In Ellen Wittlinger's *Parrotfish* (2007), set in Massachusetts, Angela has decided it's time to confirm her true gender identity: Angela is Grady, and *he* wants everyone to refer to him as such. With allies like classmates Sebastian, Russ, and Kita, as well as P.E. teacher Ms. Unger, Grady poses questions—to himself and others—that critique gender norms and help friends and family members accept his new gender expression. Similarly, short stories "Trev" by Jacqueline Woodson, "My Virtual World" by Francesca Lia Block, and "The Missing Person" by Jennifer Finney Boylan (all published in Michael Cart's 2009 edited collection *How Beautiful the Ordinary*) are told from a transgender character's perspective. While "The Missing Person" is set in Pennsylvania, a specific setting is not revealed in "Trev" and "My Virtual World," further indicating a universality of the trans* experience. In addition, Boylan herself is transgender and in 2003 published her memoir, *She's Not There: A Life in Two Genders*, a national best-seller. In Kirstin Cronn-Mills's 2012 novel *Beautiful Music for Ugly Children*, set in Minnesota, 18-year-old Elizabeth has begun to live as Gabe as high school graduation approaches. Music serves as the backdrop for the novel, and Gabe relishes the opportunity to broadcast his true self into the night air: "When you think about it, I'm like a 45. Liz is my A side, the song everybody knows, and Gabe is my B side—not played as often but just as good ... it's time to let my B side play" (p. 10).

We anticipate that in the future more authors will construct their texts in such a way as to challenge readers' expectations of both the characters and the text itself. For example, in Steve Brezenoff's 2011 novel *Brooklyn Burning*, we meet 15-year-old Kid, who is homeless after being kicked out of the house because Kid's father can't cope with Kid's gender ambiguity and undefined sexual orientation. Unlike *What Happened to Lani Garver* in which the narrator Claire assigns a gender to Lani and refers to Lani using masculine pronouns, Brezenoff never reveals Kid's sexual orientation or gender, nor those of Kid's romantic partner Scout. As Billy Merrell discloses in the notes to the reader of his 2005 coedited collection *The Full Spectrum*, "I hadn't realized how much I relied on knowing how people categorized themselves as a way of better understanding them" (np).

Brooklyn Burning forces the reader to understand Kid as a human being who refuses to be labeled.

In addition to these narrative texts, nonfiction texts offer invaluable perspective on the lived experiences of trans* and gender creative teens. Susan Kuklin's *Beyond Magenta: Transgender Teens Speak Out* (2014) offers six varying first-hand perspectives of being a trans* teen. Readers have the opportunity to learn about transgender experiences not only from the six teenagers but also from some family members and significant others. As we transition into an age of more understanding of gender creativity, these individuals seem to acknowledge the transformation that is also going on in society. We also see such shifts in Arin Andrews (2015) and Katie Rain Hill (2015) who shared their transition experiences in their memoirs *Some Assembly Required: The Not-So-Secret Life of a Transgender Teen* and *Rethinking Normal: A Memoir in Transition*. Each of the memoirs details their life, from early childhood through their teenage years in the rural Bible Belt of Oklahoma. In addition to sharing their journeys as transgender youth, Andrews and Hill reflect on their first serious romantic relationship, which happened to be with each other. Both of the books are coming-of-age stories that depict self-acceptance, the heartache of first love, and confirmation and embodiment of one's true gender identity. Collectively, each of these texts adds to the corpus and depth of understanding and recognition of trans* and gender creative youth and illustrates themes to which everyone can connect.

RATIONALE

In designing our overall suggestions for lessons, we were inspired by C.J. Pascoe's stance that all students benefit when teachers design curriculum that depicts a range of experiences and identities. In her research on masculinity in high schools, Pascoe (2007) argues that "[i]ncluding a range of sexual and gender identities in school rituals and curricula will indicate to both GLBT and nonnormatively gendered students as well as straight and normatively gendered students that school authorities don't tolerate gender- and sexuality-based harassment and violence" (p. 169).

Building from Pascoe, in our own classrooms, we regularly choose social issues books that promote reflection and spark dialog among our students. According to Lewison et al.'s (2002) work on critical literacy, "these texts give voice and visibility to those who have traditionally been marginalized, while engaging both students and teachers in more active and critical readings of texts" (p. 384). In the following lesson, we envision students and teachers engaging in critical literacy while simultaneously demonstrating both perspective and empathy (Wiggins and McTighe 2005, pp. 95–100).

These lessons seek to answer the question Miller (2015) poses in a recent *English Journal* article describing a Queer Literacy Framework: "… how can teachers move beyond discussions relegated to only gender and sexuality and toward an understanding of a continuum that also includes the (a)gendered and (a)sexuality complexities students embody?" (p. 37). By stepping up to this challenge, we hope to engage students in "ongoing critique of how gender norms are reinforced" (p. 42) in various texts, particularly YAL. This critique is particularly important in secondary schools in which heteronormative and gender normative practices often go unchecked (Pascoe 2007).

Prior to teaching these lessons, we recommend that teachers familiarize themselves with the following terms, the definitions of which can be found in the glossary of terms at the beginning of this book: *(a)gender, ally, assigned gender, assigned sex, cisgender, gender, gender expression, gender identity, gender role, label free, queer, self-determination, trans*, transgender,* and *transition*. Teachers might consider teaching these terms as they come up in the context of selected texts or discussions, by perhaps creating a Word Wall (a collection of words on a bulletin board or classroom wall that are key terms in a unit or class) or having students engage in a Vocabulary Self-Awareness activity, in which students self-assess their own understanding of key vocabulary (Fisher et al. 2015).

Lesson Descriptions

Our lessons have the potential to fit into a larger unit on self-determination, which Miller (2015) defines as "the right to make choices to self-identify in a way that authenticates one's self-expression, and which has potential for the embodiment of self-acceptance" while it simultaneously "presumes choice and rejects an imposition to be externally controlled, defined, or regulated" (p. 38). Essential questions for this larger unit might include the following prompts (see Appendix A):

- *In what ways do you find your personal, professional, and social choices being controlled, defined, or regulated by others (e.g., peers, family,*

adults, institutions)? How do you feel about the control being exerted over you? In what ways do you attempt to subvert or reject that control?
- *In what ways do you participate in controlling, defining, or regulating the choices of others? Is your participation in this control fair/just? How do you think the target of your control feels? If you don't know, how might you find out?*

In this unit, students will engage in reading and discussing YAL excerpts that feature trans* and gender creative characters. In Appendix B, we offer a range of texts and suggested excerpts as well as writing and discussion prompts that teachers can mix and match depending on time, context, and intention. Just as we do in our own teaching, we have opted to recommend passages from novels that feature transgender characters who demonstrate first-hand accounts in order to prompt critical thinking and dialog. This approach, we feel, offers multiple benefits: (1) it provides a specific illustrative example for students to consider in their thinking, writing, speaking, and listening, (2) it allows us to explore multiple texts in a relatively short time, and (3) it introduces students to a variety of texts that they may choose to read in their entirety independently. These texts are presented and scaffolded on content to develop awareness and understanding in the order that we would recommend if teachers intend to use all or just a selected few. After reading and responding to these texts, students will engage in a final project of their choice that demonstrates their efforts to promote awareness of (a)gender self-determination (Miller 2015).

Prior to reviewing any of the texts, engage students in thinking about and discussing the following questions: *What do you (think you) know about what it means to be a man or woman, a boy or girl? How did you learn this? What are the implications of these learnings?* Encourage students to consider different facets of gender performance (e.g., appearance, behavior, verbal and nonverbal language, perceived skills/attributes, and strengths/weaknesses). Then, based on students' responses, and prior to selecting the recommended texts in Appendix B, ascertain what students understand about trans* and gender creative identities.

Text Choices and Learning Activities

Embodying (a)gender identity is a key concept in David Levithan's *Every Day* (2012–2013 is the paperback). In this text, the protagonist, A, who is agender and asexual, wakes up in a different body each day and resides in that body until the stroke of midnight. Because of this, A must consider physical and personal traits of the inhabited body in order to successfully get through the day, and readers are forced to contemplate the meaning and impact of skin color, sexual orientation, and gender through A's daily journeys. After reading the initial passage in Levithan's book (see Appendix B), have students explore the following prompt: *When babies are born, they are often immediately given items that are pink or blue. Additionally, gender expectations are displayed throughout childhood. What are some of these gender norms? What is the impact of these expectations?* After the students compile responses to these queries, have them explore traits that define their own lives, including the impact if those traits changed (as A experiences in *Every Day*). End the activity by connecting the conversation to gender identity: *Why does gender matter—to you in your life?*

Parrotfish also provides opportunities for students to contemplate (a) gender expression. First, read aloud Chap. 1 (pp. 1–9), which raises questions about assigned gender, naming conventions, the importance we place on knowing gender, and what it means to "look and act" like a boy or girl. After the read aloud, ask students to review Grady's questions regarding babies' genders on pp. 3–4 as well as his thoughts on gendered appearance and behavior on pp. 8–9. Do a quick write in response to the questions posed in the text (e.g., *In your opinion, how important is it to know a baby's—or any human being's—gender? Why? What does it mean to look or act like a girl/boy?*). Excerpts from this novel can also be used to critique the culture of school sports (Cramer forthcoming).

Beautiful Music for Ugly Children features a transgender protagonist but is essentially a book about music. Gabe gets a job at a local radio station and talks explicitly about having more than one side to yourself. The "A" side is one that everyone knows (as in hit singles), but the "B" side can be just as powerful. There are numerous songs that illustrate this point: The Beach Boys' (A) "I Get Around" and (B) "Don't Worry, Baby" as well as the Beatles' (A) "I Want to Hold Your Hand" and (B) "I Saw Her Standing There." Gabe asks, "Are you a Top Forty hit, or an equally good yet potentially undiscovered gem?" Have students then contemplate what their Top 40 hit and undiscovered gem sides might be and why. After the reflection, guide the students in the following questions: *Why would Gabe ask this question? Why might he have kept his part B hidden? What are the consequences of his actions?* We would recommend using this activity as part of a book talk.

(A)gender expression is a topic for discussion in *What Happened to Lani Garver.* Read aloud pp. 12–14 in which the protagonist Claire and her friends are trying to determine the gender of Lani who is new to the school. Ask students to write about and discuss their responses to the text before reading aloud Chap. 2 (pp. 18–23) in which Claire's friend Macy confronts Lani regarding gender identity, and then cautions Claire against befriending Lani. Ask students to respond to these questions and discuss in small groups: *What kind of friend is Macy to Claire? Do you think Macy had a right to ask about Lani's gender? Do you think she has a right to criticize how Lani expresses gender? In what ways have you (or someone you know) acted in similar ways to Macy? Do you think Claire should stand up to Macy? Why or why not?*

Pairing two texts together such as *Some Assembly Required* by Arin Andrews and *Rethinking Normal* by Katie Rain Hill offers the possibility of exploring male-to-female and female-to-male transgender experiences. *Some Assembly Required* directly addresses the notion of having to work in order to make yourself whole. Andrews accomplishes this and shares his journey in the text. Have students respond in writing to the following prompts: *What assembly may still be required for you—in what ways are you not yet complete? What pieces do you need to gather? Are there mentors/guides that may help you along the way?* Comparatively, Hill's book challenges the reader to contemplate what is "normal" for a teen. Hill herself has to think through this as she examines her own gender identity. Pre-reading prompts for written reflection include *Describe a "normal" teenager. How did you arrive at your description? What are the consequences as not being "normal" in our society? What are the benefits of not being "normal" in our society?* Then, read Chap. 1 and encourage students to consider Hill's perspective on "normal" before returning to their written reflection and rethinking their own concept of "normal."

In *Jumpstart the World*, students can explore challenges faced by trans and gender creative people. Before reading, invite students to respond to this question in writing or in small groups: *Based on prior reading and/ or your own prior knowledge, what challenges do you think trans and gender creative people might face in their everyday lives?* Read aloud pp. 14–17 in Chap. 2 wherein Elle cuts off all of her hair and then is both harassed and befriended at school. Ask students to respond in writing and then in small groups: *In what ways do you notice your peers (and yourself) policing (a)gender expression and reinforcing gender norms (and perhaps punishing those who don't conform to those norms)?* Also read aloud pp. 119–128 in

Chap. 11 in which Elle learns that hospitals have the potential to be unsafe spaces for transgender people, which leads her to sneak in to watch over Frank when visiting hours end. Ask students to respond to this prompt: *In addition to hospitals, what other spaces might be unsafe for trans* and gender creative people? Are there spaces in our school and community that might be considered unsafe? What can you do to combat this injustice?* The full text of this novel is also an ideal choice for a unit of study on beauty, language and power, or finding community (Mason et al. 2012, pp. 15–17).

Assessment of Student Learning

As you wrap up readings, quick writes, and discussions of these texts, ask students to consider the following questions—in writing and in discussion with peers:

- *In what ways are gender norms constructed and enforced in our school and in the texts (both print and nonprint) we read?*
- *In what spaces and contexts have you observed people, texts, etc. challenge or disrupt gender norms?*
- *In what ways do you question (and help others to question) gender norms and demonstrate appreciation for all gender identities and expressions?*

In their responses to these questions, students may note, for example, the ways in which the language of school sports culture is often permeated by sexist, homophobic, and transphobic assumptions and insults (Cramer forthcoming). After students have had the opportunity to reflect on, write about, and discuss these questions, provide several assessment options that encourage them to demonstrate their understanding of (a)gender self-determination and how they can raise awareness of possibilities for disrupting gender normative school culture. Students might select from the following assessment options (see Appendix C):

1. Share and discuss with a particular audience a picture book with a trans* character. Lukoff (2015) has provided critiques of recent picture books, and an extensive list of picture books with trans* characters can be found on Goodreads.com.
2. Develop and carry out a plan to publicly challenge a gender normative school practice.

3. Conduct a social experiment by changing something significant about your appearance and document others' reactions.

In each of these assessment options, students should reflect on, analyze, and share their experience in writing or an oral presentation, allowing their peers to gain new insights and providing opportunities for the teacher to assess their understanding of (a)gender self-determination. This reflection should include analysis of the intended audience's reaction as well as "next steps" in critiquing and disrupting gender normative school culture.

SUGGESTIONS AND IMPLICATIONS

Although the lessons that comprise this unit align with Common Core State Standards and National Council of Teachers of English/International Reading Association Standards for English Language Arts (see Appendix A), we also recommend that teachers prepare a strong rationale that articulates clear learning objectives, as well as how the texts and activities help achieve those objectives (NCTE). In order to strive to create both internal and external safety for all students (Miller, this volume, Chap. 1), which motivates their willingness to discuss these topics, teachers should not assume heteronormative, gender normative, cisgender, and/or transphobic stances; nor should they assume any of their students maintain these stances. Whether students are or aren't "out" to teachers, it is likely that one or more students per class identifies as LGBT*IAGCQ or as an ally, or has friends or family who identify LGBT*IAGCQ. We also encourage teachers to be prepared for questions, while also recognizing that this may be a learning process for themselves. The assessment options are offered to support teachers to learn alongside students in order to model their own learning processes and challenges.

Within these lessons, young adult texts act as both windows and mirrors for all students to understand and recognize trans* and gender creative identities, and for trans* teens specifically to see themselves depicted within the pages. It is our responsibility as educators to create a culture of support and appreciation for all gender identities within our classroom and school communities, whose reach may extend far beyond what we can anticipate. In fact, MacGillivray (2000) argues that the inclusion of lesbian, gay, bisexual, transgender (LGBT) identities in the curriculum "can help to destigmatize nonheterosexual identities and can deconstruct gender role stereotypes that limit all students" (p. 305). This content doesn't just benefit our LGBT* students, it benefits *all* of our students since "[t]he fear of being perceived as gay restricts boys to making choices that will affirm what it means to be a man in our society and restricts girls to making choices that will affirm what it means to be a woman" (MacGillivray 2000, p. 305). Designing curriculum that appreciates, affirms, and recognizes all differences not only empowers classroom environments but also manifests into everyday life.

Appendix A

Essential Questions and Standards

Lesson Essential Questions
Throughout this lesson, consider the following essential questions. We will return to them as we discuss different texts and share our responses and experiences. Note how your stance shifts or is strengthened as you consider multiple perspectives—those featured in the texts and those of your classmates.

- In what ways do you find your personal, professional, and social choices being controlled, defined, or regulated by others (e.g., peers, family, adults, institutions)? How do you feel about the control being exerted over you? In what ways do you attempt to subvert or reject that control?
- In what ways do you participate in controlling, defining, or regulating the choices of others? Is your participation in this control fair/just? How do you think the target of your control feels? If you don't know, how might you find out?

Pre-reading Questions
As you respond to these questions, consider different facets of gender performance (e.g., appearance, behavior, verbal and non-verbal language, perceived skills/attributes and strengths/weaknesses).

- What do you (think you) know about what it means to be a man or woman, a boy or girl? How did you learn this?
- What are the implications of these learnings?

Common Core State Standards Addressed
Reading: Key Ideas and Details

1. Read closely to determine what the text says explicitly and to make logical inferences from it; cite specific textual evidence when writing or speaking to support conclusions drawn from the text.

Speaking and Listening: Comprehension and Collaboration

1. Prepare for and participate effectively in a range of conversations and collaborations with diverse partners, building on others' ideas and expressing their own clearly and persuasively.

National Council of Teachers of English (NCTE) Standards Addressed
1. Students read a wide range of print and non-print texts to build an understanding of text, of themselves, and of the cultures of the United States and the world; to acquire new information; to respond to the needs and demands of society and the workplace; and for personal fulfillment. Among these texts are fiction and nonfiction, classic and contemporary works.
4. Students adjust their use of spoken, written, and visual language (e.g. conventions, style, vocabulary) to communicate effectively with a variety of audiences and for different purposes.
11. Students participate as knowledgeable, reflective, creative, and critical members of a variety of literacy communities.
12. Students use spoken, written, and visual language to accomplish their own purposes (e.g., for learning, enjoyment, persuasion, and the exchange of information).

Appendix B

Text Choices and Learning Activities

Every Day by David Levithan
"I wake up. Immediately I have to figure out who I am. It's not just the body—opening my eyes and discovering whether the skin on my arm is light or dark, whether my hair is long or short, whether I'm fat or thin, boy or girl, scarred or smooth. The body is the easiest thing to adjust to, if you're used to waking up in a new one each morning. It's the life, the context of the body, that can be hard to grasp" (p. 1).

1. When babies are born, they are often immediately given items that are pink or blue. Throughout early childhood, gender expectations are taught and reinforced. What are some gender norms that you experienced as a young child?
2. What defines who you are? In the chart below, list specific traits that define you in the first column, and describe how each trait defines you in the second column. In the third column, consider this: What might it feel like if you would change one of the attributes, as A must do in *Every Day*?

Traits	How does it define you?	Impact of change

3. Why does gender matter—to you in your life?

Parrotfish by Ellen Wittlinger

1. Read Chap. 1.
2. Carefully review Grady's questions regarding babies' genders on pp. 3–4 as well as his thoughts on gendered appearance and behavior on pp. 8–9.
3. Do a quick-write in response to the questions posed in the text

   (a) In your opinion, how important is it to know a baby's—or any human being's—gender? Why?
   (b) What does it mean to look or act like a girl/boy?

Beautiful Music for Ugly Children by Kirstin Cronn-Mills
At his job at a local radio station, Gabe talks explicitly about having more than one side to yourself. The "A" Side is one that everyone knows (as in

hit singles), but the "B" side can be just as powerful. Gabe asks, "Are you a Top Forty hit, or an equally good yet potentially undiscovered gem?"

- Why would Gabe ask this question?
- What might he have been keeping his part B hidden?
- What are the consequences of his actions?
- In the chart below, list and briefly describe some of your own Top 40 Hits and undiscovered gems.

Top 40 Hit	Undiscovered gem

What Happened to Lani Garver by Carol Plum-Ucci
1. Read pp. 12–14 in which the protagonist Claire and her friends are trying to determine Lani's gender.
2. Write about and discuss your responses to the text.

   (a) Why do you think Claire and her friends are so intent on determining Lani's gender?
   (b) Is it important that we categorize people by gender? Why or why not?

3. Then read Chap. 2 (pp. 18–23) in which Claire's friend Macy confronts Lani regarding gender identity, and then cautions Claire against befriending Lani.
4. Respond to these questions and discuss in small groups:

   (a) What kind of friend is Macy to Claire?
   (b) Do you think Macy had a right to ask about Lani's gender?
   (c) Do you think she has a right to criticize how Lani expresses gender?

(d) In what ways have you (or someone you know) acted in similar ways to Macy?

(e) Do you think Claire should stand up to Macy? Why or why not?

Some Assembly Required by Arin Andrews

"You know how some toys come in a box that reads SOME ASSEMBLY REQUIRED? I can relate to those toys...It captures this sense that I've had for a long time, that if I were going to be who I wanted to be, I was going to have to literally put myself together piece by piece" (p. 237). As you consider this quote, respond to the following prompts:

- What pieces and what assembly do you think is still required for you--in which ways are you not yet complete?
- What are the pieces you need to gather/obtain?
- Are there any mentors/guides that may help you along the way?

Rethinking Normal by Katie Rain Hill

Before reading Chap. 1 of Hill's book with its challenge to the reader, contemplate what is "normal" for a teen, respond to these prompts in writing:

- Describe a "normal" teenager.
- How did you arrive at your description?
- What are the consequences as not being "normal" in our society?
- What are the benefits of not being "normal" in our society?

Read Chap. 1, and begin to rethink your concept of normal through Hill's own words. Now, return to your written reflection and rethink your concept of normal as you consider Hill's perspective.

Jumpstart the World by Catherine Ryan Hyde

1. Before reading, respond to this question in writing or in small groups: Based on prior reading and/or your own prior knowledge, what challenges do you think trans* and gender creative people might face in their everyday lives?

2. Read aloud pp. 14–17 in Chap. 2 in which Elle cuts off all of her hair and then is both harassed and befriended at school.

3. Respond in writing and then in small groups to the following prompts: In what ways do you notice your peers (and yourself) policing (a)gender expression and reinforcing gender norms (and perhaps punishing those who don't conform to those norms)?

4. Then read aloud pp. 119–128 in Chap. 11 in which Elle learns that hospitals have the potential to be unsafe spaces for transgender people, so she sneaks in to watch over Frank when visiting hours end.

5. Respond to this prompt: In addition to hospitals, what other spaces might be unsafe for trans* and gender creative people? Are there spaces in our school and community that might be considered unsafe? What can you do to combat this injustice?

APPENDIX C

Summative Assessment Options

As we wrap up our reading, writing, and discussions of these texts, consider the following questions—in writing and in discussion with peers:

- In what ways are gender norms constructed and enforced in our school and in the texts (both print and non-print) we read?
- In what ways have you observed people, texts, etc. challenge or disrupt gender norms?
- In what ways do you question (and help others to question) gender norms and demonstrate appreciation for all gender identities and expressions?

After you have had the opportunity to reflect on, write about, and discuss these questions, select one of the following assessment options. Each of these options encourages you to demonstrate your understanding of (a) gender self-determination and how you can raise awareness of possibilities for disrupting gender normative school culture:

Option 1: Picture Book Read Aloud Select a picture book with a trans* or gender creative character. An extensive list of picture books with trans* characters can be found on Goodreads.com. Select an audience (peers, younger students, siblings or other family members). Then read the picture book aloud and facilitate a discussion with that audience. Write about the experience, including your rationale for your text and audience selection, the reaction of your audience, how you facilitated the discussion, and any challenges you faced, as well as surprises and successes.

CCSS Addressed:
Speaking and Listening: Comprehension and Collaboration
1. Prepare for and participate effectively in a range of conversations and collaborations with diverse partners, building on others' ideas and expressing their own clearly and persuasively.
Writing: Range of Writing
10. Write routinely over extended time frame (time for research, reflection, and revision) and shorter time frames (a single sitting or a day or two) for a range of tasks, purposes, and audiences.

NCTE Standards Addressed:
3. Students apply a wide range of strategies to comprehend, interpret, evaluate, and appreciate texts. They draw on their prior experience, their interactions with other readers and writers, their knowledge of word meaning and of other texts, their word identification strategies, and their understanding of textual features (e.g., their sound-letter correspondence, sentence structure, context, graphics).
4. Students adjust their use of spoken, written, and visual language (e.g., conventions, style, vocabulary) to communicate effectively with a variety of audiences and for different purposes.
5. Students employ a wide range of strategies as they write and use different writing process elements appropriately to communicate with different audiences for a variety of purposes.
11. Students participate as knowledgeable, reflective, creative, and critical members of a variety of literacy communities.
12. Students use spoken, written and visual language to accomplish their own purposes (e.g., for learning, enjoyment, persuasion, and the exchange of information).

Grading Considerations:
Selection and justification for text selection, preparation of discussion, effectiveness of discussion, depth of written reflection

Option 2: Challenge Gender Normative Practices Select a gender normative school practice, and develop a plan to question or challenge it. Create an argument (print or non-print text) for a specific audience, and present it to that audience. In writing or in a presentation to the class, reflect on your experience and analyze both your performance as well as the reactions of your audience. Articulate your "next steps."

CCSS Addressed:

Writing: Text Types and Purposes:
1. Write arguments to support claims in an analysis of substantive topics or texts, using valid reasoning and relevant and sufficient evidence.
Writing: Production and Distribution of Writing
4. Produce clear and coherent writing in which the development, organization, and style are appropriate to task, purpose, and audience.
Speaking and Listening: Presentation of Knowledge and Ideas
4. Present information, findings, and supporting evidence such that listeners can follow the line of reasoning and the organization, development, and style are appropriate to task, purpose, and audience.
NCTE Standards Addressed:
5. Students employ a wide range of strategies as they write and use different writing process elements appropriately to communicate with different audiences for a variety of purposes.
11. Students participate as knowledgeable, reflective, creative, and critical members of a variety of literacy communities.
12. Students use spoken, written and visual language to accomplish their own purposes (e.g., for learning, enjoyment, persuasion, and the exchange of information).
Grading Considerations: Selection of topic, argument development, depth of analysis, viability and relevance of next step possibilities, quality of presentation (written or oral).

Option 3: Conduct a Social Experiment Similar to Elle's haircut in *Jumpstart the World,* conduct a social experiment. With your parent/guardian's permission, change something about your appearance (e.g., your clothing, your accessories, your hair, your non-verbal language). Make it something significant, ideally something you have wanted to change, and perhaps something you have been afraid to change. Observe other people's reactions to this change. Write about the experience (or share it in a presentation). What did you change and why did you wait until now to do it (what previously held you back)? In what ways do you find yourself supported or challenged as a result of this change? Compare and contrast your experience with those of characters we encountered in our reading.
CCSS Addressed:
Writing: Text Types and Purposes:
1. Write arguments to support claims in an analysis of substantive topics or texts, using valid reasoning and relevant and sufficient evidence.
NCTE Standards Addressed:

5. Students employ a wide range of strategies as they write and use different writing process elements appropriately to communicate with different audiences for a variety of purposes.
12. Students use spoken, written and visual language to accomplish their own purposes (e.g., for learning, enjoyment, persuasion, and the exchange of information).

Grading Considerations: Choice task selection/completion, observational notes, experience reflection, accurate and meaningful comparison to *Jumpstart* characters.

NOTES

1. We intentionally move back and forth between trans* and transgender based on how it is used by an author or us.

REFERENCES

Alter, A. (2015, June 6). Transgender children's books fill a void and break a taboo. *The New York Times.* Retrieved from http://www.nytimes.com

Andrews, A. (2015). *Some assembly required: The not-so-secret life of a transgender teen.* New York: Simon & Schuster.

Beam, C. (2011). *I am J.* New York: Little, Brown and Co.

Biegel, S. (2010). *The right to be out: Sexual orientation and gender identity in America's public schools.* Minneapolis: University of Minneapolis Press.

Boylan, J. F. (2003). *She's not there: A life in two genders.* New York: Broadway Books.

Cart, M. (Ed.). (2009). *How beautiful the ordinary: Twelve stories of identity.* New York: Harper Teen.

Cart, M., & Jenkins, C. A. (2006). *The heart has its reasons: Young adult literature with Gay/Lesbian/Queer Content, 1969–2004.* Latham: The Scarecrow Press.

Cramer, K. M. (forthcoming). Using YAL to interrogate the heteronormative, transphobic culture of school sports. In A. Brown & L. Rodesiler (Eds.), *Developing contemporary literacies through sports: A guide for the English classroom.* NCTE.

Cronn-Mills, K. (2012). *Beautiful music for ugly children.* Minnesota: Flux.

Fisher, D., Brozo, W. G., Frey, N., & Ivey, G. (2015). *50 instructional routines to develop content literacy.* Boston: Pearson.

Hill, K. R. (2015). *Rethinking normal: A memoir in transition.* New York: Simon & Schuster.

Hyde, C. R. (2010). *Jumpstart the world.* New York: Knopf.

Katcher, B. (2009). *Almost perfect.* New York: Delacorte.

Kosciw, J. G., Greytak, E. A., Palmer, N. A., & Boesen, M. J. (2014). *The 2013 National School Climate Survey: The experiences of lesbian, gay, bisexual and transgender youth in our nation's schools*. New York: GLSEN.

Kuklin, S. (2014). *Beyond magenta: Transgender teens speak out*. Boston: Candlewick.

Levithan, D. (2012). *Every day*. New York: Ember.

Levithan, D., & Merrill, B. (Eds.). (2005). *The full spectrum: A new generation of writing about gay, lesbian, bisexual, transgender, questioning, and other identities*. New York: Knopf.

Lewison, M., Flint, A. S., & Van Sluys, K. (2002). Taking on critical literacy: The journey of newcomers and novices. *Language Arts, 79*(5), 382–392.

Lukoff, K. (2015, May 8). Evaluating transgender picture books; Calling for better ones. *School Library Journal*. Retrieved from http://www.slj.com/

MacGillivray, I. K. (2000). Educational equity for gay, lesbian, bisexual, transgendered, and queer/questioning students: The demands of democracy and social justice for America's schools. *Education and Urban Society, 32*(3), 303–323.

Mason, K., Brannon, A., & Yarborough, E. (2012). Locating queer community in award-winning LGBTQ-themed young adult literature (2005–2010). *The ALAN Review, 39*(3), 12–20.

Miller, s. (2015). A queer literacy framework promoting (a)gender and (a)sexuality self-determination and justice. *English Journal, 104*(5), 37–44.

Morris, R. (2015, January 12). Transgender 13-year-old Zoey having therapy. *BBC News US & Canada*. Retrieved from http://www.bbc.com

NCTE. Rationales for teaching challenged books. Retrieved from http://www.ncte.org/action/anti-censorship/rationales

Pascoe, C. J. (2007). *Dude, you're a fag: Masculinity and sexuality in high school*. Berkeley: University of California Press.

Peters, J. A. (2004). *Luna*. New York: Little, Brown and Co.

Plum-Ucci, C. (2002). *What happened to Lani Garver*. Orlando: Harcourt.

Sokoll, T. (2013). Representations of trans* youth in young adult literature: A report and a suggestion. *Young Adult Library Services, 11*(4), 23–26.

Wiggins, G., & McTighe, J. (2005). *Understanding by design* (2nd ed.). Upper Saddle River: Pearson.

Wittlinger, E. (2007). *Parrotfish*. New York: Simon & Schuster.

CHAPTER 8

Risks and Resiliency: Trans* Students in the Rural South

Stephanie Anne Shelton and Aryah O'Tiss S. Lester

Queer Literacy Framework Principles:

1. Refrains from possible presumptions that students ascribe to a gender; and,
3. Recognizes that masculinity and femininity constructs are assigned to gender norms and are situationally performed.

INTRODUCTION

"We'd like to remind all you students that you can't bring firearms onto school property. It's hunting season, so don't forget to take your stuff outta your car before you come to campus. And, be sure to take any kills out before you leave the house, too. Don't want that sittin' there all day" [sic]. We looked at one another and silently giggled. The administrator's reminder was absurd; his ridiculous Southern drawl only made it sillier. We constantly bemoaned to one another the pains of living in a tiny Southern town, and an intercom reminder that our classmates—many of whom the

S.A. Shelton (✉)
The University of Georgia, Athens, USA

A.O.S. Lester
State of Florida Health Department's Transgender Work Group, USA

© The Editor(s) (if applicable) and The Author(s) 2016   143
sj Miller (ed.), *Teaching, Affirming, and Recognizing Trans and Gender Creative Youth*, DOI 10.1057/978-1-137-56766-6_8

teachers refused to trust with pens or pencils—might have ready access to rifles and deer heads was too much.

Equally painful was navigating the hallways between classes. We had to be careful of the slick red clay that streaked the school linoleum, the "Georgia mud" that everyone tracked in from outside after a heavy rain. The yellow "Caution" signs that lined the corridors did little to increase safety, only to highlight the most precarious spaces. Students seemed to be enacting intricate dance steps as we each carefully navigated the slipperiest places, our shoes squeaking and squealing through the mess.

More risky than our mud choreography, though, were our internal thoughts. Though we—Stephanie and Aryah—have known one another since fifth grade, neither of us was privy to the other's thoughts at that time. Neither of us knew how little the other felt that she belonged. We lived in a place where we had learned no vocabulary to articulate our deepest concerns and thoughts, but even if we had had the words, we were in a place where only silence was permissible.

Being "Different" in the Rural South

First, as we both still live in the Southeastern United States and have each lived significant portions of our lives in the South, we do not wish to suggest that there is a monolithic Southern identity or set of beliefs. The stereotypes that media perpetuate, as seen in shows such as *Duck Dynasty* and *Here Comes Honey Boo Boo*, are problematic and offensive to many Southerners, even as others identify with figures on the shows. However, despite the diversity and beauty present in the Southeast, the region remains highly problematic to queer populations.

Before the Supreme Court's historic ruling on marriage equality, nearly all of the states that prohibited same-sex marriages were in this region (Human Rights Campaign 2014). Since Supreme Court of the United States decision, a number of Southern states have made national news due to some state officials' refusals to recognize the federal ruling (e.g., Roosevelt 2015; Williams and Robinson 2015). Beyond marriage equality, in comparison to the rest of the USA, no state in the Southeastern region offers what *The Guardian* refers to as "maximum protection" for lesbian, gay, bisexual, trans*, and queer/questioning (LGBTQ) Americans, including equal employment protections and safeties from gender- and sexuality-based harassment inside state-funded schools (Guardian Interactive 2012). While there are certainly Southerners who celebrate people's rights to self-define, to self-identify, and to self-determine in relation to issues such as sexual orientation and gender identity, the region tends to lag behind other sections of the country in relation to civil rights.

These issues matter very much when considering Southern schools. In 2012, the Gay, Lesbian, & Straight Education Network (GLSEN) conducted a nationwide survey of more than 2300 students that evaluated LGBT middle and high schoolers' experiences in specific geographic regions. Researchers determined that discriminatory school policies and bullying behaviors toward LGBT individuals seemed "to be amplified in the South" (2012a, n.p.). The study attributed the finding to Southern cultural beliefs, which contribute to a lack of public support and resources for LGBTQ populations, including fewer teacher allies and resources such as Gay-Straight Alliances. Given this environment, Southern queer students are especially vulnerable (Whitlock 2010).

However, as two queer people who grew up not just in the South, *but* the rural South, research indicates that many students' experiences today mirror ours from over 20 years ago. The GLSEN (2012c) study also determined that, in rural sections of the country in general, students consistently reported greater degrees of biased language, such as homophobic and "negative gender expression-based remarks," and a significantly diminished sense of being safe at school (p. x). Additionally, over 80% of rural students described feeling unsafe due to self-determined or perceived characteristics related to sexual orientation, gender, and gender expression. Of those students, nearly half reported being either harassed or assaulted due to those same characteristics.

As our focus is not on rural areas in general but on the rural South, it is noteworthy that even with the degree of risk associated with being a queer student in any rural region, the survey found that "rural students in the South" were "more likely to feel unsafe than rural students" in most other regions (p. x). The lack of safety translates into the determination "that places in the South ... may be more hostile than [some other] areas" of the country to queer students (p. 1).

For trans* students specifically, the survey found that 15% of trans* students from rural areas included in the survey reported attending schools that had openly discriminatory policies, such as gender-segregated school facilities (e.g., gym, locker room) and consistent refusal from school personnel to use the proper pronouns when referring to students (p. 16). One trans* student living in the rural South described in an interview with GLSEN that his mother had declared that his gender nonconformity was "the work of the Devil," while classmates "shoved [me] into my locker and called [me] a redneck fag" (2013, n.p.). This chapter examines these risks and the ways that teachers and schools in rural Southern regions might both recognize and support this population.

TRANS* STUDENTS OF COLOR

The intersection of race with gender is as important as geographic location for trans* students. While GLSEN does not specifically report by region, they found in surveys and interviews with over 2100 LGBT students of color across the nation that transphobic language was pervasive in schools, and only about one-fifth of trans* students of color reported that teachers and administrators intervened when other students made derogatory comments about gender expression or race (Diaz and Kosciw 2009, p. xi). Additionally, over 60% were harassed because of gender expression, with some racial and ethnic groups being more susceptible than others to harassment (p. 12). African Americans, for example, reported hearing negative peer remarks about gender expression "frequently" or "often" at least 62% of the time that they were in school. In addition to verbal harassment due to gender identity and expression, students' racial and ethnic identities exacerbated peers' treatment and often led to physical violence (p. xi). While over 80% of the students in the study agreed that having supportive teachers and school personnel was critical to both safety and success, only about one-third reported having access to supportive faculty. Related, very few reported finding representation in school curricula. Only one-third reported having access to LGBT resources in their school libraries, about one-fourth could access LGBT-related information via their school Internet, and only one-tenth of LGBT students of color reported having access to any positive LGBT representations in school materials, much less positive representations of trans* people and/or LGBT people of color (pp. 38–39).

TWO DIFFERENT PERSPECTIVES ON TRANS* IDENTITY IN A RURAL SOUTHERN SCHOOL

When we wrote earlier that we were both queer students without the vocabulary to articulate those identities, we were remarking on Aryah's identity as a trans* woman of color and Stephanie's identity as a cisgender lesbian. One aim in sharing our personal perspectives is to describe the experiences that Aryah as a trans* student in the late 1990s faced in a regional climate that has traditionally been and remains hostile to trans* people and people of color; another is to describe Stephanie's frustrations with her struggles to support a friend in a space that made understanding and acknowledging trans* identity impossible.

Aryah's Struggle

When I was very young, I loved the color purple. Any item in any shade, whether it was a fanciful dress or a fluffy stuffed animal—if it was purple, I loved it. I learned very quickly that as a little boy, my color choice was questionable, off, *wrong*. I adjusted to others' expectations of what was acceptable, and I quietly selected yellow as my new favorite color. My second favorite color choice got far fewer reactions than purple, and so I began to learn to navigate gender norms in ways that protected me from others' evaluations of me as abnormal.

As I grew older, life became more complicated. My favorite color was no longer the only aspect of my life that was monitored to ensure that I was enough of a boy. While playing, I had been happiest when enjoying hopscotch, jumping rope, and playing house. For a time, those activities had been acceptable, had been excused because of my age. With each birthday, my world narrowed, and activities that had brought me joy were squeezed out of my life. Adults told me directly that I was "abnormal," that I should play games better suited for little boys. While there were certainly family and friends who policed my behaviors, I vividly remember my elementary school principal being one of the figures who brought my world of play crashing down.

During recess, I tended to gravitate to the girls' groups on the playground. They were the ones with the fun games, after all. With them, I was free to hop across a grid of squares and to pretend to cook gourmet meals, before I would rush off to jump rope to "Cinderella Dressed in Yellow" and other singsong rhymes. One day while enjoying time with friends, my elementary school principal pulled me to the side to inform me, "You are to cease playing with the girls on the playground. You are to play with the little boys, where you belong. That will be more fun for you anyway, won't it?" It was not. Suddenly I found myself in a foreign land where the games were far different from those I had participated in before, and the space between the "girl section" and "boy section" of the schoolyard might well have been miles rather than yards. I was forced into a social group where I did not belong and where I was not welcomed.

The first principle outlined in the Queer Literacy Framework (QLF) is that an educator or administrator "refrains from possible presumptions that students ascribe to a gender" (Miller 2015, Fig. 1)—but this was not the case. One of my most heartbreaking early school memories was because my principal not only assumed that all students fit within the gender binary of male/female, but he actively enforced that divide. Had he only considered the benefits of students, regardless of gender identity or expression, interacting in a non-gender-segregated way, I would have been allowed to continue to interact with peers who made me feel comfortable and safe, without being forced to adhere to stereotypical notions of masculinity.

When I entered middle school in 1990, a year after Stephanie and I had met, I found myself trapped. The enormous space that had separated me from the other section of the playground had been replaced by a tiny box into which I worked to cram myself every single day. I knew at that age what it meant to "act like a boy," so I could play the part outwardly, but internally I was awash in conflicting and complex thoughts that ran contrary to what everyone expected and believed me to be. I did not know the phrase "gender nonconformity" or any similar concept, but I did know that who I was outwardly was not who I knew myself to really be.

Growing up in the rural South, my home and school were heavily influenced by deeply conservative Judeo-Christian values, and I was horrified to find that in addition to my struggle with my gender identity, for which I had no words to articulate my inner turmoil, I was also attracted to boys in my class. Certainly that part of who I was had a label: I was a homosexual. Pastors, teachers, and peers consistently provided clear messages that being gay was a sin and that any relationship with another boy had to be a platonic and casual friendship. To want or to pursue anymore was a path to damnation.

Additionally, my religious upbringing—reinforced at home, in the church, and in my public school classrooms—prevented me from having even the most basic knowledge of sexual health and desire. For years, I had believed that babies were born from women's belly buttons. But even after I had better understandings of anatomy, I had no ways to describe to others or to resolve within myself the yearnings that I felt both for my male and female classmates. I was alarmed by my sexual attraction to other boys and by my continued need to be more like other girls. I felt my cage closing tighter and tighter, and I began to spiral into deep bouts of depression.

Not only did the rural setting limit my access to knowledge and support, but there were no means through which I might obtain quality counseling or other support systems. Most of my classmates and I had to drive at least a half-an-hour roundtrip just to pick up basic items from the nearest store; mental and emotional health resources were impossible. There were no teachers whom I believed would understand. Their curricula constantly focused on White cisgender experiences, through the authors we read and the historical figures we discussed. When a teacher included a person of color, the issue of the individual's race was a fleeting fact that the teacher cursorily mentioned. As we read Langston Hughes in sophomore English, for example, the teacher asked us to examine symbolism without ever examining how the imagery connected to Hughes' racial identity. The teacher never once mentioned Hughes' sexuality. In history, as I flipped through pictures of women dressed as men in the early nineteenth century, I imagined their happiness to be dressed as their true selves, even while the teacher skipped over that section and focused instead on bootleggers and the World Wars.

After a time, the issue of my identity not being recognized anywhere that I turned, including my school, was too much. However, when I finally confided in a high school psychologist (and later a college psychologist) my constant but strange struggles to understand myself, the counselor actively avoided discussing the issue of gender expression, so it never came up. What we did discuss was my diet. How my intake of various nutrients was upsetting my emotional stability. The experts insisted that my suicide attempts and my struggles to gain some form of equilibrium were caused by bipolar tendencies that were the result of my diet. My self-reproach, my social performances, and my desperate efforts to understand myself were a matter of eating too much or too little sugar, they said. Who I knew that I was, and who I struggled to articulate, did not exist beyond my heart and head. My home, my church, my school, and even my counselors and doctors provided no ways for me to exist as I knew that I should.

The third principle of the QLF, that an educator who supports (a) gender identities "recognizes that masculinity and femininity constructs are assigned to gender norms and are situationally performed," might have saved me during this time (Miller 2015, Fig. 1). I had no one who articulated that gender fluidity was possible, much less healthy. Everyone around me assumed that masculinity and femininity were not only normal but the only ways to gender-identify; additionally, the seeming normality of a gender binary prevented the adults in my life from understanding the ways that I was trapped into unhappily performing masculinity. Just as importantly, their unawareness prevented them from noting the ways that they and my peers were also performing specific and learned versions of masculinity and femininity.

Stephanie's Perspective

I missed a lot of school for a variety of reasons, which often required that I sit in a classroom during "break" to make up work. I learned early that keeping quiet and looking busy gave me access to private teacher talk. Having just started sixth grade, I remember puzzling over something related to Moroccan geography. Something I had missed while out the week before. While I decided what colors I needed for a map activity, Mrs. Tory tried to look official thumbing through her L.L. Bean catalog. Suddenly another teacher, Mrs. Sherman, rushed in. I knew from previous experience that now was the time to look incredibly dedicated to my map, so I did not lift my head but definitely focused on her. She glanced at me, surely to confirm that I was not paying attention, and then began whispering to Mrs. Tory. Though I had always listened intently to the teacher talk that I knew I shouldn't be overhearing, I realized that on this day the topic of the conversation was one of my close friends, O'Tiss.

"I'm telling you, Ginger," Mrs. Sherman whispered, "that boy is 'funny.' Like too-much-estrogen-funny." I had long ago mastered the art of watching without looking, and I saw Mrs. Tory nod. She glanced my way, and I guarantee that from where she was sitting, I looked fully committed to Eastern African geography. "Well, Jean, I don't know what's wrong with him. His family's a good Christian family. He's got a father figure, and they go to church every week." The two then transitioned into a conversation about their daughters' Easter dresses, apparently inspired by the mention of church. But while they discussed sashes and bows, I numbly colored in Marrakech and considered how my friend was "funny," "wrong." I didn't understand the problem with O'Tiss, but I fully understood that my teachers had very clear notions of normalcy (Meyer 2009). They'd decided that he wasn't "right," and I was unsure of what to do with this information. I certainly could not tell O'Tiss—the information would only hurt his feelings. He was my friend, and I thought that he was wonderful, but I could not fathom what it meant that two teachers had described his "wrongness" at school in front of me.

As I retrospectively consider this moment through the lens of the third QLF principle, that an educator "recognizes that masculinity and femininity constructs are assigned to gender norms and are situationally performed" (Miller 2015, Fig. 1), I realize that both teachers recognized that O'Tiss was moving outside stereotypical masculine performance while their critiques of my friend worked to reinforce gender norms and stereotypical understandings of femininity and masculinity. They were clear in declaring that my friend's gender fluidity was "funny" and "wrong." Rather than examine the ways that my friend's family and church life were a part of constructing specific versions of masculinity that O'Tiss begrudgingly struggled to embody, they treated those social constructs both as reasons that my friend had failed to be a successful boy and as essential elements of properly conforming to traditional and stereotypical understandings of gender roles.

By the end of middle school, O'Tiss and I had started hanging out with one another during the school break. Most of our peers had boyfriends or girlfriends, but we had both stayed determinedly single. It was not that I had no interest. I was very much in love—as much as a preteen might be—with "Cynthia," who sat beside me in my science and English classes. Such desires were out of the question, though. When others questioned why O'Tiss and I were unattached but still constantly together, I laughingly justified our mutual singlehood and apparently odd friendship to my parents, teachers, and friends by reminding them that we were both extraordinarily nerdy. I knew, though, that O'Tiss served as a "cover" for me—I did not have to confront my sexuality because I could retreat to the social safety of having a close male friend. Retrospectively, I realize that it was a shared front: We were both trying to navigate what were socially forbidden desires and had somehow found one another in that struggle.

"What do you think about this?" I looked up from my book to see what O'Tiss was showing me. I had assumed, given our homework assignment, that it would be an algebraic equation; instead, I found that he had sketched a woman in a fur-lined dress. "O'Tiss, why do you always draw such impractical stuff? What woman is going to wear that junk for real?" He looked at me as if I was nuts. "What do you mean 'impractical'? Fashion isn't supposed to be practical! It's not like you really know what regular girls wear anyway, ya know." I rolled my eyes and went back to my book. Overhearing teachers and peers talk about any students who were "different," who were "queer"—though I did not know the word in that way yet—had taught me a great deal. I definitely did not know terms such as "heteronormativity" and "gender conformity" at the time, but I understood the concepts. I knew, without question, that if O'Tiss and I hung out with one another in public spaces, they would assume that we were together. Boy + Girl = Couple. The end. Use the system to avoid being abused by the system. Of course, we still did not avoid controversy: O'Tiss was Black and I was White, and Spike Lee's *Jungle Fever* had just been released. But having classmates sing Stevie Wonder's song lyrics under their breath was less threatening than the alternative of public conversations about topics like the one that Mrs. Tory and Ms. Sherman had discussed.

Like Aryah, I struggled to find self-representation in the many books that I read and the classes I attended. The only instance that I can recall in school of someone mentioning a queer individual was Aryah's and my senior English teacher telling us, "Oscar Wilde was gay, put on trial, and died in prison." The rampant homophobia and heteronormativity were both confusing and infuriating. However, unlike Aryah, I did have the luxury of a teacher ally who told me about her gay son and encouraged me to read Virginia Woolf, who she said was "another super smart and awesome lesbian." My cisgender identity, though I did not know the term at the time, allowed me to fit both social situations and my own body in ways that were not afforded to Aryah. And, even the teacher ally who supported me puzzled over Aryah's high school self and suggested that I help "your friend find a boyfriend after high school." There was no moment when gender identity and gender fluidity were a part of conversation, much less curriculum. I certainly struggled, but my friend was rendered invisible in ways that I had no way of understanding or supporting.

As wonderful as my support system was for me, my teacher allies and my understandings of gender ran counter to the first QLF principle. She nor I refrained "from possible presumptions that students ascribe to a gender" (Miller 2015, Fig. 1). While I loved my friend and wanted nothing more than Aryah's happiness, it never occurred to me that she should not be confined to a specific gender role. Aryah dressed and (unwillingly) behaved as a boy throughout our childhood, and both her teachers and I took the performance at face value. She looked, sounded, and acted like a boy, so she must be male. Had any person in Aryah's life allowed that students may not have a gender, or that gender performance and gender identity were not aligned, my friend might have had a very different experience. As someone who went to the same classes, had the same teachers, hung out with the same friend group as Aryah, and valued my friendship with her very much, I can attest that we both grew up in a school and social structure that not only assumed that all people had only one of two genders but also actively policed gender performance to ensure that all adults and students fell into what were the assumed "proper" gender roles.

CHALLENGES OF THE RURAL SOUTH

We recognize that what we experienced as children—the erasure of trans* identity, the inability to articulate a queer self, and the heavily structured and oppressive social norms—are not unique to a particular region. We also recognize, however, that the South has historically and presently been more resistant to change than other areas of the country. Related to the GLSEN study discussed earlier, the political and social attitudes toward queer rights influence Southern schools' policies as well. Eight states in the nation have what GLSEN terms "no promo homo" laws, which are "local or state education laws that expressly forbid teachers from discussing gay and transgender issues (including sexual health and HIV/AIDS awareness) in a positive light—if at all" (GLSEN 2012b). Of the eight, six are in the South—including South Carolina, which adopted a marriage equality law prior to the SCOTUS ruling. One of South Carolina's laws, for example, reads that educators "may not include a discussion of alternate sexual lifestyles from heterosexual relationships including, but not limited to, homosexual relationships except in the context of instruction concerning sexually transmitted diseases" (South Carolina Legislative Services Agency 2012).

However, these six states with laws that specifically prohibit positive inclusion of gender- and sexuality-queer figures and information are not exceptional in the region. Tennessee, a state without a "no promo homo" law, recently garnered media attention due to a proposed anti-bullying law change. The alteration would have permitted students to bully queer students, if the bullying was due to religious beliefs ("Tennessee anti-bullying law" 2012). Specifically, the law "would allow students to speak out against homosexuality without punishment if that's what their religious beliefs call for."

On top of the political and cultural climates that make being a queer Southerner challenging, our experiences in rural communities add another layer of complexity. Rural communities generally have diminished access to resources, to information, and to facilities. For example, rural living sometimes means driving substantial distances to access the nearest supportive community groups. Additionally, while online communities offer support options today that did not exist when we were teenagers, many rural communities continue to have limited access to resources such as Wi-Fi (Guerin 2014). These issues with access created for both of us very isolating experiences. Even if we had had someone with whom we might have talked, which was unlikely given the circumstances, we had no words to explain. That is why Aryah had doctors examine her diet rather than discuss her efforts to articulate her struggles with gender roles and social expectations. The sociocultural and sociopolitical elements of the Southeast, coupled with the access issues of living in rural areas, make being a safe and happy nonconforming person challenging at best.

Supporting Trans* Students in Rural Schools

This book is long overdue in supporting educators, students, community members, and others in their efforts to recognize trans* experiences as being unique to each individual while considering what they might do to help. We are confident that other chapters here will support trans* populations and teacher advocates, even if the chapters are not specific to this particular section of the USA. Students in the rural South consistently report that teachers and other school members are essential to students feeling safe and empowered in school and home settings (e.g., Blackburn 2012; Mayo 2014; Miller and Gilligan 2013) and that students also report the incredible value of having resources available to teachers that bolster teacher activism and support teachers' abilities to support LGBT*IAGCQ student health.

However, because we grew up in and now work in areas of the nation where politicians, community leaders, and others actively and openly oppose permitting spaces for trans* identities, we want to consider viable teacher actions within the context of the rural South. Even without all Southern states having the "no promo homo" laws, most states restrict discussions of queer topics in school, and research shows that many teachers feel that queer topics have no place in classrooms (e.g., Blackburn 2012; DeWitt 2012; Thein 2013). Therefore, while the QLF discussed in the Introduction and elsewhere will be extremely helpful to many educators, not all actions are feasible in all contexts.

There is justifiable fear and genuine risk for educators who choose to adopt the QLF in particular settings and contexts. Stephanie, who was a high school teacher in the rural South for seven years, had an influential local pastor complain to the school district superintendent, for example, when the pastor learned that Stephanie was incorporating queer topics and theories into her curriculum. Though not a student's parent, the pastor's concerns required that Stephanie attend multiple meetings, and she ultimately had to threaten her administration with legal intervention through her membership in a state-level educators' association. The proposed course of action had the intended effect: the school administration ultimately thanked the pastor for his concern while supporting Stephanie's curricular decisions. This experience is intended to remind those teachers working in socially and politically conservative contexts that there are numerous resources available through state-level organizations, national-level organizations such as the National Council of Teachers of English's (NCTE) LGBT Strand and Gay/Straight Educators' Alliance (GSEA), and online communities. Stephanie often had to find advice and support from Internet allies, as there were none available at the school level.

Additionally, as the most recent GLSEN research shows (2012c), sociocultural context matters very much both in terms of what students experience and what teachers may accomplish. When teachers who adopt the QLF work in contexts where administrators actively subscribe to rigid gender roles and colleagues use language and curriculum that reinforce gender stereotypes, they do important work, but often in professional and social isolation or even hostility. However, educators should be aware of school-, state-, and federal-level hate crime and bullying laws, as well as Title IX protections, that permit educators to support non-gender-conforming students without fear of reprisal (e.g., Meyer 2009).

However, to focus solely on the risks of doing this sort of work is to potentially leave teachers hesitant to act, and for students such as Aryah, left to feel unsupported and alone. We have both grown and learned too much to allow fear to trump justice, and we choose instead to focus on what can and should be done—now, tomorrow, and beyond. The first principle of the QLF asks that teachers adjust their thinking and "never presume that students have a gender" (Miller 2015, Fig. 1). Given the sociocultural contexts and realities of teaching in the rural South or other equally problematic settings, it may be impossible for teachers to ask students directly about pronoun usage, for example. However, we would recommend that teachers actively reflect on what it means to live in a society that assigns gender to everything—even pens and phone cases—when not all people accept the gender that they are assigned and not all people self-assign a gender at all, and then encourage their students to do the same. For example, teachers might use a short story in which the author does not assign gender to a character and ask students to consider why they tend to ascribe a gender to the character anyway. One story that Stephanie has used with great success is "The Fabulous Story of X," a fictional story about an agender child who grows up to be the happiest and most well-adjusted student in the school. Discussion might then shift to the implications of assigning and assuming gender, with the teacher or students examining personal experiences when others have made gender-based assumptions about them, based on their clothing, their voice, their mannerisms, or other characteristics. Such a conversation would permit opportunities to examine gender as both a performance and a social construction. Because these conversations begin with a curriculum-relevant short story—which the teacher selects because of the likelihood of it permitting conversations about (a)gender expression and identity—and shifts to students' personal experiences, there is minimal risk to the teacher. Teachers tend to know which texts are low-risk in their particular contexts, and the lesson becomes an academically defensible one about making gender-based assumptions without textual support, which can easily shift to personal experiences that help the students connect directly with the text.

Additionally, the third QLF principle is a means of both navigating limiting school contexts and actively serving as an ally to trans* students. The principle states that an educator "recognizes that masculinity and femininity constructs are assigned to gender norms and are situationally performed" (Miller 2015, Fig. 1). One recommendation for teachers who wish to help students appreciate the social constructions and performativity of "male" and "female," which most people take for granted as "normal," is to have students list out behaviors, clothing, and other characteristics that they deem to be specifically masculine or feminine. Over the course of the semester or year, students could return to this list and, through the lenses of various assigned texts, consider the ways that particular authors reinforce or challenge these gender norms. Importantly, the teacher could use the discussions as opportunities to examine gender performance fluidity, particularly in novels, plays, or longer works during which students have extended opportunities to chart how various characters' gender performances shift. A traditional and "safe" author at the secondary level, William Shakespeare provides ample opportunities to examine issues of gender performance and fluidity. The Shakespearean standard of men-dressed-as-women and men-dressed-as-women-performing-as-men, in plays such as *Twelfth Night* and *The Merchant of Venice*, provide important opportunities for students to consider multiple ways of performing gender, both within the context of the play and in their own lives. And neither the author nor the texts create significant risk for classroom teachers in most school contexts.

A final recommendation comes in relation to helping trans* students feel safe and healthy. Miller (2015) wrote, "[O]ur personhood depends on recognition, which is connected to social norms. Yes, some of these conditions make life unlivable" (p. 38). Both Aryah in this chapter and Miller in the Introduction describe suicide attempts as part of their efforts to fully actualize themselves. When students are not given spaces in which they have autonomy over their identities, they live in a state where constant "social, institutional, or political violence" is visited on their persons (Miller 2015, p. 38). Though state and school policies may prevent direct conversations about trans* identity in some spaces in this region of the country, it is reasonable to ask that teachers permit students to have writing opportunities and safe spaces in which they might recognize and be recognized by others for their in situ self-determined (a)gender and (a)sexuality identities. Teachers who adopt the QLF can permit these writing spaces with no public risk at all.

Coming Home to Our Younger Selves

This chapter started with the two of us giggling over an intercom announcement about hunting season. Though we both very much felt the confines forced upon us as we moved through school, there were certainly times of happiness that we found with one another and our peers. The friendships that allowed Aryah to fashion and model dresses from hotel sheets during a field trip gave her small moments when she could feel at peace with herself, and helped her childhood friends to love her in such a way that they readily embrace and celebrate her trans* activism as an adult. Stephanie's access to a teacher ally both made her transition to being an out lesbian possible and facilitated her identity as an educator who readily adopted a queer pedagogy that examines issues such as gender construction, fluidity, and performance. However, there were a number of ways that we both might have been better served as children, and we hope that our experiences and reflection will empower other educators and administrators to act when the ones we had access to did not. Each of us had a key moment when, had we had the knowledge and bravery that we have now, we would have spoken up to challenge ourselves and the adults in our lives.

Aryah's Response

In reflecting on my elementary school principal declaring, "You are to cease playing with the girls on the playground. You are to play with the little boys, where you belong. That will be more fun for you anyway, won't it?" I recognize that moment as one of the key turning points in my unhappy efforts to constantly maintain a convincing public performance as a male student. If there were a time machine that would allow me to go back and advocate for my younger self, I would demand of the principal, "Why do you want the playground divided so completely into a 'boys' section and girls' section anyway? Wouldn't it be better if you helped all of us to play and learn together? Wouldn't the boys benefit from the challenges of the girls' jump rope games, and wouldn't the girls enjoy the strategies required in some of the boys' sports? And, if the answer to all of those questions is an irresponsible and unbelievable 'No,' then help me to understand what the harm is in an eight-year-old choosing what games to play and which peers to befriend? What is the purpose of recess for elementary children, if not to exercise and to learn to form social relationships? I'm getting both opportunities no matter where I am on the playground, am I not?"

As I consider the QLF, and especially the two principles that we focus on in this chapter, I realize that the biggest challenge that I faced was that everyone around me "presume[d] that students have a gender" and that that gender correlated with the sex assigned at birth (Miller 2015, Fig. 1, Principle 1). Had a single administrator, teacher, counselor, psychologist, family member, or friend recognized that I did not need to change sides on the playground, I did not need to change my dietary intake of sugar, I did not need to change me at all, then my childhood, adolescence, and young adulthood would have been dramatically different, I believe. No single person should ever underestimate their potential impact on a life. I certainly had family, friends, and school personnel who loved me and whom I loved, but it was a long and arduous process to be able to articulate my authentic self. One person who understood gender beyond stereotypes would have made that journey a far less rocky path.

Stephanie's Response

As Aryah and I wrote this chapter, I had ample time to reflect on our shared experiences and my position as her friend. In looking back, I realize that there were significant ways in which I might have supported her, except that I did not have the vocabulary or awareness to do so. I am cisgender and so I never had a reason to push against gender constructions until much later in life. I fit into the gender system that Aryah and I were navigating, and my gender privilege prevented me from seeing the ways I did not and could not support my friend. If I could borrow the time machine that Aryah imagined, I would say the following to her: "I do not understand what it means to live as a person who is gendered against her will in ways that force you to adopt mannerisms and dress that run counter to who you know yourself to be, but I will work to understand so that I might better support and love you." My only wish would have been to keep my friend healthy and happy, and neither she nor I had the words to make that possible.

The third principle of the QLF is key to my reflections on my experiences: "Recognizes that masculinity and femininity constructs are assigned to gender norms and are situationally performed" (Miller 2015, Fig. 1). To the teachers who gossiped about my friend and who made LGBT issues in the curriculum either invisible or negative, I would say, "I understand, having been a classroom teacher myself now, that one can never have all of the knowledge and freedom to do what best serves all students. However, it is necessary to recognize that gender norms and stereotypes hurt all people, not just trans* people. All people constantly perform gender, based on societal assumptions of what it means to be female or male. But no one performs the same way all of the time; we all adopt at least a degree of gender fluidity in our performances. Recognizing these performances and fluid movements in yourselves, in the students you teach, and in the literature you assign can help all students to examine limiting social structures that keep us tied to confining notions of gender." As someone who graduated in 1997, I recognize that much of the vocabulary and awareness that is possible now was not as readily available then, but like Aryah, I recognize teachers' importance in taking the information here in this book, especially in relation to the QLF to support the mental, emotional, social, and physical well-being of trans* students like Aryah.

Closing Thoughts

We both insist that gender is only as confining and powerful as our society allows it to be, and educators are key in helping students value themselves and others without gender being a prison, as it is for many. We would also remind educators that trans* students of color are at increased risk of harassment and bullying, given the many intersections of race and gender (Diaz and Kosciw 2009). We acknowledge that teachers who work in extremely sociopolitically conservative regions risk livelihood and even safety in advocating for, recognizing—believe it or not—understanding, and supporting all trans* and gender creative students. However, as Miller (2015) suggests, "no one personhood is of any more or less value than any other" (p. 38), and teachers' words, actions, and lessons have the power to demonstrate to trans* and gender creative students that their identities are not only valuable but validated. There are risks in this work, but the resistance and resiliency make efforts both possible and imperative. This is important work that literally has the power to save lives. It is time to shift ways of thinking to provide different ways of being in our schools.

REFERENCES

Blackburn, M. V. (2012). *Interrupting hate: Homophobia in schools and what literacy can do about it.* New York: Teachers College Press.

DeWitt, P. M. (2012). *Dignity for all: Safeguarding lgbt students.* Thousand Oaks: Corwin.

Diaz, E. M., & Kosciw, J. G. (2009). *Shared differences: The experiences of lesbian, gay, bisexual, and transgender students of color in our nation's schools.* Retrieved from http://www.glsen.org/learn/research/national/report-shared-differences

GLSEN. (2012a, September 05). *2011 National School Climate Survey: Lgbt youth face pervasive, but decreasing levels of harassment.* Retrieved from http://www.glsen.org/cgi-bin/iowa/all/library/record/2897.html

GLSEN. (2012b). *"No promo homo" laws.* Retrieved from http://glsen.org/learn/policy/issues/nopromohomo

GLSEN. (2012c, December 11). *Strengths & silences: The experiences of lesbian, gay, bisexual and transgender students in rural and small town schools.* Retrieved from http://www.glsen.org/cgibin/iowa/all/library/record/2916.html?state=research&type=research

GLSEN. (2013, May 03). *Strengths & silences: A transgender life in rural America.* Retrieved from http://www.glsen.org/blog/strengths-silences-transgender-life-rural-america

Guardian Interactive Team. (2012, May 8). *Gay rights in the US, state by state.* Retrieved from http://www.guardian.co.uk/world/interactive/2012/may/08/gay-rights-united-states

Guerin, E. (2014). *Rural Americans have inferior internet access.* Retrieved from https://www.hcn.org/issues/46.2/rural-americans-have-inferior-internet-access

Human Rights Campaign. (2014). *Marriage center.* Retrieved from http://www. hrc.org/campaigns/marriage-center

Mayo, C. (2014). Preparing teachers and leaders to be advocates. In J. A. Banks (Ed.), *LGBTQ youth & education: Policies & practices.* New York: Teachers College Press.

Meyer, E. J. (2009). *Gender, bullying, and harassment: Strategies to end sexism and homophobia in schools.* New York: Teacher College Press.

Miller, s. (2015). A queer literacy framework promoting (a)gender and (a)sexuality self-determination and justice. *English Journal, 104*(5), 37–44.

Miller, s., & Gilligan, J. R. (2013). The distressing realities about queer-related (LGBTQGV) bullying. In s. Miller, L. D. Burns, & T. S. Johnson (Eds.), *Generation bullied 2.0: Prevention and intervention strategies for our most vulnerable students* (pp. 33–48). New York: Peter Lang.

Roosevelt, K. (2015). *Can Texas defy Supreme Court's same-sex marriage ruling?* Retrieved from http://www.cnn.com/2015/07/01/opinions/ roosevelt-same-sex-marriage-enforcement/

South Carolina Legislative Services Agency. South Carolina Legislature. (2012). *South Carolina code of laws unannotated current through the end of the 2012 session* (SECTION 59-32-30-5). Retrieved from website: http://www.scstatehouse.gov/code/t59c032.php

Tennessee Anti-Bullying Law Change Could Allow Students to Speak Out Against Gays for Religious Reasons: Report. (2012, January 05). *The Huffington Post.* Retrieved from http://www.huffingtonpost.com/2012/01/04/tennessee-anti-bullying-law-change-gays-religion-_n_1183915.html

Thein, A. H. (2013). Language arts teachers' resistance to teaching lgbt literature and issues. *Language Arts, 90*(3), 169–180.

Whitlock, R. U. (2010). Getting queer: Teacher education, gender studies, and the cross-disciplinary quest for queer pedagogies. *Issues in Teacher Education, 19*(2), 81–104.

Williams, P., & Robinson, K. (2015). *Federal judge: Alabama judges must issue same-sex marriage licenses.* Retrieved from http://www.nbcnews.com/news/ us-news/federal-judge-alabama-judges-must-issue-same-sex-marriage-licenses-n385141

CHAPTER 9

Introducing (A)gender into Foreign/ Second Language Education

Paul Chamness Miller and Hidehiro Endo

Queer Literacy Framework Principles:

2. Understands gender as a construct, which has and continues to be impacted by intersecting factors (e.g., social, historical, material, cultural, economic, religious);
6. Engages in ongoing critique of how gender norms are reinforced in literature, media, technology, art, history, science, math, and so on;
7. Understands how Neoliberal principles reinforce and sustain compulsory heterosexism, which secures homophobia; and how gendering secures bullying and transphobia;
8. Understands that (a)gender intersect with other identities (e.g., sexual orientation, culture, language, age, religion, social class, body type, accent, height, ability, disability, and national origin) that inform students' beliefs and, thereby, action; and,
10. Believes that students who identify on a continuum of gender identities deserve to learn in environments free of bullying and harassment.

P.C. Miller (✉) • H. Endo
Akita International University, Akita, Japan

© The Editor(s) (if applicable) and The Author(s) 2016
sj Miller (ed.), *Teaching, Affirming, and Recognizing Trans and Gender Creative Youth*, DOI 10.1057/978-1-137-56766-6_9

Why Challenging Gendernormativty Matters to Us

Paul is a former high school French teacher, who has become a secondary education teacher educator and a writing/composition professor in an English for Academic Purposes (EAP) program of a small liberal arts college. Hidehiro was a university undergraduate Japanese language teacher, followed by being a high school English teacher in Japan, and is currently a teacher educator for a high school English language teaching licensure program at the same small liberal arts college. We have often heard pre- and in-service teachers, classroom teachers, as well as faculty say that their job is to teach only their content. In our case as language teachers, that usually means teaching one or more of the four skills of language (i.e., speaking, listening, reading, and writing). However, language teaching and learning goes beyond these skills to include what the American Council on the Teaching of Foreign Languages (ACTFL 2015) has outlined in their commonly called *5 Cs*: Communication, Cultures, Connections, Comparisons, and Communities. Despite these standards not specifically including sexual and (a)gender identities among their goals, there is a recurring theme within these standards that includes using languages to engage with global communities, understand difference, and develop critical thinking. There are similar expectations in the standards put forth by the Teaching English to Speakers of Other Languages International Association (TESOL 2006). Even though the TESOL standards are organized and worded very differently from ACTFL's standards, the emphasis of using language to engage in globalization, diversity, and critical thinking is similar.

While there are similarities between these two leading organization's standards, the problem and benefit of these standards is that they are vaguely written. The problem is that the obscurity in the language of standards allows for those at state and school district levels to determine what can and should be included in the curriculum. State governments and local school boards that are largely run by socially conservative individuals may deliberately limit curriculum to exclude the possibility of queering the classroom. The benefit, however, is that the ambiguity in the language of the professional organizations' standards affords teachers the ability to meet targeted language standards and include in the curriculum components that challenge gendernormative binaries.

Though these standards target grades K-12, the examples we provide here are perhaps most appropriate for junior and senior high school classrooms. Additionally, our examples illustrate how to take the same goals and apply them to a freshman intensive writing course at a university setting. Of course, this is not to say that one should not trans*cend the curriculum in earlier grades using similar activities, but the learners' linguistic ability must be taken into consideration when planning such activities. This is particularly important when working with language learners, as they are also processing language as well as content at the same time. If the tasks are too taxing on their language ability, they are likely to not meet content goals the teacher has as the aim for the lesson.

Many language teachers may question why it should be up to them to challenge and queer the curriculum. After all, they were hired to teach French, German, Spanish, English, or others, right? But as (Miller, this volume, Chap. 1, p. 8) points out, youth in the USA who do not conform to one label or the other of the gender binary are at the highest risk for suicide (Ybarra et al. 2014), academic struggles, and bullying, among many other difficulties (Kosciw et al. 2014). Unfortunately, in Japan the educational experiences of Lesbian, Gay, Bisexual, Trans* (LGBT) youth mirror that of the USA, with nearly 70 percent of LGBT youth having experienced bullying, of which about half have attempted suicide (Aoki 2014). Additionally, because high school is not compulsory in Japan, it is even easier for youth who are bullied and struggling to not finish secondary education. Sadly, both the number of bullying cases and dropout rate are on the rise in Japan (MEXT 2012).

Unfortunately, there is no data like that of Kosciw, Greytak, Palmer, and Boesen that is broken down by grade level, or even to compare from one year to the next about LGBT youth. Only one attempt was made to collect similar data across schools in Japan, but the Tokyo Education Bureau ordered the organization to stop and to shred any data they had already collected (Maruko 2015), despite teachers, activists, parents, and citizens' concerns over the number of youth suicides in Japan. It is unclear exactly why the Bureau put an end to the study, despite having claimed they are concerned for the welfare of LGBT youth in Japan. Many interpret this action (or rather the lack thereof) on the part of government as a disinterest in the plight of LGBT children and adolescents.

Given that bullying is universal, we believe it is the ethical duty of *every* teacher to provide a safe, positive learning environment for *all* students (Miller 2010), irrespective of the content one teaches. Integrating Miller's (2015) QLF into teacher's disposition, its application to classroom practice can help to ensure that school is a safe, embracing milieu for every child or adolescent, regardless of the subject matter one teaches. In order to nourish this framework, achieving such a school climate must come from within each classroom, which goes beyond a set of superficial classroom rules that are broken daily by students and teachers alike. This type of environment comes from a commitment of the language teacher to engage learners with not only the development of their linguistic skills but also connecting that curriculum to *all* aspects of the lives of the students, including their (a)gender identity, as well as those whom they call family— noting that "family" is a common theme that repeatedly appears in second language curriculum. In so doing, the teacher will have implemented all ten of the Principles of the framework, especially Principles 2, 6, 7, 8, and 10. The example we provide in this chapter illustrates and generates possibilities to achieve these goals on a regular basis in our own classrooms.

It is imperative that language teachers be committed to making their classrooms and curriculum inclusive for all learners, because many second language learners have not come from a culture of understanding the concepts of discrimination or social justice. In some cases, such as Japan, such topics are not even a part of conversations in schools, at home, nor in the community. This ideology comes from the fact that Japan is largely a conformist society, where everyone is expected to think and act the same (at least superficially). Furthermore, most Japanese believe the myth that the Japanese society is homogeneous, despite the fact that society is evolving before their very eyes. Consequently, the government does not recognize the fact that the nation needs to further promote diverse human social identities, including the curriculum. Thus, students in Japan have few opportunities to think about the experiences of people from underrepresented groups who are living right next door to them. Accordingly, second language learners who come from environments where social justice is not a part of daily discourse tend to find it difficult to fully engage in discussions about social justice issues in class because not only are they unfamiliar with the issues, but they do not possess the language to express their views.

The challenge for teachers who wish second language learners to participate in discussions of social justice and diversity is to consider other methods besides only using words to allow learners to express themselves. One such example is to consider coupling a reduced amount of writing with other media for expression, such as creating artistic projects with drawing, painting, collages, and other tasks that reduce the amount of language necessary to achieve the goals of the lesson. Such activities provide opportunities for individuals to express themselves beyond words not in their vocabularies and can reduce the cognitive load that processing language significantly requires above their current abilities (Al-Shehri and Gitsaki 2010; Leahy and Sweller 2004; Paas et al. 2010). In so doing, the second language learner is able to use cognitive resources on the content of the lesson, while simultaneously learning new vocabulary, linguistic structures, and other aspects of language.

Not only are there linguistic benefits in using art in educational settings that include second language learners, but such methods are also a unique yet important method in gaining information about how an individual makes sense of a social issue (Leavy 2009). Knowles and Cole (2008) note that the in-depth exploration of artwork enables people to produce an insightful description that words just cannot always convey. Furthermore, Adams (2002) found that artistic expression could have a positive impact on the growth of social justice movements. Specific to language learners, Berho and Defferding (2005) discovered that incorporating a visual practice into English as a Second Language (ESL) lessons plays an important role in creating a positive learning atmosphere for language learners. We have found that the engagement in an artistic project provides learners who may not be so outspoken with more effective opportunities to freely express their feelings about social justice issues.

CHALLENGING GENDERNORMATIVITY IN THE SECOND LANGUAGE CLASSROOM

The setting of our work is a small liberal arts university in rural Japan that is ranked among the top five universities in Japan. There are two majors: global studies and global business. The entire curriculum, university wide, is taught in English, in an effort to prepare students to be global citizens and to be highly sought in the job market upon graduation. As a result, all students on the campus speak English (of varying degrees of ability); however, the majority of students are native speakers of Japanese, learning English as a second, third, or fourth language. All of the students, except for a very small percent of native English speakers, must first pass the EAP program before moving into their major. In this program, students are to take three separate courses: Academic Writing, Academic Reading, and Speaking and Listening, with the goal of ensuring that their linguistic skills are advanced enough to be successful in their electives and courses for their major. Depending on the level of linguistic ability, students are in this program for a single semester or up to two additional semesters, provided they pass each set of courses. Students who fail could be in the program for two or more years before being able to move into general education courses. The activities we describe in this chapter took place in Academic Writing, one of the three required courses. In this course, the primary goals are to help students develop the skills to write academic essays and to develop critical thinking skills, but it is up to the instructor to decide how to achieve these goals. Another unique requirement of all students at the university is that they are required to study abroad for one year. Japanese K-12 education does not teach students about issues of social justice, equity, or even critical thinking. As a result, in addition to a focus on developing language skills in our English writing courses, there is also a goal of teaching our students how to think critically in preparation for their year abroad and as part of our mission of fostering global-minded citizens of the world.

Although we teach in two different programs at the same university (Paul teaches the Academic Writing course; Hidehiro teaches in the Teacher Licensure Program), we both have the same goals in our courses for our students, who are in their first semester, after graduating from high school one month earlier. The university's general goal is to prepare global citizens, which some faculty, including us, interpret to include promoting an understanding of and commitment to social justice and challenging gendernormativity, among other topics. We decided to collaborate given we have many students in common (i.e., they are often enrolled in both of our courses), but we use the writing course as the context for the work with our students.

This particular project that we designed takes place over two days and combines an emphasis on two primary goals for the course: developing writing skills in English and fostering critical thinking. On the first day, we ask the students to read *Michael's Diary* (Bryant 2013). This story, presented in a shortened diary format, is about a ten-year-old boy named Michael whose dream is to receive a sewing machine for his birthday. This story offers a critical opportunity to challenge gendernormativity in a second language classroom, not only because of the story but also because of the way in which it is written. In diary format, the sentences are short, written in conversation style, and each "entry" of the diary is its own topic. These features of the reading will afford a second language reader the ability to process the language more easily than a typical story written in narrative style. For the lesson, the students were asked to read the piece on their own. After students completed the reading, we led a group discussion where they were asked to think about the meaning behind the reading, what it means to be *bullied*—a term that is, unfortunately, becoming all too common across cultures—at school, what it means to have supportive parents, especially when a child is trans* or gender creative (Miller, this volume, Chap. 1), and how this story might have been received if the family were Japanese. There were several guiding questions to facilitate the discussion, displayed in Table 9.1. Once our class discussion was complete, students broke up into small groups of three or four where they drew and colored (with colored pencils, markers, or crayons) anything they wanted about their understanding of the topic and themes of the story. Students were also encouraged to talk to each other while they were working. Additionally, they were asked to write a short description of their drawing.

To illustrate the product that comes from this activity, see Fig. 9.1, which is a sample of one of our students.

While some of the students often choose to depict a summary of the entire reading, which is acceptable in this particular context, many students choose to focus on one aspect of the story that is particularly salient at the moment. In this case, the student focused on the idea of acceptance, as can be seen in the drawing and in the description provided. The drawing depicts Michael with a balloon image of his sister accepting him, another picture in the upper-right corner of his peers not accepting him, and another of his parents in the upper-left corner unhappy that he does not enjoy activities that are socially constructed for boys to like. The student also noted in the writing that "people around him can't accept this fact easily" but that "his father is trying to accept the fact and allow him to live as he is."

As another illustration (Fig. 9.2), this particular student chose to focus on what makes Michael sad and what makes him happy, demonstrating an understanding of the importance of doing things not because they are typical of the gender binary construct that society imposes on us but because they bring us joy and fulfillment. For example, this student divided the drawing into two sections: things that make Michael sad and things that make him happy. On the "sad" side are pictures depicting sports, scissors to represent cutting his hair (because Michael likes to keep his hair long), and peers making fun of him. On the "happy" side, one finds a sewing machine, clothes he has made, and the love of his parents. The student's words reveal an understanding that "even though his preferences are different from others, the love of the people around him will never change."

Fig. 9.1 Sample of *Michael's Diary*: acceptance

Fig. 9.2 Sample of *Michael's Diary*: what makes him happy?

Along with this revelation, this student has shown through the drawing and caption the importance of doing what makes us happy, not doing what is socially constructed by society.

However, it is a challenge for some students to fully grasp the point of the lesson. As evidenced in Fig. 9.3, this particular student, while perhaps accepting and understanding some of the ideas behind the lesson, still attributes certain activities and characteristics to one particular gender (e.g., pink is for girls, blue is for boys; sports are for boys; sewing is for girls). The student's drawing displays this way of thinking where we see a bow on top of Michael's head that is half blue and half pink. Inside the lightning, the student has attributed certain activities to either boys or girls, based again on a small person with either pink or blue. The drawing is explained in the caption, where the student wrote, "he is a boy, but he like [sic] things that girls like." At the same time, the student acknowledges the love of Michael's parents, irrespective of his interests, but again

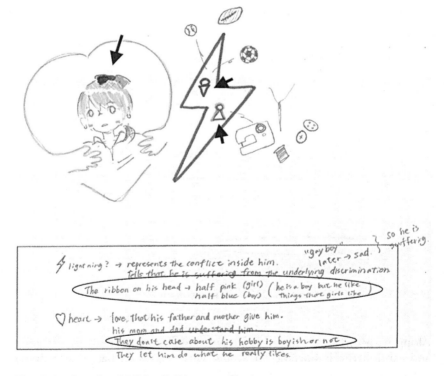

Fig. 9.3 Sample of *Michael's Diary*: conflict

couched in the stereotypical attributes of what it means to be a boy: "They don't care about [sic] his hobby is boyish or not." While this example might appear to be a lack of success, we are able to use such examples to help us monitor the progress that our students are making with the challenges to gendernormative ideas with our activities.

The second session takes place in the same manner, on the next class session, where students read *Death by Bullying* (Lockette 2009). This is a short blog post that discusses the rise in the number of teenagers who are committing suicide because of bullying, and in particular remembers the death of Carl Hoover, who was bullied not because he identified as gay or trans* but simply because his peers perceived him as such. This story is a great contrast to the reading in the first lesson, because, unlike Michael, Carl conformed to what society expects of a boy; he was involved in several sports and even the Boy Scouts. But somehow, his peers believed that he failed to fully conform to the social construct of what a boy is supposed to be. Sadly, he ended his own life right before his twelfth birthday. Again, this particular reading is ideal for non-native speakers of English because the reading is short and the paragraphs are manageable. Perhaps even more important is that the author provides simple examples and statistics and even suggests resources that students and teachers can take to help counter bullying and hopefully save a life. Once the students read the article, we lead a short whole-class discussion in which students talk openly about bullying, and especially whether they think bullying is a problem in Japan or not, and specifically on their campus. Then in small groups, students use the remaining class time to draw and color a response to the reading in the same way as the previous day's tasks. They also write a short narrative to describe the drawing once they have finished their artwork. Once again, during the small group activity, students are encouraged to talk about the reading and their drawings as they work (see Table 9.1).

Figure 9.4 is an example of the type of product that results from this lesson.

This student emphasized the importance of the role that adults (i.e., teachers and parents) play in the prevention of bullying. One of the questions raised in the reading is whether students should be left to fend for themselves or if it is adults' responsibility to help protect them. This particular question was salient to this student at that particular time. As the drawing indicates, this student believes that it is the teacher's job to protect students at school. Furthermore, parents can also play a role in

Table 9.1   Overview of the lesson

	Overall theme	Lesson steps	Guiding questions
Day 1	Challenging gendernormativity	Read *Michael's Diary* Whole class discussion	N/A What does it mean to be bullied? Why are students bullied? Does bullying happen on our campus? What kinds of expectations does society have on boys and girls? What happens when someone does not fit the stereotype of a boy or girl? Do you think Japanese parents would be supportive like Michael's parents? Why or why not? What about Japanese classmates? Would they bully a boy for wanting a sewing machine? Why or why not? What does it mean to have supportive parents, especially when a child doesn't conform to gender stereotypes?
		Drawing/writing activity Small group discussion	N/A Discuss what you drew and why? What does this represent to you?

protecting their children. As noted in the student's caption, "teachers' and parents' actions can help children."

Figure 9.5 illustrates a darker understanding of the issue of bullying on this particular student's mind. She noted that "nothing could have helped him from bullying," which she connects in her drawing to his sports and Boy Scouts, suggesting that perhaps there is no hope for students who are bullied, even when they are doing everything society says they should do. As noted in Table 9.1, one of the topics discussed in class around this reading is what we can do as teachers, parents, classmates, and members of society to change what is happening, especially in situations such as Carl's,

Table 9.1 (continued)

	Overall theme	Lesson steps	Guiding questions
Day 2	Bullying and gendernormativity	Read *Death by Bullying*	N/A
		Whole class discussion	Is bullying a problem in Japan?
			How are students bullied?
			How (if at all) do teachers respond to bullying?
			Do teens use Facebook or other media to bully?
			What happens if a student bullies someone else? Do they get punished?
			Do you think teenage suicide is a problem in Japan?
		Drawing/writing activity	N/A
		Small group discussion	Discuss what you drew and why?
			What does this represent to you?

where what he does is just not good enough for his peers to accept him. One of the purposes of this story is to lead students to see that bullying is often about perception, because many students (especially in cultures where conformity is emphasized) think, before taking our courses, that to stop bullying, students should just stop whatever behavior is making others want to bully them. This student demonstrated her beginning of understanding this idea.

The last example, Fig. 9.6, exemplifies a similar way of thinking to that displayed in Fig. 9.3, namely the difficulty in letting go of the gender binary of male and female. We see this in his drawing, where Carl is seen with a basketball and a soccer ball and then he is seen in a dress. This student referred to his actions that reflected what is typically perceived as a girl in his textual description. As the student noted in the caption, "He was being bullyed [sic] because of his actions like a girl [sic]." Students who have been engrained to believe that certain behaviors are for girls and certain behaviors are for boys often grapple with changing their ideas of these social constructs for a very long time. Some may never accept that there are other views of (a)gender identity because of very rigid constructs about how one should behave. Students who do not conform to society's

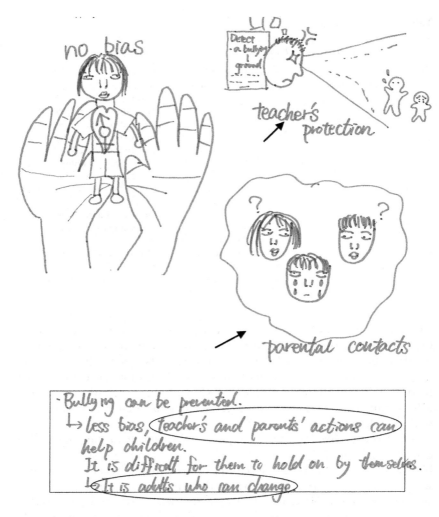

Fig. 9.4 Sample of *Death by Bullying*: adults can help

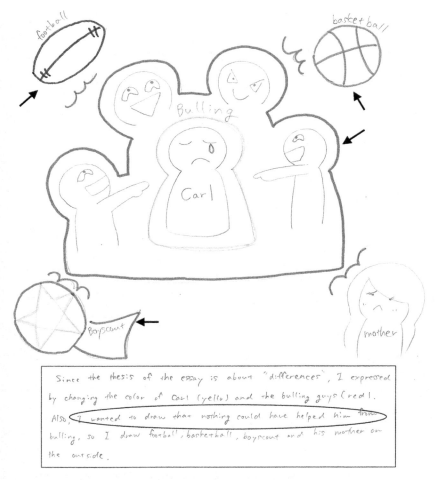

Fig. 9.5 Sample of *Death by Bullying*: nothing can help

construct of what it means to be a boy or a girl tend to be blamed when they are victimized, as if society is saying, "Well, if you would act like everyone else does, you wouldn't be bullied." This example alludes to this way of thinking, almost implicitly blaming Carl for his own death.

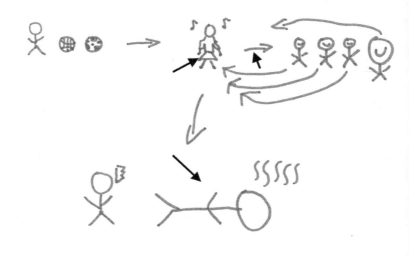

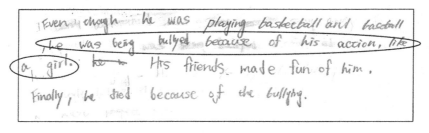

Fig. 9.6 Sample of *Death by Bullying*: blaming the victim

These lessons, given early in the semester, clearly show that by combining reading, writing, and artistic work, students can not only develop the linguistic skills necessary to express their understanding of social justice issues but also challenge their ways of thinking about such important concepts as (a)gender identity. Obviously, this is only the beginning of thinking about such topics for most of our students, and two lessons that take place in a two-hour period of time twice is hardly sufficient for having a lasting impact on students.

In order to continue challenging students' preconceived social norms in general, it is imperative to continually and consistently embed opportunities to challenge gendernormative ideology throughout the semester. Since challenges to such ideologies underscore objectives for the course, several other writing projects deepen what students have learned from these lessons. Students are expected to write three "traditional" essays throughout the course, including compare and contrast, argumentation, and cause and effect. Even though students are able to choose a topic that interests them, we steer students in the direction of topics related to social justice issues, such as LGBT rights, women's rights, racial/ethnic discrimination, and Islamophobia, among other social concerns. Even if a student chooses not to focus on such topics, they will continually have exposure to these themes through peer editing, group presentations, and other readings that we select for the course that exemplify the rhetorical modes that are studied in the course.

BEING A TEACHER IS MORE THAN TEACHING CONTENT

The language classroom is a place for so much more than a mere focus on listening, speaking, reading, and writing, because language is one component of a society's composition. It is, therefore, not logical to study just the surface aspects of language; one must, while learning *about* the language, *use* the language to learn about culture, society, and its issues. In order to achieve the goals that have been put forth in Miller's (2015) QLF, second and foreign language teachers must incorporate all ten principles included in this framework.

As this chapter has described, it is possible to develop language lessons that incorporate many of the principles for queering literacy and, most important, to support our students in recognizing that there are people who trans*cend gendernormativity. By selecting queer readings and centralizing challenges to gendernormativity in the lessons, we have illustrated examples about how students can develop different perspectives about (a)gender. Through our in-class discussions of the readings about how (a)gender identity falls outside of the binary, students demonstrated a growing awareness that there are different (a)gender identities altogether. Finally, by having these discussions in a language class, we demonstrated how topics related to (a)gender identity intersect with culture, language, and other aspects of humanity while building students' linguistic ability.

As is the case for many English language learners, whether teaching in an English-as-a-Second-Language setting or an English-as-a-Foreign-Language setting like us, thinking critically about social justice issues, including gendernormativity, is commonly a new experience for the learner. Consequently, the teacher must be careful not to assume any level of background knowledge on the part of the students, especially topics related to sexual behavior, (a)gender identity, and so forth, because in many countries, such topics are considered highly taboo, including Japan. In Japanese, most terms describing (a)gender or sexual identity are borrowed from the English word. They are pronounced using following Japanese phonetic rules: transgender (トランスジェンダー—"Toransujendā"), gay (ゲイ—"Gei"), and lesbian (レズビアン—"Rezubian"). Given that these terms are borrowed from English, one cannot assume that they are commonly known or understood. Furthermore, on Japanese television we see trans* individuals, cross dressers, and others; despite their being visible in the public, that aspect of their life is not discussed, and they are often portrayed in a comic way. Therefore, lessons must be carefully scaffolded to build vocabulary and language skills necessary to engage in topics of (a)gender identity and sexual identity, among others.

Out of deference to students and their families, while also accounting for cultural and social more, we were careful to scaffold our lesson carefully by selecting texts and crafting discussion questions that required no background knowledge. We used the discussion as an opportunity to build in key terms such as trans*, (a)gender, and identity; we allowed these terms to come up organically in our discussion, rather than having a predetermined list of "vocabulary words," because our primary goal in this first experience for our students was to discuss these issues and foster the beginning of critical thinking related to these topics. Artwork and other creative expression give English language learners the opportunity to convey their critical ideas and recognize and expand their awareness about identities beyond their own.

Whether teaching language classes in a middle/junior high level or a high school setting, integrating lessons such as ours is a great way to introduce the concept of (a)gender to preteens and teens, by integrating the topic into lessons where learners use all four language skills (i.e., reading, speaking, listening, and writing) while learning about this concept. Teachers can start with asking students to read an authentic text in the target language, such as *Michael's Diary*, that is suitable for the linguistic ability and age of the learners. To engage students in speaking and listening, crafting discussion questions that are manageable for the age and linguistic level about the reading is a great activity. Such discussions can also connect the reading of their own lives and the world around them and will guide their thinking toward the concept of (a)gender. Finally, as our lesson demonstrated, by allowing students to use art coupled with writing that is appropriate for the age and linguistic ability of the learners will enhance their language skills, while using such activities to monitor the language learners' growth in understanding a concept that may be difficult for them. With students who are younger or limited in language proficiency, having them write a short caption is ideal. For those with higher ability, students could, instead, write their own short stories, essays, or even research papers. The advantage to this type of lesson is that students develop their linguistic skills in real, meaningful ways, while simultaneously learning about important concepts that will make them better citizens by understanding and celebrating difference.

Furthermore, as language teachers and teacher educators, we can emulate through our own actions and the choices we make with our curriculum that, regardless of the content that we are teaching, social justice issues can become an integral part of the classroom. Although cliché, in such instances, our actions do speak louder than our words. Our students see what we believe, not necessarily by what we say but by what we do. It is through our actions, actually living out these ten principles of the framework, that students will then know which teachers, even the French teacher, Japanese teacher, or ESL teacher, truly believe "that students who identify on a continuum of (a)gender identities deserve to learn in environments free of bullying and harassment" (Miller 2015, p. 42).

References

Adams, J. (2002). Art in social movements: A case from Pinochet's Chile. *Sociological Forum, 17*(1), 21–56.

Al-Shehri, S., & Gitsaki, C. (2010). Online reading: A preliminary study of the impact of integrated and split-attention formats on L2 students' cognitive load. *ReCALL, 22*(3), 356–375.

American Council on the Teaching of Foreign Languages (ACTFL). (2015). *World readiness standards for learning languages.* Alexandria: Author. Retrieved from ACTFL website: http://www.actfl.org/sites/default/files/pdfs/WorldReadinessStandardsforLearn ingLanguages.pdf

Aoki, M. (2014, May 8). LGBT bullying rife in schools: Survey. *Japan Times*. http://www.japantimes.co.jp/news/2014/05/08/national/lgbt-bullying-rife-in-schools-survey/?#.VcCrgChR4sy

Berho, D. L., & Defferding, V. (2005). Communication, culture, and curiosity: Using target-culture and student-generated art in the second language classroom. *Foreign Language Annals, 38*(2), 271–277.

Bryant, T. (2013). Michael's diary. *Teaching Tolerance, 44*. Retrieved from http://www.tolerance.org/magazine/number-44-summer-2013/department/michael-s-diary

Knowles, J. G., & Cole, A. L. (2008). *Handbook of the arts in qualitative research: Perspectives, methodologies, examples and issues*. Thousand Oaks: Sage.

Kosciw, J. G., Greytak, E. A., Palmer, N. A., & Boesen, M. J. (2014). *The 2013 National School Climate Survey: The experiences of lesbian, gay, bisexual and transgender youth in our nation's schools*. New York: GLSEN.

Leahy, W., & Sweller, J. (2004). Cognitive load and the imagination effect. *Applied Cognitive Psychology, 18*, 857–875.

Leavy, P. (2009). *Method meets art: Arts-based research practice*. New York: Guilford.

Lockette, T. (2009, April 13). Death by bullying. *Teaching Tolerance* [Web log post]. Retrieved from http://marioncountyschoolcounselors.blogspot.jp/2009/04/death-by-bullying-article-from-teaching.html

Maruko, M. (2015, February 20). Officials pull plug on teacher survey about LGBT students. *Japan Times*. Retrieved from http://www.japantimes.co.jp/news/2015/02/20/national/social-issues/officials-pull-plug-on-teacher-survey-about-lgbt-students/#.VcRAMChR4sw

Miller, P. C. (2010). An elephant in the classroom: LGBTQ students and the silent minority. In M. Fehr & D. Fehr (Eds.), *Teach boldly* (pp. 67–76). New York: Peter Lang.

Miller, s. (2015). A queer literacy framework promoting (a)gender and (a)sexuality self-determination and justice. *English Journal, 104*(5), 37–44.

Ministry of Education, Culture, Sports, Science & Technology (MEXT). (2012). *Koukousei no futoukou chutotaigaku no genjou* [The current truancy and drop-out situation of high school students]. Tokyo: Author. Retrieved from http://www.mext.go.jp/b_menu/shingi/chukyo/chukyo3/047/siryo/__icsFiles/afieldfile/2012/03/21/1318690_02.pdf

Paas, F., van Gog, T., & Sweller, J. (2010). Cognitive load theory: New conceptualizations, specifications, and integrated research perspectives. *Educational Psychology Review, 22*, 115–121.

Teaching English to Speakers of Other Languages International Association (TESOL). (2006). *TESOL Pre-K-12 English language proficiency standards framework*. Alexandria: Author. Retrieved from TESOL website: http://www.TESOL.org/docs/books/bk_prek-12elpstandards_framework_318.pdf?sfvrsn=2

Ybarra, M. L., Mitchell, K. J., & Kosciw, J. G. (2014). The relation between suicidal ideation and bullying victimization in a national sample of transgender
and non-transgender adolescents. In P. Goldblum, D. Espelage, J. Chu, &
B. Bognar (Eds.), *Youth suicide and bullying: Challenges and strategies for prevention and intervention* (pp. 134–147). New York: Oxford University Press.

CHAPTER 10

Exploring Gender Through *Ash* in the Secondary English Classroom

Paula Greathouse

Queer Literacy Framework Principles:

6. Engages in ongoing critique of how gender norms are reinforced in literature, media, technology, art, history, science, math, and so on.

How can texts be vehicles through which youth challenge gender roles, expectations, and gender norms within specific cultures and time periods? How can this process then shape and inform youth to challenge their own and others' beliefs? And, how can the ensuing understandings influence their beliefs about the criticality of being both recognized and recognizing the other? These questions guide the work for this chapter by drawing on the revisionist story of Cinderella in Malinda Lo's young adult novel, *Ash* (2010), to explore the importance of recognition of trans*, gender creative, intersex, and/or gender flexible youth within a secondary English classroom.

Identity's role "in adolescent development has been particularly important as youth come to know and define themselves in ways that were not possible during their childhood" (Huffaker and Calvert 2005). This process can become a struggle for adolescents in finding the balance between who they want to be, who others think they are, and who they really are. For lesbian, gay, bisexual, trans*, intersex, or questioning (LGBTIQ)

P. Greathouse (✉)
Tennessee Technological University, Cookeville, USA

© The Editor(s) (if applicable) and The Author(s) 2016
sj Miller (ed.), *Teaching, Affirming, and Recognizing Trans and Gender Creative Youth*, DOI 10.1057/978-1-137-56766-6_10

adolescents the process is even more stressful as they are often forced to create false façades in an effort to be recognized as socially acceptable (Miller 2016). Within school contexts the need to create and sustain these false fronts become more prevalent as those that do express gender outside of the gendernormative school culture often find themselves victims of bullying and other aggressions. The emotional labor (Hochschild 1983) experienced as a result of these aggressions is so taxing that often the focus of school days for LGBTIQ becomes surviving rather than success (Miller and Gilligan 2014). In remedying this problem, we must ask ourselves what we can do as teachers to combat such a stigmatic social issue whose repercussions can be life altering and damaging for any adolescent. The question most often asked is "how?"

Within school contexts, some LGBTIQ adolescents experience ignominy, especially when gender-biased, heterosexually instructional guided classrooms do not support exploration or dialog with reference to other manifestations of sexual orientations or gender expressions; thus, the repercussions of homophobia, transphobia, and cisnormativity are felt and at times with such a force that adolescents find it easier to pretend they are something they are not in fear of retaliation, both physically and mentally, by their peers and their teachers (Ressler and Chase 2009). This homophobic anxiety has impacted the high school climate significantly, and as a result, secondary teachers are reluctant to include texts and dialog surrounding "non-normative" identity and gender in their curriculum. This reluctance has sent a silent yet powerful message to all students that any orientation outliers that do not reinforce heterosexuality, cisnormativity, and/or binary forms of gender expression is demeaned, devalued, made inferior, and determined invisible and thereby, unrecognizable.

In my conversations with secondary English educators, this absence has been attributed to not only a lack of knowledge and exposure to literature that affords students opportunities to explore gender and identity, but also educators are still not clear on ways in which they can engage students in socially responsible dialogs about identities outside of the heterosexual, gender-biased, cisnormative, world in which they teach. Within secondary English classrooms teachers have powerful opportunities to use texts to explore different expressions of (a)gender and its manifestations. Course standards in the Secondary English language arts (SELA) call for the examination, evaluation, and analysis of texts across time periods and cultures with similar themes according to the Common Core Standards, RL.6, RL.7, RL.9 (National Governors Association Center for Best Practices [NGA Center] & Council of Chief State School Officers [CCSSO] 2010).

Through literature, SELA teachers can draw upon texts as both revision and evolution by exploring and dialoging with youth about trans* and gender creative identities and gender expressions in meeting these standards.

QLF Principle 6: The Use of Literature to Explore Identity and Gender

The use of literature as a pedagogical tool for teaching and discussing gender and identity can be very beneficial. Not only does literature allow us to meet our students where they are, it provides us an accessible instrument in encouraging them to make meaning from text that supports or challenges particular ways of thinking about what it means to be a man or a woman, male or female, masculine or feminine. Asking students to explore gender assumptions can encourage them to question and challenge the "norms" they see and often openly accept. Furthermore, literature that focuses on the recognizability of trans* and gender creative expressions in the SELA classroom is a crucial site for initiatives that can be spatialized into the larger school community and society writ large.

The power of literature can support readers to experience worlds in which they can "find" themselves and where the opportunities to experience life alongside of those who have lived and are living it. Literature becomes a world in which students can submerge their beings in order to better understand and accept themselves and the society they live in. For adolescents, readings and discussion about trans* and gender creative youth can provide both a sense of recognition of self and of other. The use of LGBTIQ literature, which tends to be saturated with stories of youth whose identities fall outside of binaries, can become a valuable instrument for all students, where each can discover their own beliefs, values, gender expressions, and sexual identities, while simultaneously addressing social injustices and misconceptions that surround each. This work goes far beyond the cliché of tolerance; "For education to be empowering, teachers and learners must strive toward understanding differences and use them to create new ways of being in the world" (Allen 1995, p. 136).

When teachers attempt to address gender identities and expressions through literature with characters and events that do not fit the *heteronormal,* gender identities that fall into society's norms (Blackburn and Buckley 2005; Crisp and Knezek 2010; Ellis 2009), they often face scrutiny from parents, administrators, and even other teachers. Perhaps the "tendency of any perspective to position people as either insiders or outsiders in exaggerated social dichotomies where differences are emphasized at the expense of similarities" (Blackburn and Buckley 2005, p. 203) places educators in unfamiliar territory, which in turn, may be the cause for reluctance in using LGBTIQ texts or within their classrooms. I purport that this fear stems from an anxiety that when teachers leave the heterosexual, gender-binary world and enter into a world where characters with sexual orientations and gender identities and expressions are present and even celebrated, it threatens status quo beliefs. This in-between state faced by teachers is indicative that teacher preparation must step up to better prepare teachers who experience a reluctance and/or uncertainty about how to address these themes within the SELA curriculum (Clark 2010).

Though, in order for SELA teachers to be effective in how they draw upon LGBTIQ literature, they need to be willing and able to lead dialog about real-world, sensitive issues, and in particular here, about (a)gender identities. While some educators avoid the topics all together, others just graze the surface in a superficial and safe manner. Teachers who do provide students opportunities to study, unlearn, and relearn about LGBTIQ issues move students toward greater acceptance, affirmation, and recognition about preconceived and hostile beliefs, which offers opportunities to clear up any misconceptions about lesbians, gays, bisexuals, trans*, gender creative, or intersex adolescents. Presenting LGBTIQ literature as part of, not outside, the SELA curriculum can challenge our students to recognize, dialog about, and reflect on their personal beliefs and perceptions about those who express identities outside of their own identities. Drawing on the QLF to mediate this process, teachers are provided a foundation for facilitating responsible discussion around trans* and gender creative identities, gender expressions, and gender norms in a responsible and mindful way. What follows is a thematic unit that incorporates LGBTIQ literature into a high school English class. Drawing upon Miller's (2015) QLF, this unit presents how gender and identity can be effectively explored.

CINDERELLA ACROSS TIME PERIODS AND CULTURES IN THE HIGH SCHOOL ENGLISH CLASS THROUGH THE QLF

Our culture, past and present, is full of fairy tales. What makes fairy tales so powerful are the lessons that accompany them. However, the world depicted in fairy tales does not reflect the real world of our students; rather they represent gender norms, gender expectations, gender expressions as they intersect with cultural beliefs of the time period written through the lens of the author. But what if *these* realities were challenged? What if we read fairytales, specifically the tale of Cinderella, in an effort to discover how cultures and contexts shape gender? How does this tale challenge gender when Cinderella is male? Students will listen to and read several children's cultural versions of the popular fairy tale and a young adult novel version of the tale in an effort to not only evaluate gender roles, expectations, and gender norms within the culture and time period they were written, but as a way to challenge one's own beliefs about gender and how these expressions may or may not influence one's gender perceptions and identity today.

The choice to explore the tale of Cinderella results from the many issues surrounding gender roles and stereotypes presented within. Drawing on Principle 6 of the QLF, and through the reading of several variations across cultures and time periods, students will examine and analyze concepts of gender and gender disruptions, to explore how cultural forces impact gender as a construct as presented within literature.

Pre-reading Activities

In an effort to prepare students to read and explore the tale of Cinderella, educators must first tap into students' perceptions and definitions of gender, gender expectations, and gender norms in order to comprehend the messages surrounding gender within the tales. One way to motivate students to participate in a dialog surrounding these themes is to first allow them time to reflect on their own stances and perceptions of gender and its manifestations. In other words, explore how they define gender, what it means to them, and the various ways they support or fail to support their peers who are gender creative or trans*. Through the activity of journaling, students are given an opportunity to spend time examining their beliefs and perceptions in an authentic and safe way. For teachers, the use of student journals to begin planning the exploration of gender affords them an opportunity to examine students' perceptions prior to facilitating class discussions, allowing them to clear up any misconceptions surrounding gender, gender identity, gender expressions, and gender stereotyping that may be present. Drawing on Miller's exploration of gender markers presented in Chap. 2 (Miller 2015, p. 40), the following are sample journal prompts:

1. Define gender.
2. What is the difference between gender and sex?
3. What does it mean to be male or female/masculine or feminine?
4. What does it mean to express gender?
5. What does it mean to be gender creative?
6. Define gender roles and gender expectations. Provide examples you recognize in school and how gender roles/expectations are disrupted.
7. What is trans*?
8. What happens to people who are gender flexible? (provide them with Miller's definition—"behave in a gender that is different than their assigned text" (Miller 2015, p. 39).

Teachers who employ a QLF take up a commitment to offer students opportunities to "explore, engage and understand how gender is constructed" through "ongoing and deep discussions about how society is gendered" (Miller 2016, Fig. 2.1). As such, class dialog surrounding these prompts becomes an imperative part of this unit. However, discussions on (a)gender and gender identity can place classroom teachers in a unique position. A teachers' natural tendency to judge, evaluate, and approve or disapprove students' contributions (Rogers 1961) can work against a climate in which new and innovative ideas flourish. Therefore, I suggest that the teacher steps back and allow the discussion to be student led and student run, interjecting only when a misconception or a direct question arises. If relinquishing participation is something that a teacher may not wish to do, then I would suggest limiting input to only offer responses such as "I see", "Tell me more...," or "Please elaborate". By doing so, students are given a chance to expand their thinking without judgment, which encourages them to go further in their reflection.

Because gender is socially constructed and influenced by the attitudes and values of society, as well as each individual's own personal understanding of gender, it is important that we keep track of students' verbal responses to the journal prompts that will lead the class discussions. One way teachers can address this while creating a discussion starting point is through the creation of visuals. These visuals will not only track student verbal responses to prompts posed, but will also allow these responses to remain visible during the entire unit as frames of references. Using chart paper, begin by writing the word "gender" at the top. Ask students to draw on their journal responses to share how they defined the word gender. Once all students have shared these responses, move on to the next journal prompt, also charting responses. As you work your way through the journal prompts, stop periodically and ask students to reflect on how the responses to each prompt support the notion that gender is socially constructed. Ask students to begin reflecting on these constructed norms and how they reflect our current culture. As an extension, encourage them to begin charting ways in which one can disrupt these constructions. Continue this process until all prompts have been discussed.

Finally, before we even begin to examine the texts in this unit, consistency in definitions across the unit is important. Table 10.1 provides the terms and definitions adapted for this unit.

The Reading of Several Cultural Versions of "Cinderella"

Because the use of the QLF lens will be a first for most, if not all students, it is important for teachers to model the analysis process for this unit. One way to accomplish this is through an interactive read aloud. Research shows that interactive read alouds offer opportunities for teacher-led modeling that promotes student-led discussions (Alor and McCathren 2003). Furthermore, the dialogic nature of the interactive read aloud provides opportunities to develop complex thinking and learning as students construct the meaning of gender in both text and self. Since the most popular version of the Cinderella tale stems from Perrault's rendering, and since the other tales that will be explored are variants of this particular adaptation, students will listen to the teacher's reading of *The Little Glass Slipper* (Perrault 1697). Again, since gender is socially constructed, it is important that during this read aloud the teacher stops and demonstrates his/ her thought process in analyzing gender as expressed within the tale and encourages students to contribute to this meaning making. Teachers can do this through asking open-ended questions, charting student responses, and then building on their responses to facilitate in the exploration of gender within the text.

After the teacher models the QLF approach through the reading of *The Little Glass Slipper* (Perrault 1697), students will begin to explore several cultural adaptations of this tale. The following are several versions that can be traversed: *The Irish Cinderlad* (Climo 1996), *Joe Cinders* (Mitchell

Table 10.1   Common definitions (Miller 2016, ix–xxii)

Terms	Definitions
Assigned gender	The gender one is presumed or expected to embody based on assigned sex at birth
Assigned sex	The sex one is assigned at birth based on genitalia
Chosen gender	The gender one feels most comfortable embodying and how one sees the self
Cisgender	A person who by nature or by choice conforms to gender based expectations of society
Gender	Socially constructed roles, behaviors, and attributes considered by the general public to be "appropriate" for one's sex as assigned at birth
Gender creative	Expressing gender in a way that demonstrates individual freedom of expression and that does not conform to any gender
Gender expression/ presentation	The physical manifestation of one's gender identity through clothing, hairstyle, voice, body shape, etc., typically referred to as feminine or masculine. Many transgender people seek to make their gender expression (how they look) match their gender identity rather than their birth-assigned sex
Gender identity	One's personal sense of his or her correct gender, which may be reflected as gender expression
Gender nonconforming	A term for individuals whose gender expression is different from societal expectations related to gender
Gender role/expression	How one performs gender in the world as it relates to social expectations and norms
Heteronormative/ Heteronormativity	A culture or belief system that assumes that people fall into distinct and complementary sexes and genders and that heterosexuality is the normal sexual orientation
Heterosexism	The assumption that all people are or should be heterosexual
Sex	Sex refers to the biological traits, which include internal and external reproductive anatomy, chromosomes, hormones, and other physiological characteristics
Transgender (TG)	The experience of having a gender identity that is different from one's biological sex

2002), *The Rough Face Girl* (Martin 1998), *Mufaro's Beautiful Daughters: An African Tale* (Steptoe 2008), *Yeh-Shen: A Cinderella Story from China* (Louie 1996), and *Adelita* (dePaola 2004).

As students read each rendering, they should log places within the text and illustrations where gender norms and gender expectations are defined, as well as places where these are interrupted (Miller 2015, p. 42). Using a graphic organizer (Fig. 10.1), students can keep track of each culture's

Title:_____

Culture & Time Period	Author Gender	Beauty	Gender Expectations/Norms	Disruptions of Gender	Message about Gender Story Sends
			·		
Reflection					

Fig. 10.1 Graphic organizer: Cinderella across time periods and cultures

version as told through the author's gender perspective. These graphic organizers will serve as the foundation for whole class dialogs. As an extension of their reading of these children's versions, students could be challenged to rework each tale in an effort to re-tell the story disrupting the gender norms and expectations presented within.

THE INTRODUCTION OF *ASH*

Once students have explored the concepts of beauty, gender norms, gender expectations, and disruptions, as they appeared within these popular children's versions of Cinderella, students should be given the novel *Ash* (Lo 2010) by Malinda Lo to read. *Ash* provides segue into exploring such topics through the tale of Cinderella and generates opportunities for deeper exploration about individuals who might be trans*, gender creative, intersex, or gender flexible. This novel is a twist on the fairy tale Cinderella, with Cinderella questioning her sexuality in a world that disrupts gender roles. Many directions can be taken with the reading of this novel. For instance, in my own 10th grade English class, students read this novel independently. They were given two weeks to complete the reading outside of school. As students read, they continued using the graphic organizer to record their interactions and intersections. Other teachers might offer students time to explore the intersection of their own gender and the text as well as time to explore other identities that may influence their perceptions and beliefs about how they express their gender through assigning the text as an independent reading task.

POST-READING ACTIVITIES

In an effort to demonstrate learning while simultaneously meeting SELA standards for secondary English students, the culminating activity for this unit required students to complete a written literary analysis answering the following: Discuss the varying perceptions of gender and gender roles presented within at least three of the children's texts read and in *Ash* (Lo 2010). In what ways were gender norms and expectations reinforced and/or disrupted within the texts explored? How has the story of Cinderella influenced our perceptions of gender in terms of expectations and norms today? In what ways can you become a change agent in supporting the recognition of your trans* and gender creative peers?

For these questions to be completed at the end of the unit, dialog is vital. According to the Principle 6 of the QLF, a commitment of educators who use this framework is to "provide ongoing and deep discussions about how society is gendered and thus invite students to actively engaged in analysis of cultural texts and disciplinary discourses" (Miller, p. 39). Therefore, as educators we need to allow students an opportunity to share their experiences, perceptions, and beliefs regarding gender, gender expectations, and gender norms expressed within the Cinderella stories with their peers if we are to fulfill our commitment to help students become "change agents" when it comes to gender expectations and gender flexibility in our own culture (p. 39).

The discourse aroused in a classroom from literature can greatly influence the culture of that classroom (Schein 2008). Schein (2008) purports that in classrooms which promote discussion of text on deeper levels (levels that connect to the participants' current contexts), communities are formed that responsively address the many situations of students' lives that are culturally created. Since a key component of this unit asks students to explore their beliefs and values regarding gender, gender expectations, gender norms, and those that express gender outside the cisnormative in order to gain insight into their own being and the being of others, a culminating discussion of all texts explored in this unit is key. Furthermore, all student voices must be heard! There are several approaches to how discussion surrounding the texts in this unit can be employed. One way is through what I coin a "silent discussion". Because dialog must include all members of the class, I suggest the use of an online discussion medium. Given the sensitivity that some may have toward the subject of gender and identity, this medium allows students to remain anonymous, thus encouraging the authentic sharing of perspectives and beliefs. Additionally, the use of an online discussion removes the teacher in the conversation, allowing students to discuss and dialog among themselves. As the teacher monitors this discussion, any misconceptions or questions posed by the students can be addressed in a follow-up, debriefing activity.

As a way to facilitate and guide the online discussion, ask students to address the following prompts:

1. Describe gender roles, gender expectations, and gender norms presented within *Ash* (Lo 2010). How were these socially constructed?
2. How were these roles, expectations, and norms encouraged? How were they disrupted?
3. At the beginning of the novel, Ash is presented as cisgender. As the novel progresses, she becomes gender creative. Describe two examples from the text to support each of these identities and discuss her transformation.
4. Describe and discuss at least two characters, other than Ash, who are presented as gender nonconforming within the text. How were these characters treated and why? What message do you think the author is sending through the inclusion of these characters?
5. Discuss how this version of Cinderella challenges heterosexuality, cisnormativity, and/or binary forms of gender expression? In what ways does this version parallel our culture, if any?
6. In what ways has the story of Cinderella, as examined through the literature in this unit, support or challenge your personal beliefs and perspectives about what is considered the "norm" about gender?
7. In what ways can you be a change agent in helping others recognize your trans* and gender creative peers?

Gleanings from *Cinderella* and *Ash*

As English educators, we can impact the literature selection that our students draw upon for use in classroom practice. We need to encourage our teachers to become literary pioneers, to challenge and examine gender norms, expressions, and myriad (a)gender identities, so they can come to discover ways to disrupt dangerously held beliefs in classroom contexts. As teachers become more comfortable in their own use of LGBTIQ literature, they can seek out resources in their various contexts about how to more effectively teach, affirm, and recognize trans* and gender creative youth.

Ash could offer students a freedom to explore literature in ways they had never done before. As a teaching profession, whether at the university, preservice or in-service level, and across grade levels and disciplines, when we begin to actually recognize the developing adolescent in all of their beautiful and multiple identities, we are bound to send a powerful message for those who still live in worlds of intolerance, hatred, and ignorance. We must strive to empower each and every person who enters our classrooms and at the end of any text or unit we teach, students should be inspired to express that *all* humans are entitled to the same dignities (Miller, this volume, Chap. 16).

REFERENCES

Allen, J. (1995). *It's never too late: Leading adolescents to life long literacy.* Portsmouth: Heinemann.

Alor, J. H., & McCathren, R. B. (2003). Developing emergent literacy skills through storybook reading. *Intervention in School and Clinic, 39*(2), 72–79.

Blackburn, M., & Buckley, J. (2005). Teaching queer-inclusive English language arts. *Journal of Adolescent and Adult Literacy, 49*(3), 202–212.

Clark, C. (2010). Preparing LGBTQ-allies and combating homophobia in a U.S. teacher education program. *Teaching and Teacher Education, 26*(3), 704–713.

Climo, S. (1996). *The Irish Cinderlad.* New York: Harper Collins.

Crisp, T., & Knezek, S. (2010). Challenging texts: "Just don't see myself here": Challenging conversations about LGBTQ adolescent literature. *English Journal, 99*(3), 76–79.

DePaola, T. (2004). *Adelita.* London: Puffin Books.

Ellis, S. (2009). Diversity and inclusivity at university: A survey of the experiences of lesbian, gay, bisexual, and trans (LBGT) students in the UK. *Higher Education, 57*(6), 723–739.

Hochschild, A. (1983). *The managed heart: Commercialization of human feeling.* Berkeley: University of California Press.

Huffaker, D. A., & Calvert, S. L. (2005). Gender, identity, and language use in teenage blogs. *Journal of Computer-Mediated Communication, 10*(2), 1–26.

Lo, M. (2010). *Ash.* Boston: Little, Brown and Company.

Louie, A. (1996). *Yeh-Shen: A Cinderella story from China.* London: Puffin Books.

Martin, R. (1998). *The rough face girl.* London: Puffin Books.

Miller, s. (2015). A queer literacy framework promoting (a)gender and (a)sexuality self-determination and justice. *English Journal, 104*(5), 37–44.

Miller, s. (2016). *Teaching, affirming, and recognizing trans and gender creative youth: A queer literacy framework*. New York: Palgrave Macmillan.

Miller, s., & Gilligan, J. (2014). Heteronormative harassment: Queer bullying and gender non-conforming students. In D. Carlson & E. Meyer (Eds.), *Handbook of gender and sexualities in education* (pp. 217–229). New York: Peter Lang.

Mitchell, M. (2002). *Joe Cinders*. New York: Henry Holt and Company.

National Governors Association Center for Best Practices & Council of Chief State School Officers. (2010). *Common core state standards for English language arts and literacy in history/social studies, science, and technical subjects*. Washington, DC: Authors.

Perrault, C. (1697). *The little glass slipper*. Retrieved from http://www.pitt.edu/~dash/perrault06.html

Ressler, P., & Chase, B. (2009). Sexual identity and gender variance: Meeting the educational challenges. *The English Journal, 98*, 15–22.

Rogers, C. (1961). *On becoming a person*. Boston: Houghton Mifflin.

Schein, B. (2008). *If Holden Caulfield were in my classroom: Inspiring love, creativity, and intelligence in middle school kids*. Boulder: Sentient Publications.

Steptoe, J. (2008). *Mufaro's beautiful daughters: An African tale*. London: Puffin Books.

CHAPTER 11

Transitional Memoirs: Reading Using a Queer Cultural Capital Model

Summer Melody Pennell

Queer Literacy Framework Principles:

10. Believes that students who identify on a continuum of gender identities deserve to learn in environments free of bullying and harassment.

INTRODUCTION

As an advocate for lesbian, gay, bisexual, trans*, intersex, agender/asexual, gender creative, and questioning youth (LGBT*IAGCQ) and education, I frequently talk with preservice teachers about ways they can provide safe and welcoming environments and foster a "belie[f] that students who identify on a continuum of gender identities deserve to learn in environments free of bullying and harassment" (Miller, Chap. 2, p. 25). Part of creating these environments is providing opportunities for students to discuss gender and sexuality in the classroom. One way to facilitate these discussions is through texts by and about LGBT*IAGCQ people. This chapter provides a sample four-week unit for high school English teachers, using two memoirs written by transgender teens: *Some Assembly Required: The not-so-secret life of a transgender teen* by Arin Andrews (2014) and *Rethinking Normal: A memoir in transition* by Katie Rain Hill (2014).

S.M. Pennell (✉)
The University of North Carolina- Chapel Hill, Chapel Hill, USA

© The Editor(s) (if applicable) and The Author(s) 2016   199
sj Miller (ed.), *Teaching, Affirming, and Recognizing Trans and Gender Creative Youth*, DOI 10.1057/978-1-137-56766-6_11

Because of the authors' youthful writing style; presence on social media; and relatable teen experiences such as dating, school dances, and working with teachers, these memoirs are a strong match for high school students. It is my hope that by reading these memoirs, students can be transformed into trans* allies and will gain a better understanding of the complexities of trans* youth experiences.

Students will read excerpts from each memoir drawing from a *queer cultural capital* framework (Pennell 2016), which emphasizes strengths embodied by queer populations rather than focusing only on negative aspects such as bullying. In this unit, students will find examples of queer cultural capital in each memoir, write their own memoir that showcases their own cultural capital, and critique media portrayals of Andrews and Hill using a queer cultural capital framework. By seeing trans*[1] youth as well-rounded individuals who possess many strengths and positive quali- ties, students and teachers can create a safe classroom environment where everyone is valued. In a welcoming classroom, bullying and harassment of transgender and gender creative youth is not the norm. If Andrews' and Hill's teachers had understood the queer cultural capital they each possessed, perhaps these teachers would have recognized their strengths instead of seeing them as outcasts unworthy of support.

In this chapter, I will first outline Andrews' (2014) and Hill's (2014) memoirs. Next, I provide a summary of queer cultural capital and its theo- retical foundation. Then, a unit plan template and narrative are provided along with suggested student handouts. Lastly, implications for using queer cultural capital in high school and English methods classrooms are discussed.

Memoir Synopses

Authors Andrews (2014) and Hill (2014) are both from small towns out- side of Tulsa, Oklahoma, and transitioned (meaning they began outwardly identifying as their gender identity rather than their gender assigned at birth) during high school. Their memoirs focus mainly on their teen years, though they also discuss earlier childhood memories of not feeling com- fortable with their bodies. The two teens met at a queer youth center in Tulsa, and became a couple before they each underwent gender-affirming surgery. Prior to their first meeting, Hill was an advocate for transgender youth in her community and was featured in a local newspaper (Spinwall 2011a, b). As a couple Andrews and Hill became viral media sensations.

They appeared on news shows and were the subject of a series of short videos from 2012 to 2014 focusing on their relationship and transitions (Barcroft TV 2012, 2013, 2014). In their memoirs, both teens discuss their interactions with the media and the pressure it put on their relationship. Hill wanted to be seen as an individual, not just one half of a transgender teen couple. Andrews felt that the films produced a false version of their relationship, especially when they were having problems. They are also currently active on social media, particularly Andrews, and often attend book signings in support of their memoirs and other events as part of their activist work.

Though both Andrews and Hill chose to have surgeries and take hormones, this is not true of all trans* people and is not something most teens can access. They identify as part of the gender binary, meaning that Arin is male and Katie is female. Some trans* people do not define themselves as part of the gender binary, instead seeing their (a)gender as fluid. Thus every trans* story is unique, illustrating the diversity within the trans* population. For example, though both Andrews and Hill received medical treatment to support their transition, their medical results were not parallel. Andrews' doctor, when testing his hormone levels so that he could begin taking testosterone, found that his testosterone levels were actually low for an average biological female. This exemplifies the fact that trans* people are not defined by their pre-existing hormone levels. Some people may assume, for example, that a trans* man wants to be male because he already has a high level of testosterone, or that a trans* woman had lower levels of testosterone before she began transitioning. However, Andrews was not transgender because of his biology; he was transgender because he *felt* male. Hill's doctor discovered she is likely intersex, meaning that she had some biological traits that fit with both male and female characteristics, though she did not complete enough medical tests to determine this for certain. However, an intersex identity did not resonate with her and she chose to continue identifying as trans. As she stressed in her memoir,

> Often trans narratives might focus on how—in the case of a male-to-female, for instance—a child born male loved pink, or only wanted to play house, and this is used to 'prove' the child's true female identity. I want to be clear that my love of stereotypical girl toys…is not what makes me female…What makes me female is something I felt in the core of myself: that my external body did not match up with how I felt inside, and that I was being seen by others as something I was not. (Hill 2014, p. 44)

Furthermore, while Andrews and Hill did date, their relationship did not indicate that they identify as heterosexual. By the end of Andrews's memoir he is dating a male, and discusses how he was initially attracted to a person's spirit rather than their exterior. This illustrates that trans* people have different sexual orientations, just as cisgender people do, and reinforces the idea that gender and sexual orientation are not inherently tied. By reading about Andrews' and Hill's diverse and intertwined experiences, students can avoid having a singular perception of trans* people. If students see that there are multiple ways to be trans*, they may be less likely to police and judge the behavior of their trans* and gender creative classmates. Through a wider perception of trans* communities, the classroom environment can begin to move away from harassment and bullying. One way to facilitate this movement is by introducing a queer cultural capital framework, which allows all youth to see the strengths in queer communities.

QUEER CULTURAL CAPITAL

Queer cultural capital (Pennell 2016) is built from work by Yosso (2005) on cultural capital found in communities of color, who drew upon Bourdieu's (1986) theory of cultural capital. In general, cultural capital is a sociological theory used to describe the knowledge, skills, and privileges associated with a person's background and life experiences (Bourdieu 1986). In Bourdieu's (1986) work (as well as Yosso's), capital does not primarily refer to monetary wealth but to intangible social wealth and knowledge. e.g., a middle class person in the USA who has a college degree will have *institutional capital* (Bourdieu 1986) and knows how to navigate the institutions and privileges an educational pedigree provides such as a career and a social circle of other educated individuals. Bourdieu (1986) outlined two additional forms of cultural capital: *embodied* and *objectified*. Embodied capital refers to mindsets and dispositions. Knowing how to speak professionally and shake hands firmly at a job interview is embodied capital. Unlike the other forms of cultural capital, objectified capital does refer to material goods. However, Bourdieu (1986) is clear that these objects only have capital in combination with embodied and institutional capital. If one owns an item of couture clothing, for example, one must also know how to wear it properly and talk about designers to have objectified capital. Though Bourdieu (1986) did not intend for cultural capital to apply only to privileged white individuals that is how his theory is often interpreted (Yosso 2005).

Yosso's (2005) work is used by education scholars and teacher educators to move away from a deficit model of People of Color. In response to the false perception that only white people possess cultural capital, Yosso detailed five forms of cultural capital possessed by Communities of Color: *aspirational, linguistic, familial, navigational,* and *resistant.* These forms of capital illustrate that Communities of Color are not deficit. Aspirational capital refers to a prevailing sense of hope maintained through adversity. The contemporary Black Lives Matter movement (Garza 2014), which continues to work for Black equality in the USA, despite continued violence against them, is an example of aspirational capital. Linguistic capital indicates the skills and knowledge gained from speaking more than one language. For instance, for students of color who are learning English, linguistic capital views their multilingual abilities as a strength. Yosso uses the term familial capital to describe the cultural knowledge, history, and memory gained through kinship. This is seen in Communities of Color that support one another through a shared cultural history. Navigational capital demonstrates the way People of Color maneuver through institutions (e.g., education and legal systems) that were not created for them or designed to intentionally exclude them. For example, Ruby Bridges demonstrated navigational capital as the first African-American child to attend a white school in the segregated south (Biography 2015). Lastly, resistant capital refers to the skills gained from oppositional behavior in response to unequal treatment. The Black Lives Matter movement is also an example of resistant capital, as participants work to protest police violence and learn about the judicial system. Yosso's (2005) detailed discussion demonstrates that People of Color in the USA are not lacking in cultural capital, but are in fact rich in community cultural wealth, even if it is unrecognizable by whites.

My work demonstrates that Yosso's (2005) identified forms of capital are also found in queer communities. Queer cultural capital uses 'queer' as an umbrella term to describe all LGBT*IAGCQ people. In queer communities, aspirational capital is demonstrated when activists continue to work for legal employment protection, despite setbacks from local or national government. Linguistic capital can refer not only to established verbal languages like English or Spanish, but also to less-formalized languages that queer individuals use to define themselves in culturally specific ways (Boellstorff and Leap 2004), as well as nonverbal communication (Knofler and Imhof 2007; Nicholas 2004). For example, trans* individuals may choose or create their own pronouns if they feel that she/her or he/him do not accurately describe their personal identity. As institutions were not necessarily created for queer people, navigational capital applies to queer people as well. Trans* students exemplify navigational capital when they negotiate gendered school spaces such as restrooms and locker rooms. Such facilities are designed with the presumption that everyone is cisgender, and as a result, trans* students are typically disallowed from using the facility that corresponds to their gender identity. Resistant capital may be the most visible form in queer communities, especially if one is familiar with queer activist movements. Examples of queer resistance include protests and marches, which may give participants organizational and public speaking skills.

Building from Yosso, I add an additional form of capital—*transgressive* (Pennell 2016). Resistant capital is related to transgressive capital, but I argue that it is useful to view them as separate (Pennell 2016). While resistant capital comes from *reactions* to oppression and inequality, it does not describe capital that stems from *proactive* demonstrations. To transgress means to go around and beyond border and boundaries, rather than to resist, which indicates a reaction to something perceived as oppositional. Moving beyond boundaries gives transgressive capital a focus on space, further distinguishing it from resistant capital. Additionally, scholars discussing the nature of transgressions have described its incorporation of play (White and Stallybrass 1986) by playfully crossing and subverting cultural norms. This playful, boundary-crossing response to cultural normalities aligns transgressive cultural capital with queer theory, which works to critique and respond to societal norms (Britzman 1995). Transgressive cultural capital is not limited to queer communities; it can be found in any group or individual who proactively moves away from dominant societal norms.

Queer transgressive cultural capital is evidenced when queer communities deconstruct normative borders of gender to create their own methods of expression that do not align with the gender binary. Another example of queer transgressive cultural capital can be seen in the Undocuqueer movement (Pennell 2016). Undocuqueer activists are members of several intersectional (Crenshaw 1991) communities including undocumented US immigrants and People of Color (Chávez 2013). Demonstrating transgressive capital in combination with linguistic capital, leaders in the movement playfully combine rhetoric from multiple activist movements, such as decorating their "undocubus" with images of butterflies (http://nopapersnofear.org). The bus itself hearkens to the busses used by the

Freedom Riders during the Civil Rights Movement; butterflies were used by some trans* people as a symbol for transformation. When resistance is not enough to stop oppressive behaviors, transgression is used to get around oppression and express alternative realities. In the case of the undo-cubus, it was a transgressive form of capital used hand in hand with resis-tance, as participants in the movement drove it to different sites of protest.

Just as Yosso (2005) was frustrated with the deficit view of people of color, so am I frustrated with those who only view LGBT*IAGCQ communities from a deficit perspective. While I believe it is important that educators know of the struggles LGBT*IAGCQ youth face, I do not wish this emphasis to give them a negative view of these students. By using a queer cultural capital model to 'read' LGBT*IAGCQ identities and experiences, educators and students may gain a more well-rounded perspective and learn to see the strengths these individuals possess (see Table 11.1).

TRANSITIONAL MEMOIRS UNIT

Rationale

In this four-week unit, students will complete four major tasks in response to *Some Assembly Required* (Andrews 2014) and *Rethinking Normal* (Hill 2014): (1) Analyze the memoirs using a queer cultural capital framework; (2) Write a memoir highlighting their own cultural capital; (3) Analyze media portrayals of Andrews and Hill using the queer cultural capital framework; and (4) Create their own media project of the teens. The academic goals are to practice supporting analysis with textual evidence, write a personal narrative, and create a multimodal project. These goals easily align with curriculum standards. For example, reading the memoirs aligns to the 9th and 10th grade "informational text" category of the Common Core State Standards (CCSS), which reads "RI.1: Key Ideas and Details: Cite strong and thorough textual evidence to support analysis of what the text says explicitly as well as inferences drawn from the text" (Common Core State Standards Initiative 2015). The social goals are to teach students about trans* people, in order to foster a welcoming envi-ronment free of bullying. It is my hope that if teachers facilitate a unit such as the one described here, they will show students the diversity and strength of trans* people, which may in turn encourage students to be open minded about (a)gender diversity.

Table 11.1   Forms of cultural capital from Yosso and Pennell

Name	Definition	Queer example
1. Aspirational	"The ability to hold onto hope in the face of structured inequality and often without the means to make dreams a reality" (Yosso 2005, p. 77)	Queer activists working for employment protection despite government resistance
2. Linguistic	"Intellectual and social skills attained through communication experiences in more than one language or style" (Yosso 2005, p. 78)	Communication in queer communities may be conducted nonverbally (Knofler and Imhof 2007; Nicholas 2004) and is also culturally specific (Boellstorff and Leap 2004)
3. Familial	"Cultural knowledges nurtured among *familia* (kin) that carry a sense of community history, memory, and cultural intuition" (Yosso 2005, p. 79)	Queer people often have "chosen families" and strong social networks
4. Navigational	"The skills of maneuvering through social institutions" (Yosso 2005, p. 80)	Transgender students must navigate school spaces, such as locker rooms, that were not designed for their needs
5. Resistant	"Knowledges and skills fostered through oppositional behavior that challenge inequality" (Yosso 2005, p. 80)	Kiss-ins, Pride parades, demonstrations at government institutions, and other forms of protest in unwelcoming environments build organizational and public speaking skills
6. Transgressive	Skills gained through playfully and proactively moving beyond boundaries to deconstruct oppressive structures (Pennell 2016)	Undocuqueer movements go beyond boundaries of "immigrant" and "queer" to discuss the overlap of these groups and the people who fit into both categories, playfully combining and altering symbols from each activist movement

Unit Plan for Unpacking and Recognizing the Multitude of Trans Identities*

All activities described in this section are listed on the unit plan calendar (see Appendix: Transitional Memoirs Unit Plan Calendar: Teacher Reference). The unit should be used as a guideline rather than as a rigid plan as each teacher will need to make adjustments for their students' needs and the length of their class periods. This plan does not detail how to teach narrative structure or multimodal projects, as the focus of this chapter is on the inclusion of transgender teen memoirs into an existing high school English curriculum rather than on discipline-specific instructional strategies.

Weeks 1 and 2

In the first two weeks, students will learn about the social construction of gender and vocabulary related to trans*/transgender identities and the memoirs, and read excerpts from Some Assembly Required (Andrews 2014) and Rethinking Normal (Hill 2014). It is best that students already have prior experience conducting Internet research and know how to discern if sources are credible.

Day 1

1. Introduce the unit by having students complete the anticipation guide (Table 11.2), which asks them if they agree or disagree with the following statements: (1) All high school students are entitled to a high-quality education. (2) School should be a safe and welcoming place. (3) School administrators and teachers are always right. (4) Everyone is born either male or female. (5) Gender is flexible. (6) Everyone has the right to feel comfortable in their own body. These questions will spark students' thinking about gender roles and society. After students are finished, facilitate a class discussion based on their responses.

2. Next, facilitate an activity that illustrates the social construction of gender. On the board, or on opposite sides of the room if possible, write "male" and "female." Either as a class conversation, or in two groups, ask students to name expectations that our society has for each gender. Phrasing it this way allows students to name stereotypes and ideas without fear of reprisal. For example, a student may say women are expected to be caregivers for children, whether they personally agree with that or not. When the lists are complete and have been seen by everyone, ask all students to stand up. Tell students that they should imagine a line between male and female and stand where they fall, based on the lists. Suggest that they can only stand completely on one side if they fit every characteristic on one list and none of the characteristics on the other. Essentially, every-

Table 11.2   Anticipation guide

Name_____ Period_____ Date_____

Directions: Read each statement, and then check the box under the answer that best describes your response.

	Agree	Maybe	Disagree
1. All high school students are entitled to a high quality education.			
2. School should be a safe and welcoming place.			
3. School administrators and teachers are always right.			
4. Everyone is born as either male or female.			
5. Gender is flexible.			
6. Everyone has the right to feel comfortable in their own body.			

Directions: Choose **one** statement to write about, briefly (2-3 sentences) explaining your answer choice.

Statement number _____.

Explanation for answer choice:

one ends up somewhere in the middle. Once everyone has chosen a spot, facilitate a discussion asking students to talk about their choice. Point out that our society has expectations for gender that were created by people, not biology, and that most people do not fully live up to these expectations.

3. Now that students are familiar with the idea that gender is a social construction, tell them that they are going to read parts of two memoirs by transgender teens from Oklahoma. Explain that these memoirs are interesting to read together because the writers know each other and dated for a time, which they each describe from their own perspective.

4. Introduce students to vocabulary words, such as *transgender* and *transition*, using the definitions provided in the book's glossary. Even if students are familiar with this vocabulary, a review is a good way to clear up any misconceptions. One way to introduce the vocabulary is by writing the words on chart paper and having students walk around the room writing their ideas and questions under each word. Teachers may also want to bring in a counselor, Gay-Straight Alliance (GSA) advisor, or other expert who can answer questions.

5. Wrap up the lesson by facilitating a discussion on gender and sexual orientation, driven by student comments and questions. Remind students about the social construction of gender in society.

Day 2

1. Introduce the concept of cultural capital to students as the knowledge and skills gained from one's background experiences. Ask them to come up with examples from their own lives. At this point it is not necessary for the students to know how to categorize the forms of capital. They might think of things like knowing how to speak in public from the debate team, knowing how to survive the outdoors from scouting experiences, or knowing how to travel in a city from using public transportation.

2. Once assured the students have a basic understanding of cultural capital, introduce them to the concept of queer cultural capital. Explain that this refers to the skills and strengths possessed by LGBT*IAGCQ communities. If resistance from students or administration is present or anticipated, teachers may wish to call this cultural capital and leave out the word 'queer.' Give students the queer cultural capital handout (Chart 11.1) and review with students.

3. Ask students to find examples of each form of capital in trans* and/ or gender creative people or communities. You may want to have students work individually or in pairs, using a computer with Internet access to conduct their research. Ask students if they know of any trans* or gender creative people they could research. If not, teachers should suggest examples, such as Laverne Cox (a trans woman, actress, and activist), Caitlyn Jenner (a transgender woman, former athlete, and reality television star), or Chaz Bono (a transgender man, activist, and writer).

Directions: Read the following definitions and examples.

Type of Queer Cultural Capital	Definition	Example
1. Aspirational	Maintaining hope in the face of inequality.	LGBT*IAGCQ activists working for protections for LGBT*IAGCQ students, despite laws failing to pass in local and national governments.
2. Linguistic	Skills and knowledge gained through speaking more than one language. This can include verbal and non-verbal languages, and words invented by LGBT*IAGCQ people to describe themselves.	Learning to use "gaydar" to find other queer people. Choosing (or even inventing) your own pronouns that affirm your gender identity (such as ze/hir instead of she/he or him/her).
3. Familial	Family history and community memories, social networks and resources. Family can mean families united by kinship or chosen families (common in LGBT*IAGCQ communities).	LGBT*IAGCQ people often have "chosen families," and strong social networks of friends from which they draw support.
4. Navigational	The ability to steer through institutions (schools, legal systems, etc.) that were not designed in consideration of LGBT*IAGCQ people.	Trans*students must navigate school spaces, such as locker rooms, that were not designed for their needs.
5. Resistant	Skills and knowledge gained through opposition to inequality.	LGBT*IAGCQ people must learn a lot about government and law to protest discrimination. Protests require strong organizational and public speaking skills.
6. Transgressive	Skills and knowledge gained by proactively (and often playfully) challenging and going around boundaries that limit LGBT*IAGCQ people.	Undocuqueer movements go beyond boundaries of "immigrant" and "LGBT*IAGCQ" to discuss the overlap of these groups and the people who fit into both categories. Undocuqueer activists playfully combine and alter symbols from each activist movement, showing great creativity.

Chart 11.1   Queer cultural capital definitions and examples

Directions: Using the internet, look up stories on trans*and/or gender creative people, communities, and activist movements. Be sure that your sources are legitimate. As you research, fill out the chart below with examples of the different forms of queer cultural capital.

Type of Queer Cultural Capital	Example	Source
Aspirational		
Linguistic		
Familial		
Navigational		
Resistant		
Transgressive		

Chart 11.1 (*continued*)

4. Monitor students as they work to answer questions, clear up misconceptions, and ensure that they are using suitable sources. If this is the first time students have discussed trans* identities, they may use troubling terms or mis-gender trans* individuals (for example, referring to a transgender woman as 'he'). Respectfully correct any misconceptions while encouraging the students to continue learning about transgender experiences.

Day 3

1. Tell students that today they will begin reading excerpts from one of the memoirs, *Some Assembly Required* (2014) written by Arin Andrews, a teen trans male. Introduce students to the following terms and acronyms that they will encounter in their reading throughout the unit:

OKEQ: Oklahoma Equality Center	A community center in Tulsa, Oklahoma, that works to support LGBTQ people
OYP: Open Arms Youth Project	A center for LGBTQ teens in Tulsa, Oklahoma. Arin and Katie first meet here at a transgender youth support group
Two-spirit	This is a Native American term (only used by some groups) to describe people who have both male and female spirits. Arin's therapist mentions the term to him and his mom, and it helps his mom understand his trans identity. However, it is not recommended that anyone use this word casually as it is not used by all Native American groups. It is very specific and should only be used if a person tells you they identity as two-spirit
Transgenders	Katie often writes 'transgenders' rather than 'transgender person.' Using 'transgenders' is generally considered incorrect by most people, so unless quoting her specifically it is recommended that you always use 'transgender person,' as you would say 'disabled people' rather than 'disableds.' This may be different where Katie lives. It is always best to use the term people ask you to use, or that you hear them using, If unsure, it is best to respectfully ask about chosen terms and (a)pronouns

2. Tell students that they will read the first chapter of Arin's memoir (pp. 1–14), where he describes going to his junior prom, and that they will use the queer cultural capital model discussed yesterday to analyze the memoir, looking for moments where Arin showed strength. Give each student a copy of the "student reading handout" (Chart 11.2) and instruct them to note examples of queer cultural capital as they read. They do not need to identify every form each day, but by the fourth and final day of reading from this memoir they should have identified at least one example of each form of capital.

3. Depending on time, allow students to complete the reading and work on their queer cultural capital charts in class. Before the end of the class, facilitate a discussion on the reading. Can they relate to any of Arin's experiences? Ask students what stood out or surprised them and what forms of capital they noticed. See Table 11.3 for examples of queer cultural capital in each memoir.

Directions: As you read the memoirs, complete the table citing examples of each type of queer cultural capital in each memoir (additional chart on back). You must have at least one example from each memoir for each form of capital.

Type of queer cultural capital	Examples in *Some Assembly Required* by Arin Andrews
Familial	
Aspirational	
Navigational	
Linguistic	
Resistant	
Transgressive	

Chart 11.2 Student reading handout for memoirs

214   S.M. PENNELL

Type of queer cultural capital	Examples in *Rethinking Normal* by Katie Rain Hill
Familial	
Aspirational	
Navigational	
Linguistic	
Resistant	
Transgressive	

Chart 11.2 (*continued*)

Day 4

1. Tell students that they will continue reading from Arin's memoir. Explain that while his memoir started at his junior prom, today's excerpt is from an earlier time when he attended a private school.

Table 11.3 Queer cultural capital in trans memoirs

Types of capital	Examples in Andrews (2014)	Examples in Hill (2014)
Familial	Arin and his mother's relationship improves with the help of a therapist who supports Arin's transition (pp. 127–128)	Katie finds a close group of friends at her local LGBTQ center's youth group (p. 171)
Aspirational	Arin continues to hope that his mom will accept his identity (p. 103)	Katie hopes for a college education and gender-affirming surgery despite the expenses (pp. 117–118)
Navigational	Arin navigates the teen rituals of prom as a male, when he has not been socialized to play this role (p. 5)	Katie returns to her high school despite the bullying and is the first transgender student to graduate high school in Oklahoma. She and her mother show the school documents that prove they have to educate Katie despite their discomfort and prejudice (pp. 150–151)
Linguistic	Arin learns the words transgender and cisgender, which shows him that he does not have to be labeled as "other" nor are non-transgender people "normal" (pp. 87–89)	Katie chose her name, and to use female pronouns, to reflect her gender identity (pp. 6, 11)
Resistant	When Arin's teacher at a private Christian school says that gay marriage is wrong, he resists by pointing out that Jesus preached love and not discrimination (p. 86)	When Katie is discriminated against at a camp that is supposed to advocate for diversity, she and her mother complain to the camp director and the counselor who outed her without her consent is fired (p. 135)
Transgressive	Before Arin has top surgery, he wears a binder to give him a flat chest (p. 3)	Katie speaks at events in support of transgender people, in order to create space for herself as a trans woman (pp. 168–169)

2. Have students read pp. 86–90 and pp. 100–104. The first section describes Arin's experience at a private Christian school and discovering the word transgender. The second section narrates the moment Arin tells his mom he is trans.
3. As with the previous day, instruct students to fill out their queer cultural capital chart as they read.

4. To end class, discuss the reading. Ask students what they think of his experiences at school, what they think about his relationship with his mother, and what forms of queer cultural capital are evident?

Day 5

1. Today students will read pp. 118–128. In this section Arin begins trans-affirming therapy, transfers to an academically lax public high school and begins transitioning to male.
2. Instruct students to fill out their queer cultural capital chart as they read.
3. Discuss the reading. Ask if they think this new school is better than his old school, how his relationship with his mother is developing, what he has learned about his own identity, and what forms of queer cultural capital are evident?

Day 6

1. Today students will read one more excerpt from Arin's memoir, pp. 203–211. In this section Arin has top surgery (where his breasts are removed) and discusses his relationship problems with Katie.
2. By the end of the class, students should have at least one example for each type of queer cultural capital.
3. Facilitate a discussion about Arin's memoir. Ask how their own experiences compare to Arin's, how might Arin have felt if he had attended their school, what forms of queer cultural capital did he show throughout the excerpts, and how did this help him during his transition?

Day 7

1. Today students begin reading excerpts from Katie's memoir: pp. 5–14. In this section Katie begins college and enjoys making new friends.
2. Instruct students to fill out their queer cultural capital chart as they read.

3. Facilitate a class discussion. Ask how Katie's experiences are similar and different to a cisgender college freshman, and what forms of queer cultural capital are evident?

Day 8

1. Students read pp. 29–31 and 108–117. In the first section Katie navigates college life and choosing between being 'just Katie' and 'activist Katie.' The second section jumps back in time to Katie's transition in high school, going to meetings at OKEQ and OYP, and talking to a trans-affirming doctor.
2. Instruct students to fill out their queer cultural capital chart as they read.
3. Facilitate a class discussion. Ask how students respond to Katie's high school experiences and what forms of queer cultural capital are evident?

Day 9

1. Students read pp. 132–135, in which Katie attends a summer camp with a mission of diversity, and pp. 140–153, in which Katie tries virtual high school due to the bullying she faced at school. Ultimately she finds the experience isolating and returns to high school the next semester.
2. Instruct students to fill out their queer cultural capital chart as they read.
3. Facilitate a class discussion. Ask how students respond to Katie's high school experiences and what forms of queer cultural capital are evident?

Day 10

1. Students read pp. 168–174, in which Katie speaks on a panel on LGBTQ issues at a local college, writes about dating, and discusses getting gender-affirming surgery.
2. By the end of class, students should have a completed queer cultural capital chart for the memoir.

4. Facilitate a discussion on the memoir as a whole. Ask how their own experiences compare to Katie's, how her story differs from Arin's, what forms of queer cultural capital she shows throughout the excerpts, and how this helped her during her transition?

Week 3

This week, students will begin by wrapping up their discussions on the memoirs and then will write their own memoir. Student memoirs will showcase a moment where they exemplified cultural capital. This will work best if students already have experience with narrative structure. Teachers may wish to include this in a larger unit on writing memoirs and may wish to include specific lessons on writing, which are not detailed here. This week aligns with one of the CCSS writing standards for 9th and 10th grade: "Use precise words and phrases, telling details, and sensory language to convey a vivid picture of the experiences, events, setting, and/or characters" (Common Core State Standards Initiative 2015). Some teachers may wish to end the unit with the memoir assignment.

Day 11

1. Have students describe and compare examples of queer cultural capital in both memoirs. One way to conduct this is a gallery walk. Write each form of capital on chart paper, and create two columns, one for each memoir. Have students write in examples on the chart paper. When finished, facilitate a discussion on what they observed. Possible discussion questions include:
   (A) What forms of queer cultural capital did Arin and Katie use at school?
   (B) How did they use their queer cultural capital to find information about trans people?
   (C) What were the benefits and negative effects of being labeled on Katie and Arin?
   (D) Was their relationship a form of queer cultural capital? Why or why not?
   (E) How did they navigate the pressures and obstacles they faced?
   (F) How did their experiences differ, and was that affected by their cultural capital?

2. Lastly, to relate the memoirs to their own schooling experiences, teachers may ask:
   (A) How would Arin and Katie feel at our school?
   (B) What spaces are welcoming to trans students? What spaces are unwelcoming?
   (C) What action can be taken to improve our school for trans students?
   By couching these questions in Katie and Arin's experiences, teachers can avoid singling out and potentially harming trans or gender creative student individuals at their school. Talking about the memoirs can allow high school students to voice questions and concerns without fear of outing themselves or their friends, and can also allow students to voice stereotypes. The teacher can then facilitate conversations to help dissipate stereotypes and prejudices in a productive way, with the texts as reference, again preventing students from being targeted.

Day 12

1. Introduce the memoir assignment. Teachers should decide on the specifications for the assignment. Tell students that they will be writing a memoir that shows their own cultural capital. Students do not have to identify as queer to demonstrate the forms of cultural capital; anyone can possess cultural capital.
2. Ask students to brainstorm events in their life that are particularly memorable. Ask them if something meaningful happened to them, did they overcome a hardship, or have a life-changing experience?
3. Once they have ideas, ask students to consider how cultural capital is evident in their examples. Teachers may wish to ask students to work with a partner for this activity. Each student should be able to identify at least one form of cultural capital in their memoir idea.

Day 13

1. Students outline their memoir.
2. Students begin writing their memoir. Teachers may wish to have students complete a draft in class or at home. This may take more than one class period.

Day 14

1. Students should finish working on their drafts.
2. Facilitate peer review. Do their peers identify the same forms of cultural capital they intended to express? Are other forms evident?

Day 15

1. Students finish final drafts. This may take more class periods and/or homework time depending on the students and length requirement.
2. In pairs, trade final drafts. Students should evaluate their peer's memoirs for evidence of cultural capital. Do their peers identify the same forms of cultural capital they intended to express? Are other forms evident?
3. Facilitate a class discussion comparing the students' memoirs to Arin's and Katie's.

Week 4

For the final week of the unit, students will analyze the portrayals of Andrews and Hill by various media outlets and compare these portrayals to the authors' descriptions of interacting with the media. This will illustrate media bias and help with students' critical analysis skills. This week's activities align with the following CCSS for "informational text": "analyze various accounts of a subject told in different mediums (e.g., a person's life story in both print and multimedia), determining which details are emphasized in each account" (Common Core State Standards Initiative 2015). Teachers should plan a multimodal project suited to their school's resources in which students will create their own media portrayal of Katie and/or Arin, using the memoirs to guide their work.

Day 16

1. Introduce this week's lessons by explaining to students that they will continue reading about Arin and Katie, this time focusing specifically on how the media portrayed them. Ask students to discuss their opinions on the media, and ask for examples of media bias.

2. Students read pp. 185–187 and 195 from Arin's memoir. In these pages, Arin talks about being filmed with Katie for a British producer and their segment on *Inside Edition*.
3. Next, have students reread p. 29 from Katie's memoir, which talks about being filmed for *Inside Edition* and pp. 160–162, where Katie writes about being filmed for *Tulsa World*.
4. Briefly discuss with students how Arin and Katie felt about these experiences, and explain that now they will watch two short videos about them.
5. Watch *Becoming Katie*, from *Tulsa World* (tulsaworld 2012)
6. Watch *Transgender love story: Transgender couple fall in love* (Barcroft TV 2012).
7. Discuss differences in Katie and Arin's memoirs compared to the videos. What forms of queer cultural capital are evident? What are missing?

Day 17

1. Read pp. 212–221 from Arin's memoir, in which Arin and Katie have relationship problems and make another video.
2. Read pp. 213–215 from Katie's memoir in which they film a video after Arin's top surgery.
3. Briefly discuss how Katie and Arin felt about being filmed, and how they described their relationship.
4. Watch *Transgender love story: Life after surgery.* (Barcroft TV 2013)
5. Discuss differences in Katie and Arin's memoirs compared to the videos. What forms of queer cultural capital are evident? What are missing?

Day 18

1. Read pp. 226–228 in Arin's memoir. Here, Arin and Katie are in a campaign for Barneys department store, and make a video about breaking up.
2. Read pp. 224–228 and 237–242 in Katie's memoir. In these excerpts Arin and Katie film a talk show segment, are photographed for the Barneys campaign, and break up.

3. Briefly discuss how Katie and Arin felt about being filmed, and how they described their relationship.
4. Watch *Transgender love story: Arin and Katie break up* (Barcroft TV 2014)
5. Watch *Brothers, sisters, sons, & daughters-Introducing Katie and Arin.* (Barneys New York 2014)
6. Discuss differences in Katie and Arin's memoirs compared to the videos. What forms of queer cultural capital are evident? What are missing?

Day 19

1. Facilitate a wrap-up discussion on the week's reading and videos. Ask questions such as: What forms of capital did they use when interacting with the media? What forms of capital were enhanced by this interaction? What forms of capital were hindered?
2. Introduce the media project that shows Katie and Arin in a new light and illustrates at least one form of queer cultural capital. The details will be decided by each teacher depending on available resources, but students might create projects such as: an online slideshow using images inspired by the memoirs; a video where students act as Katie and Arin and discuss their true feelings for each other; a video focusing on one of the teens telling their version of events; or a video that uses existing footage of the pair edited in a new way that students feel tells a more honest story.
3. Students should begin working on their project in groups. This work may take multiple days depending on the complexity of the assignment.

Day 20

1. When students have completed their assignments, they should present them to the class.
2. Discuss the projects. What new stories were told? How do these relate to the memoirs? What forms of queer cultural capital were illustrated?

Assessment

The queer cultural capital handout, memoir, and multimodal project are all assessments, each designed to allow students to demonstrate their understanding of the memoirs and queer cultural capital. The queer cultural capital handout assesses if students successfully identified each form of capital in both memoirs. The student-written memoir can be assessed in terms of writing style, narrative structure, and mechanics as well as for their understanding of cultural capital. Students should demonstrate how they used their own cultural capital (queer or otherwise) and how their cultural capital is a strength. While all students may not have undergone hardship, or may not want to share their vulnerabilities, the variety of forms of capital should allow all students to successfully write their own memoir. Students may write how their familial capital allows them to have confidence in their abilities, for example, without writing about a struggle. The multimodal project allows them to highlight the queer cultural capital possessed by Arin and/or Katie and support their analysis with textual evidence, rather than relying on biased media portrayals.

While these assessments allow students to practice technical skills, they will also hopefully show students that transgender people are deserving of kindness and respect and have strengths created by their experiences transitioning, thus helping students create a welcoming classroom environment for all students. Sometimes non-LGBT*IAGCQ people can undergo a broadened mindset merely by learning about LGBT*IAGCQ experiences, and if teachers use these memoirs in the classroom they may be introducing their students to transgender lives for the first time. After completing this unit, students may notice when things are inhibitive or exclusive of trans* people at school; may comment on trans* representations in the media with a respectful and critical lens; or may ask for trans* inclusive spaces and practices at their school and in the community. This will help teachers who are practicing the tenth principle from the queer literacy framework "believe that students who identify on a continuum of gender identities deserve to learn in environments free of bullying and harassment" (Miller, Chap. 2, p. 25).

IMPLICATIONS

For classroom teachers, these memoirs can both inform cisgender students about trans* experiences and also show any trans* or gender creative students that they are not alone. The lessons have potential to establish that the teacher is a safe person to talk to about (a)gender identity issues. In fact, these teachers may find their classroom becomes a haven for students questioning or struggling with (a)gender identity. Additionally, showing high school students two memoirs written by teens may help them identify as writers (Gallagher 2006). If teachers face resistance from administrators or parents for using these texts in the classroom, they can demonstrate how this unit aligns with curriculum standards and research-based practices.

Teacher educators may also want to use these memoirs with their preservice teachers. Introducing these books in an English methods course will likely increase the chance that they will use it in their future classrooms. If a teacher educator feels their students do not have time to read both memoirs in full, they can read the same excerpts detailed in the high school unit. When I have used these memoirs with future secondary English teachers, the response was highly positive. The preservice teachers felt that these memoirs were easier to relate to than academic texts on transgender experiences and helped them think through how they might help future students. By giving preservice teachers examples written by trans youth, they gain a fuller picture of the day-to-day experiences of trans youth. Ideally, this exposure will instill a belief that all students, no matter their (a)gender identity or expression, deserve a safe and welcoming classroom free from harassment. Beyond believing in this, hopefully they will act on this belief by working to create these environments in their classrooms and schools at large. When the memoirs are coupled with an analysis drawing upon queer cultural capital, teachers develop the strengths of trans*, gender creative, and all youth and instill them with the ideal that difference should be celebrated and revered, not feared or shamed.

ADDITIONAL RESOURCES

Articles on Katie Hill from *Tulsa World*

- Spinwall, C. (May 7, 2011a). "Part One: Katie Hill finds herself after 16 years living as a boy." *Tulsa World*. Accessed at http://www.tulsaworld.com/.
- Spinwall, C. (May 8, 2011b). "Katie Hill braves returning to school, finds love." *Tulsa World*. Accessed at http://www.tulsaworld.com/.

- Spinwall, C. (June 3, 2012). "Much has changed in year for Bixby transgender teen" *Tulsa World*. Accessed at http://www.tulsaworld.com/.

Media about Arin Andrews and Katie Hill:

- [Auritt]. (December 2, 2014). *Katie Rain Hill & Arin Andrews— "Re-thinking Normal" & "Some Assembly Required"*. [Video file]. Retrieved from https://www.youtube.com/watch?v=oFdSwMfey_g.

Social media:

- Arin Andrew's YouTube channel: [Rockclimber712]. https://www.youtube.com/user/Rockclimber712/videos.
- Arin Andrews twitter: @arin_andrews, https://twitter.com/arin_andrews.
- Katie Hill's twitter: @KatieRainHill, https://twitter.com/KatieRainHill.

Other trans youth writings:

- *I Don't Do Boxes: Queer stories from the South*. Accessed at http://www.idontdoboxes.org/we-dont-do-boxes/. Written by teens, published in Greensboro, NC.
- *I Am Jazz* (2014) by Jessica Herthel and Jazz Jennings. Jazz is a transgender child and transgender activist.

Teacher and student resources:

- Gay, Lesbian, & Straight Education Network (GLSEN) has lesson plans, research, and student resources on their website: http://www.glsen.org/.
- LGBTQIA Resources for Educators is an online resource for teachers and students created by a collaboration between LEARN NC and Safe Schools NC. http://www.learnnc.org/lp/editions/LGBTQIA-resources/.

APPENDIX : TRANSITIONAL MEMOIRS UNIT PLAN
CALENDAR: TEACHER REFERENCE

Day 1-Gender and LGBTQIA	Day 2-Queer cultural capital	Day 3-*Some Assembly Required*	Day 4-*Some Assembly Required*	Day 5-*Some Assembly Required*
Unit introduction (anticipation guide)	Introduce queer cultural capital (student cultural capital handout)	Memoir introductions	SAR pp. 86–90; 100–104. Arin's experience at a private Christian school and first discovering the word transgender; Arin tells his mom he's trans	SAR pp. 118–128: Arin begins trans-affirming therapy, starts at an academically-lax public school and begins transitioning
Gender line activity	Practice finding evidence of queer cultural capital	*Some Assembly Required* (SAR) pp. 1–14. Arin goes to prom	Students work on queer cultural capital chart in class or for homework	Students work on queer cultural capital chart in class or for homework
Vocabulary activity		Students work on queer cultural capital chart in class or for homework (student reading handout)	Small group and/or whole class discussion on reading	Small group and/or whole class discussion on reading
Whole class discussion about gender, sexual orientation, and society's expectations		Small group and/or whole class discussion on reading		

Day 6-*Some Assembly Required*	Day 7-*Rethinking Normal*	Day 8-*Rethinking Normal*	Day 9-*Rethinking Normal*	Day 10-*Rethinking Normal*
SAR pp. 203–211: Arin's top surgery and relationship problems with Katie	*Rethinking Normal* (RT) pp. 5–14. Katie begins college and enjoys making new friends	RT pp. 29–31: Katie navigates college life and choosing between being 'just Katie' and 'activist Katie'	RT pp. 132–135: Katie attends a summer camp with a mission of diversity	RT pp. 168–174: Katie speaks on a panel on LGBTQ issues at a local college, dating, discussion of gender-affirming surgery

Students finish SAR side of queer cultural capital chart in class or for homework	Students work on queer cultural capital chart in class or for homework	RT pp. 108–117; Katie's transition in high school, bullying, unhelpful administration; going to OKEQ & OYP; talking to a trans-affirming doctor	RT 140–153: Katie tries virtual high school due to the bullying she faces, but finds it too isolating and returns to high school the next semester	Students work on queer cultural capital chart in class or for homework
Whole class discussion on Arin's memoir	Small group and/or whole class discussion on reading	Students work on queer cultural capital chart in class or for homework Small group and/or whole class discussion on reading	Students work on queer cultural capital chart in class or for homework Small group and/or whole class discussion on reading	Whole class discussion on reading
Day 11-Memoir discussion	**Day 12-Memoir writing**	**Day 13-Memoir writing**	**Day 14-Memoir writing**	**Day 15-Memoir writing**
Gallery walk: write the forms of queer cultural capital on individual sheets of paper and hang around the room. Have students walk around and write examples	Introduce memoir assignment (decide on length and other requirements)	Students outline memoir	Finish working on drafts	Work on/finish final draft
Whole class discussion (see lesson narrative for suggested questions)	Brainstorming- Ask students to think of a memorable life event	Begin writing	Peer review	In pairs, trade memoirs, write how the memoir shows evidence of cultural capital
	Map out how memoir idea relates to cultural capital			Discuss how student memoirs relate to Arin and Katie's stories

Day 16-Media	Day 17-Media	Day 18-Media	Day 19-Media	Day 20-Media
SAR pp. 185–187; 195. Arin talks about being filmed with Katie for a British producer and *inside Edition* RT: p. 29 (reread paragraph about *Inside Edition*) 160–162	SAR pp. 212–221. Arin and Katie have relationship problems, make another video RT: pp. 213–215. Katie and Arin make a video after Arin's top surgery	SAR pp. 226–228. Arin and Katie are in a campaign for Barneys, make a video about breaking up RT pp. 224–228; 237–242. Arin and Katie film a talk show segment, Barneys campaign, and break up	Introduce media project	Finish creating media project Share projects with the class
Watch *Becoming Katie* (link in lesson narrative)	Watch *Transgender love story: Life after surgery.* (link in lesson narrative)	Watch *Transgender love story: Arin and Katie break up.* (link in lesson narrative)	Students begin working on project in groups	Discuss evidence of cultural capital in media projects
Watch *Transgender love story: Transgender couple fall in love.* (link in lesson narrative)	Discuss differences in Katie and Arin's memoirs compared to the videos. What forms of queer cultural capital are evident? What are missing?	Watch *Brothers, sisters, sons, & daughters-Introducing Katie and Arin.* (link in lesson narrative)		
Discuss differences in Katie and Arin's memoirs compared to the videos. What forms of queer cultural capital are evident? What are missing?		Discuss differences in Katie and Arin's memoirs compared to the videos. What forms of queer cultural capital are evident? What are missing?		

NOTES

1. This chapter utilizes trans* in spaces when not directly referencing Andrews and Hill, but uses *trans* when referencing their memoirs because of how they identify or write on trans issues in their memoirs. Transgender will be used in places when it is more appropriate to the context in which it is being used.

REFERENCES

Andrews, A. (2014). *Some assembly required: The not-so-secret life of a transgender teen*. New York: Simon and Schuster.

Barcroft TV. (2012, November 14). *Transgender love story: Transgender couple fall in love*. [Video file]. Retrieved from https://www.youtube.com/watch?v=g35kGQGwwM8

Barcroft TV. (2013, July 22). *Transgender love story: Life after surgery*. [Video file]. Retrieved from https://www.youtube.com/watch?v=hRKQJCC_RSM

Barcroft TV. (2014, January 10). *Transgender love story: Arin and Katie break up*. [Video file]. Retrieved from https://www.youtube.com/watch?v=LQ4bmxcSNDU

Barneys New York. (2014, January 31). *Brothers, sisters, sons, & daughters-Introducing Katie and Arin*. [Video file]. Retrieved from https://www.youtube.com/watch?v=M9FL3cwdhFo

Biography. (2015). *Ruby Bridges biography: Civil rights activist*. Retrieved from http://www.biography.com/people/ruby-bridges-475426

Boellstorff, T., & Leap, W. (2004). Introduction: Globalization and "new" articulatoins of same-sex desire. In W. Leap & T. Boellstorff (Eds.), *Speaking in queer tongues: Globalization and gay language* (pp. 1–22). Urbana/Chicago: University of Illinois Press.

Bourdieu, P. (1986). The forms of capital. In J. G. Richardson (Ed.), *Handbook of theory and research for the sociology of education* (pp. 241–258). Westport: Greenwood Press.

Britzman, D. (1995). Is there a queer pedagogy? Or, stop reading straight. *Educational Theory, 45*(2), 151–165.

Chávez, K. (2013). *Queer migration politics: Activist rhetoric and coalitional possibilities*. Chicago: University of Illinois Press.

Common Core State Standards Initiative. (2015). *English language arts standards*. Accessed at http://www.corestandards.org/ELA-Literacy/

Crenshaw, K. (1991). Mapping the margins: Identity politics, intersectionality, and violence against women. *Stanford Law Review, 43*(6), 1241–1299.

Gallagher, K. (2006). *Teaching adolescent writers*. Portland: Stenhouse Publishers.

Garza, A. (2014, October 7). A herstory of the #BlackLivesMatter movement. *The Feminist Wire*. Retrieved from http://thefeministwire.com/2014/10/blacklivesmatter-2/

Hill, K. (2014). *Rethinking normal: A memoir in transition*. New York: Simon and Schuster.

Knofler, T., & Imhof, M. (2007). Does sexual orientation have an impact on non-verbal behavior in interpersonal communication? *Journal of Nonverbal Behavior, 31*, 189–204.

Nicholas, C. (2004). Gaydar: Eye-gaze as identity recognition among gay men and lesbians. *Sexuality & Culture, 8*(1), 60–86.

Pennell, S. M. (2016). Queer cultural capital: Implications for education. *Race Ethnicity & Education, 19*(2), 324–338.

Spinwall, C. (2011a, May 7). Part one: Katie Hill finds herself after 16 years living as a boy. *Tulsa World*. Accessed at http://www.tulsaworld.com/

Spinwall, C. (2011b, May 8). Katie Hill braves returning to school, finds love. *Tulsa World*. Accessed at http://www.tulsaworld.com/

tulsaworld. (2012, April 5). *Becoming Katie*. [Video file]. Retrieved from https://www.youtube.com/watch?v=Xktfuvg2dyc

White, A., & Stallybrass, P. (1986). *The politics and poetics of transgression*. Ithaca: Cornell University Press.

Yosso, T. (2005). Whose culture has capital? A critical race theory discussion of community cultural wealth. *Race Ethnicity and Education, 8*(1), 69–91.

CHAPTER 12

Trans* Young Adult Literature for Secondary English Classrooms: Authors Speak Out

Judith A. Hayn, Karina R. Clemmons,
and Heather A. Olvey

Queer Literacy Framework Principles:

5. Opens up spaces for student to self-define with chosen (a)genders, (a)sexuality, (a)pronouns, or names; and,
6. Engages in ongoing critique of how gender norms are reinforced in literature, media technology, art, history, science, math, and so on.

Trans* teens, perhaps more than any other nonprivileged group of adolescents, live in a world fraught with misinformation and misunderstanding. The English language arts (ELA) classroom ought to be one venue where fears and lack of knowledge by both trans* youth and also their classmates can be safely addressed. Preservice teachers and experienced practitioners need the motivation to prioritize and advocate for including trans* pedagogy in the English language arts high school curriculum. The authors of this chapter advocate the implementation of trans* young adult literature

J.A. Hayn (✉) • K.R. Clemmons • H.A. Olvey
University of Arkansas, Little Rock, USA

© The Editor(s) (if applicable) and The Author(s) 2016
sj Miller (ed.), *Teaching, Affirming, and Recognizing Trans and Gender Creative Youth*, DOI 10.1057/978-1-137-56766-6_12

(YAL) as one pathway to begin to open minds and hearts in secondary English classrooms. Changing attitudes, reexamining perceptions, and gaining understanding about trans* issues and other social justice topics are directly addressed in the revised NCTE (National Council of Teachers of English) Standards for the Initial Preparation of Teachers of Secondary English Language Arts (NCTE 2012).

For the first time, a standard devoted entirely to the integration of social justice as a critical component of a teacher education program is a mandate. Standard VI, officially approved by CAEP in 2013, reads as follows:

Professional Knowledge and Skills VI. Candidates demonstrate knowledge of how theories and research about social justice, diversity, equity, student identities, and schools as institutions can enhance students' opportunities to learn in English Language Arts.

Element 1: Candidates plan and implement English language arts and literacy instruction that promotes social justice and critical engagement with complex issues related to maintaining a diverse, inclusive, equitable society.

Element 2: Candidates use knowledge of theories and research to plan instruction responsive to students' local, national and international histories, *individual identities* (e.g., race, ethnicity, *gender expression*, age, appearance, ability, spiritual belief, sexual orientation, socioeconomic status, and community environment), and languages/dialects as they affect students' opportunities to learn in ELA (NCTE 2012).

Infusing this standard into ELA teacher education programs, especially Element 2 which identifies the importance for teacher candidates to know how to plan instruction responsive to individual identities, e.g., gender expression, is now not only a moral imperative, but also a requirement for all who prepare future educators. As Alsup and Miller (2014) remind us: "[Social justice] is a way of approaching public education, and teacher education, that ensures that it will be as open and equitable as possible to all children, regardless of their identities, biologies, or experiences" (p. 199).

WHY TRANS*FORM?

Along with the commitment to social justice with teachers, preservice candidates, and their students comes the obligation to include dedication to equity for all. Munoz-Plaza et al. (2002) reported that youth who identify as lesbian, gay, bisexual, or transgender are especially susceptible to high levels of verbal and physical harassment. Even more recently, Sokoll in her 2013 article, "Representation of Trans* Youth in Young Adult Literature: A Report and a Suggestion," documents the need for using YAL to increase awareness of and to lead to the understanding of trans* youth among adolescent readers. She analyzed some of the relevant results of the 2011 National School Climate Survey: The Experiences of Lesbian, Gay, Bisexual and Transgender Youth in Our Nation's Schools conducted by the Gay, Lesbian, and Straight Education Network:

> Transgender students experienced more hostile school climates than their non-transgender peers—80 percent of transgender students reported feeling unsafe at school because of their gender expression.... Compared to other LGBT students, transgender students faced the most hostile school climate.... In addition, gender nonconforming students experienced more negative experiences at school compared to students whose gender expression adhered to traditional norms. (p. 24)

This disturbing data urges us that adopting curriculum that creates a safe environment for all our students is a key component of actively engaging in socially just pedagogy.

Dank et al. (2013) in their landmark study, "Dating Violence Experiences of Lesbian, Gay, Bisexual, and Transgender Youth," surveyed 5,647 youth in 20 schools; 3,745 responded that they were in a dating relationship or had been in a recent one. Predictably, the results showed that LGBT youth "...are at higher risk for all types of dating violence victimization (and nearly all types of dating violence perpetration), compared to heterosexual youth" (p. 846). Few transgender teens responded, but for those who did, the results are troubling: "[They]...reported the highest rates of victimization with regard to all forms of dating violence compared to male or female youth" (p. 855). The danger of being a transgender teen in society, and thus in school, is real and needs immediate and serious attention.

Schieble, in her 2012 article, "A Critical Discourse Analysis of Teachers' Views on LGBT Literature," examines a discussion thread created during a web-based forum maintained through a children's literature course as part of a teacher education program. She asserts that teacher conservatism, including among teacher educators, creates an unwillingness to engage in discussion about sexual orientation and gender identity with students. Hermann-Willmarth (2010) contends that K-6 preservice teachers view

LGBT topics as inappropriate to discuss with children. She further maintains that harassment involving sexual orientation toward both teachers and students coupled with censorship of literature selections combines to create an exclusionary school climate. Hermann-Willmarth (2010) asserts that it is the duty of all teachers to create an environment in which all students feel safe as well as included, and Kitchen and Bellini (2012) agree when they state "Whatever one's personal beliefs, a teacher has a moral and legal obligation to respect every student and prevent harassment and bullying" (p. 457). Yet, the imperative for teaching trans* and gender creative literature to teens is clear as an integral part of the LGBT*IAGCQ aspect of social justice. As English educators assume responsibility for building our preservice teachers' skills and dispositions concerning social justice issues, the expectation of what that means in its varied aspects cannot be ignored.

Williams and Deyoe (2015) cite several reports and policy statements recommending that schools and libraries focus on LGBTQ youth and their families. Yet, their survey results show that libraries in schools with teacher preparation and/or library science programs "...have few or no holdings of recently published LGBTQ-themed youth literature" (p. 67). Another study focusing on teen access to LGBT-themed literature in 125 high school libraries in one state found the same trend. School libraries were not providing students with this literature that focuses on LGBTQ needs; the average number of LGBTQ titles in the libraries surveyed was 0.4% (Hughes-Hassell et al. 2013). The same disillusioning results occurred on a smaller scale when Meixner (2006) reports on the result of an experiment with her undergraduate students in teacher education during an independent study on LGBTQ YAL. Five students investigated teen access to books like those they read in class by examining local school and public library collections. Their action research found that LGBTQ library resources in their communities were not available for adolescents; therefore, teachers would also not have access. These studies conducted on YA library collections examined all LGBTQ literature, but it is apparent that if there are limited books for students and teachers for LGBTQ youth, then trans* and gender creative youth are also being denied access, and therefore the possibility to be affirmed and/or recognized in, by, and through school curriculum.

Rockefeller (2007) reminds us in his article, "The Genre of Gender: The Emerging Canon of Transgender-Inclusive YA Literature":

Contemporary young adult literature is a remarkably open universe, integrating controversial subjects and allowing topics earlier considered inappropriate for teen readers to become legitimate areas of exploration, conversation, and debate. Today's teen readers are accustomed to novels containing drinking and drug use, gay and lesbian characters, active sexuality, teen pregnancy, and violence. Yet all of these topics were at some point considered taboo, and most made hesitant first appearances in books that were heavy-handed and issue-driven. (p. 519)

Rockefeller, the Chief of Young Adult Services at the Martin Luther King, Jr. Memorial Library in Washington, DC, cites media coverage and popular culture as covering transgender issues; this trend continues eight years after he wrote the article. For example, recently Caitlyn Jenner appeared on the cover of *Vanity Fair* and drew countless viewers in a Diane Sawyer special interview; she received the ESPY Arthur Ashe Award for Courage and stars in her own reality series, *I am Cait.* Series produced by Internet companies, like *Orange Is the New Black* and *Transparent,* have made transgender topics more present in the media. An ABC Family docuseries, *Becoming Us,* follows Ben—an Evanston, IL, teen—as he copes with his parents' divorce and his father Charlie's transitioning into Carlie. Jazz Jennings, one of the youngest people at age five ever to be diagnosed with gender dysphoria, now 14, has her own reality show, *I am Jazz* on TLC. *Big Brother* had its first trans* houseguest/ contestant, Audrey Middleton.

Though popular media has begun to introduce trans* themes, as Rockefeller laments, earlier YA literature with trans* themes tended to be unbalanced and didactic. Rockefeller (2007) indicated hope that more authors and texts would adhere "to a respect for atypically gendered characters" (p. 520). He, like us, seeks those novels that "...craft believable, multidimensional characters who embody or face transgender themes in a plausible way" (p. 521). The authors of this chapter continue that search by asking students to connect with the authors who reveal why they wrote the trans* YA books that they did.

WHO AND WHAT TRANS*FORMS? HOW TO TRANS*FORM?

As a common practice in the ELA, teachers and their students routinely investigate author intent and purpose in writing texts. The most popular YA trans*-focused books explicated and discussed in previous chapters offer the same potential. Students might be curious about why an author chose trans* issues when choosing character and plot. Several resources in this section offer authentic conversations with writers about those books that other chapters in this text discuss as viable for classroom use. Classroom connections for these materials are described in detail in the Appendix and serve as a valuable resource for teachers, librarians, and teacher educators.

When Julie Ann Peters' *Luna* was released in 2004, there was little beyond case studies and psychology texts in mainstream fiction that dealt with the subject. This novel, for probably the first time, offers credible characters who face transgender[1] themes in a believable way. Regan narrates her experience as her brother Liam transitions into Luna, and she chronicles the story with love and growing awareness. Peters (Smith 2012) relates in an interview that she envisioned the book's concept in bed, where she says she often works out how her novels will progress.

> That particular morning I remember so vividly, a strong presence woke me. She was a girl, sixteen or so, with shoulder-length blonde hair and bangs. Characters don't usually come to me so visually distinct and fully formed…
>
> She said, 'Write about me….'
>
> 'No,' I said. 'But who are you?'
>
> She replied, 'I am Luna'

Peters knew nothing about transgender or gender-variant persons and began to research the topic. She sought authentic voices, which almost derailed the book, because she is not a trans* person, but a self-identified lesbian. In fact, the main character is not a trans* teen, but readers access Luna through her sister's narrative.

In *Parrotfish*, by Ellen Wittlinger (2007), the first YA novel to feature a female-to-male transgender teen, Angela changes her name to Grady and begins to deal with his medical transition. Grady finds bigotry but also encounters allies like Sebastian and Kita in his quest for identity, just as most adolescents do. Wittlinger, in an interview on the Young Adult Library Services Association website (Calkins 2012), sees herself as poised to offer every teen realistic characters and stories that can lead to their own self-awareness. In the interview after she won the Printz Award in 2012, Wittlinger explains why she focuses on gender uniqueness: In my mid-twenties I was fortunate enough to live in Provincetown, Massachusetts, for three years as a fellow of the Fine Arts Work Center. I'd always had a few gay friends, but usually they weren't out to their family or co-workers.

But in the early 1970s I was at ground zero for people who were "out and proud" and it affected me profoundly. Because of my own difficulties with my family, I'd always felt I had a lot in common with my gay and lesbian friends, but it was in P'town that I first began to think of myself as an advocate as well as an ally.

> ... I hadn't met anyone before that who was transgender and it seemed likely to me that most teens hadn't either. People become more comfortable with those they think are unlike them once they actually meet them and get to know them. We fear what we don't understand... (Calkins 2012).

In another YA text, *Double Exposure*, by Bridget Birdsall, she uses her own life-long experiences about socially gendered expectations. This is the story of 15-year-old Alyx Atlas, who was raised as a boy. Born with ambiguous genitalia, "she" and her mother move from California to Milwaukee to start a new life where Alyx identifies as a girl. In Birdsall's (2014) moving letter on the website *Dear Teen Me*, she posts as an adult a letter to herself when she was an adolescent who lived in her own private hell as she struggled to find who she was. She writes:

> All this will change, I promise.
>
> You'll start to understand that your parents aren't bad people, they're just sick. Super sick. You'll learn about alcoholism, mental illness, emotional incest, and the definition of a sociopath. Though it will take awhile, you'll even figure out who you are, what you like, and what it means to love and accept yourself—exactly as you are.

Yet another text, by Meagan Brothers, *Debbie Harry Sings in French*, takes a deep look into cross-dressing. The main character Johnny becomes obsessed with the group Blondie, and he enters a drag contest portraying the lead singer Debbie Harry. Johnny feels comfortable as a woman, but he does not admit his emerging trans* identity. In an interview on the Bookbandit's Blog, "Shootin' the Breeze with Meagan Brothers" (2010), the author discusses the character Johnny:

> I think it's kind of a big thing, especially in the South, for young guys to flaunt their masculinity. In my hometown, it was all about how big your pickup truck tires were, and how many mudholes you could drive that sucker through. Hunting was an obvious rite of passage. But here's a very female

thing, putting on this dress. Guys down there don't kid around about that kind of stuff. (2010)

In Cris Beam's *I am J* (2011), J knows that he mistakenly is a boy living in a girl's body. The struggles he encounters in seeking a sense of self take him to uncomfortable and even dangerous places. *I am J* was named a Kirkus Best Book and Library Guild Selection and is the first book with a transgender character to land on the state of California's recommended reading list for public high schools (Beam 2011). In an interview (Wilson 2011), Beam discusses the influence her trans* partner and trans* foster child have had on her writing. She shares how she purposefully created J to become the character who can change attitudes and perceptions about trans* persons:

> As for misconceptions, different people have different ones—depending on who they are, how they were raised, where they live, whether they're gay or straight or trans or cisgender and on and on. I guess one misconception—and one that I struggled with writing the book—is the idea that trans or gender variant people experience themselves as one gender: an opposite gender to the one assigned to them at birth. I thought a lot about this when I was writing J, because my partner, for instance, often feels like neither gender or like both.

Brian Katcher expounds on his ability to write on the trans* experience as a heterosexual man, answering readers' doubts in an interview with Laura Lam (2012). Katcher's, *Almost Perfect* (2010), a Stonewall Children's and Young Adult Award winner, features brokenhearted Logan, who is obsessed with his ex-girlfriend. Then new girl Sage appears at Logan's high school. She doesn't date, but won't say why; Sage is really a trans* person. Katcher defends his position as a writer of fiction:

> Other readers have stated that a heterosexual guy has no business writing about such issues, and LGBT novels should be written by those who have experienced these things personally. Well, by definition a novelist is someone who writes about things that they've never experienced, fiction is all about inventing characters. Otherwise, I could only write about phenomenally handsome librarians from Missouri. Creating Sage was a challenge, but she's my favorite character, and I'm proud of her. (Lam 2012)

While transgender readers will find support here, the book's focus on a bystander broadens its appeal, and the message of acceptance is conveyed.

A burgeoning selection of trans* memoirs has emerged and includes *Rethinking Normal: A Memoir in Transition* by Katie Rain Hill (2014) and *Some Assembly Required: The Not So Secret Life of a Transgender Teen* by Arin Andrews (2014). Their romantic relationship was chronicled on an episode of 20/20, although the couple has since split. A discussion and interview with Hill appears on the *Daily Mail* website (see Elliott 2014): "'I was spat on, laughed at and stolen from': Transgender woman's harrowing account of having a sex change in the Bible Belt" (Elliott 2014). Born Luke in Okay, Oklahoma, Katie knew she was a boy at age four. Her story is both realistic and fascinating. Many teens can identify with both her struggles to please her parents and the desire to become invisible and disappear. The website features Hill in a video discussion about her relationship with Andrews.

Arin Andrews' memoir chronicles his transition from female to a trans* male teen. His journey is factual and informative in itself, and he includes a list of resources, including ones he used during the process. In an interview (Ongley 2015), Andrews discusses where he is now, his life in college, and his relationships.

Finally, *Beyond Magenta: Transgender Teens Speak Out* by Susan Kuklin (2016) offers the stories of six trans* and gender-neutral teens who speak in the gender of the young person's current self-identity. Kuklin provides helpful context in understanding the transitioning processes in the interviews; the author's photos add realism, poignancy, and knowledge to the text. In an interview in School Library Journal (Toth 2014), Kuklin discusses what she hopes to accomplish with this powerful nonfiction work:

> I think that's what all my books are about. It's writing about people who don't have a voice. If you give them a voice, then maybe there will be more understanding. I want to know who these people are and not just lump them into a sound bite or into generic category. By giving people a voice, we acknowledge that they are complicated, interesting human beings. I hope these are nuanced portraits.

In a two-part interview on The Pirate Tree: Social Justice & Children's Literature site (Kokie 2014b), Kuklin describes her process of using photography and taped interviews to grant significance to populations who might not ever be understood.

When to Trans*form

This evidence tells us as teachers that there is a clear, imperative, and urgent need for introducing trans* and gender creative teens and their experiences to others like them in order to ensure that *all* students are affirmed, recognized, and are able and capable of affirming and recognizing the other. Not only does our role as social justice educators demand such a moral imperative, but it also calls upon our humanity to embody empathy and care for the well-being of our students. We may be like many of the authors listed above and have to do a great deal of research to make sure we are factual and open in our approaches. The stereotypes are there; we want to do nothing to add to those images.

The difficulty in locating YA texts with trans* and gender creative characters or topics has been discussed above. For resources though, librarians and teachers can access the American Library Association Rainbow Project (http://glbtrt.ala.org/rainbowbooks/) which provides an annual bibliography of LGBTQ books for children and young adults to discover titles. Goodreads (https://www.goodreads.com/shelf/show/lgbtq) also maintains a shelf devoted to popular LGBTQ books; in fact, during the summer of 2015, the Booklist for Trans* Teens listed 158 and was selected by 222 voters.

Award lists of nominees and winners can be important tools for becoming familiar with quality trans* and gender creative literature. One example is the Lambda Literary Awards, which is the nation's most comprehensive collection of awards for LGBT writing, including fiction, poetry, mystery, and nonfiction, for adults as well as for children and young adults. The Stonewall Children's and Young Adult Literature Award is presented annually for LGBT works. Although this chapter focuses on trans* YAL, Miller (2015) notes that there are other YA texts coming into our awareness that focus on intersex and asexual youth, and among lesser known (a) gender identities.

Though Rockefeller (2009) noted prior that there were limited YAL focused on trans* topics, in his article, "Selection, Inclusion, Evaluation and Defense of Transgender-Inclusive Fiction for Young Adults: A Resource Guide," he says that, as the trans* experience expands in popular culture, trans* teen fiction is growing. He reminds us of the power these books have for all of us:

Youth can benefit from contact with transgender-inclusive fiction, regardless of their personal identity, for several reasons. First, it offers validity of experience by clearly showing that those youth questioning their gender identity are not alone. Second, transgender-inclusive fiction models inclusiveness and celebrates diversity. Third, fiction can be an effective gateway to investigate nonfiction information. (p. 288)

He recommends utilizing library and youth services journals, award lists, the Internet as a connection tool, blogs, online library collections, and word of mouth. In this important piece, he also discusses several trans*-inclusive books and short stories including many named in this chapter.

Teachers and teacher educators who seek out trans* YAL and determine to include these books in their teaching are adopting the essence of NCTE's social justice oriented Standard VI, which includes creating a climate of acceptance and openness in secondary English classrooms. The discussions generated before, during, and after students engage with text that offers "...literacy instruction that promotes social justice and critical engagement with complex issues related to maintaining a diverse, inclusive, equitable society" (NCTE 2012). Coupling social justice with the literature suggested in this chapter offers teachers opportunities, "...to answer the call that brought so many of us to the profession—to engage with young people in exploring and making sense of the human experience, in all of its diversity" (Lin 2014, p. 45).

Trans* teens like Katie Rain Hill, Arin Andrews, and those whose stories are related in *Beyond Magenta* remind us of the importance of the teacher's role in modeling acceptance and understanding in their classrooms. Hill tells of her horrific experiences in high school that led her to leave; she offers this to those who want to change behaviors, their own and thus their students:

> My advice to educators is that they talk to their trans student and make sure that s/he is being treated *equally*. Check in with the kids from time to time to ensure s/he feels comfortable and safe in and out of the classroom. Make sure she/he has teachers or counselors to talk to, adults who understand the child's problems and who will not judge him or her. Transgender people want to be treated just like everyone else while at the same time having our individual personalities respected and nurtured. I would have given anything to have such treatment while I was in high school. (Trimmer 2015, p. 21)

Hill's statement is a clear call to action to educators to not only offer YAL that is inclusive of LGBT*IAGCQ individuals, but to also use the classroom connections offered in the Appendix to engage students in reflective activities that help develop more inclusive and welcoming communities.

APPENDIX: TRANS* YA LIT CLASSROOM CONNECTIONS

Luna *by Julie Anne Peters*

To develop more background and understanding about how Peters developed her characters, students should read the compelling interview from Cynthia Leitich Smith's website, "The Story Behind the Story: Julie Anne Peters on *Luna*" (2004). Students should also listen to and discuss the Nangeroni and Gordene interview of Peters on Gender Talk Webreadio (2005). Direct students to compare and contrast the two interviews. Students should draw conclusions about Peters' purpose in writing for children and teens and provide evidence for their conclusions.

After discussing with students that *Luna* was the first YA text to examine the transgender adolescent in a realistic way, ask them to reflect on their own reactions and discuss whether they would consider *Luna* a controversial book, and how they would defend the book's inclusion in their classroom or library.

Parrotfish *by Eileen*

Direct students to read Wittlinger's complete interview (Brothers 2008). After reading the interview, ask students to respond to Wittlinger's comments for discussion. Wittlinger discusses the importance of forgiveness as a theme in her books. Have students consider the term forgiveness as a gift that can be given and how it affects both the giver and the recipient. Lead students through a self-examination as they consider their attitudes toward Grady and his experiences.

The author also mentions the impact of her book on LGBT*IAGCQ teens as providing a lifeline for navigating adolescence. Ask students to consider the components of their own personal lifeline. Prompt students to consider their role in providing support for their classmates who need similar support.

Guide a group discussion about the importance of having safe spaces in classrooms and libraries. Have students consider the behaviors of the specific bullies in the book, like Danya, Kleinhorst, and Whitney. Direct students to brainstorm how the specific bullying situations in the book could be best handled. Have students brainstorm feasible strategies to help ensure a more secure climate at school and in the community.

Dear Teen Me *by Bridget Birdsall*

In her *Dear Teen Me* letter, Birdsall writes about having and finding real friends. Have students identify their roles in their families like Birdsall does in her letter and consider whether there are parts of themselves that are as painful to confront as the author noted. Ask students to list characteristics of good friends and supportive friendships, and then consider what it is like for those who don't fit in and struggle to find friends.

Have students watch the video at https://vimeo.com/115617585 which describes why Birdsall wrote it. Ask students to discuss the issue of empowerment, what empowerment means to them, and how the sense of empowerment may differ for those who are not part of normative culture.

Debbie Harry Sings in French *by Meagan Brothers*

Prepare an anticipation guide for students prior to reading the book that includes questions about the terminology they will encounter. After reading the book, have students revisit the questions and discuss growth in knowledge and empathy. Have students consider how labels define and limit personal expression, and ask students to discuss how they can learn to change perceptions through understanding.

After reading Brothers' full interview (2008), initiate a class discussion about stereotypes and cultural expectations of what it means to be a man or a woman. Direct students to discuss and reflect on gender roles, the portrayal of gender in their lives, the role of society in determining gender roles, and ways to reduce societal limitations based on gender stereotypes.

Music is important to Johnny and Maria, and the songs Brothers chooses as chapter titles help reflect the themes of each chapter. In the interview, Brothers says that teens use music to soothe their loneliness. Ask students to create a playlist for their own lives to share with the class through a classroom wiki with multimedia links.

I am J *by Cris Beam*

Wilson's (2011) interview with Cris Beam offers opportunities for teachers and students to correct misunderstandings and deal with the realities of the trans* individual struggling to come to terms with who she or he is. After students read the interview, have them discuss what can be learned from Beam's discussion of misconceptions. Ask students to describe their own communities in terms of intolerance or tolerance specifically related to LGBT*IAGCQ individuals.

As an authentic writing activity, students can compose brief letters of feedback to Beam explaining what they learned and gained in understanding of LGBT*IAGCQ teens by reading her book. Letters can be emailed to Beam's email address available on her author website.

Almost Perfect *by Brian Katcher*

Have students read Katcher's interview (Lam 2012) and react to a passage in the book as they think the author might have done as he was creating Sage. Invites students to offer evidence from the interview that supports their portrayal of the author's perspective.

Ask students to brainstorm what they can do to educate themselves and improve their awareness and attitude about LGBT*IAGCQ issues. Have students investigate resources in their communities that could help with the process of knowledge acquisition. Students can compile the resources to share on a class wiki or on another media-based platform such as a Prezi.

Rethinking Normal: A Memoir in Transition *by Katie Rain Hill*

After reading the book, assign students to review Katie Rain Hill's social media page (www.facebook.com/katierainhill). Direct students to examine Hill's recent posts and prepare a draft of a Visitor Post to let Hill know how her experiences affected them and what insights they gained about the trans* experience from reading Hill's story.

Hill's high school experiences were dominated by bullying and exclusion. Have students reflect on their experiences with exclusion and brainstorm what they would change about their own school and community culture to prevent similar instances from happening again. Assign students to develop an anti-bullying multimedia presentation that could be shared with students, teachers, and administrators.

Rethinking Normal: A Memoir in Transition *by Katie Rain Hill and,* Some Assembly Required: The Not-So-Secret Life of a Transgender Teen *by Arin Andrews*

After students have read both books, ask students to discuss similarities and differences between the two. Direct them to read the interview (http://candieanderson.com/2014/10/transgendered-teens-arin-andrews-and-katie-rain-hill-talk-memoirs-gender-reassignment-challenges-they-face-interview.html) and then have them discuss their insights and reactions.

Andrews and Hill are both activists for trans* awareness building. Have students research additional resources in the school and community that support LGBT*IAGCQ teens, and encourage students to reflect on how to be an advocate for supportive and inclusive communities.

Beyond Magenta: Transgender Teens Speak Out *by Susan Kuklin*

Kuklin combines photography with interviews to tell the stories of selected trans* teens. Ask students to select one teen's story from the book that moved them. Have them reflect on the emotional reactions they had as they read and the impact this experience had for them.

As an extension activity, direct students to consider another person who may need an advocate and create a photo essay through a similar process of pictures and words as the author used. Students should share their insights and discoveries through the relationship between image and text.

NOTES

1. When *Luna* was written, transgender was the preferred identity marker for transgender people. Trans* is a more recent term used to more broadly encompass that there is no single transgender identity or experience.

REFERENCES

Alsup, J., & Miller, s. (2014). Reclaiming English education: Rooting social justice in dispositions. *English Education, 46*(3), 195–215.

Andrews, A. (2014). *Some assembly required: The not so secret life of a transgender teen.* New York: Simon & Schuster Books for Young Readers.

Beam, C. (2011). *I am J.* New York: Little Brown.

Birdsall, B. (2014, October 16). Dear teen me from author Bridget Birdsall. (Web log comment). Retrieved from http://dearteenme.com/?p=8367

Bookbandit's Blog. (2010, June 13). Shootin' the breeze with Meagan Brothers. (Interview). Retrieved from https://thebookbandit.wordpress.com/2010/06/13/debbie-harry-sings-in-french-take-twopart-one-the-interview/

Brothers, M. (2008). *Debbie Harry sings in French.* New York: Henry Holt.

Calkins, E. (2012, November 15). A different light: An interview with Ellen Wittlinger. Retrieved from http://www.yalsa.ala.org/thehub/2012/11/15/a-different-light-an-interview-with-ellen-wittlinger/

Dank, M., Lachman, P., Zweig, J. M., & Yahner, J. (2013). Dating violence experiences of lesbian, gay, bisexual, and transgender youth. *Journal of Youth and Adolescence, 43*(5), 846–857.

Elliott, A. F. (2014). 'I was spat on, laughed at and stolen from': Transgender woman's harrowing account of having a sex change in the Bible Belt. http://www.dailymail.co.uk/femail/article-2828770/I-spat-laughed-stolen-Transgender-woman-s-harrowing-account-undergoing-sex-change-living-Bible-Belt.html. Published: 13:16 EST, 10 November 2014 | Updated: 06:13 EST, 11 November 2014

Hermann-Willmarth, J. M. (2010). More than book talks: Preservice teacher dialogue after reading gay and lesbian children's literature. *Language Arts, 87*(3), 188–199.

Hill, K. R. (2014). *Rethinking normal: A memoir in transition.* New York: Simon and Schuster Books for Young People.

Hughes-Hassell, S., Overberg, E., & Harris, S. (2013). Lesbian, gay, bisexual, transgender, and questioning (LGBTQ)-themed literature for teens: Are school libraries providing adequate collections? *School Library Research, 16,* 1–18.

Katcher, B. (2010). *Almost perfect.* New York: Delacorte.

Kitchen, J., & Bellini, C. (2012). Addressing lesbian, gay, bisexual, transgender, and queer (LGBTQ) issues in teacher education: Teacher candidates' perceptions. *Alberta Journal of Educational Research, 58*(3), 444–460.

Kokie, E. M. (2014b, March 20). *Beyond magenta*: An interview with Susan Kuklin part II. (Interview). Retrieved from http://www.thepiratetree.com/2014/03/20/beyond-magenta-an-interview-with-susan-kuklin-part-ii/

Kuklin, S. (2016). *Beyond magenta: Transgender teens speak.* Somerville: Candlewick Press.

Lam, L. (2012, January 11). Author interview: *Almost perfect*—Brian Katcher. (Interview). Retrieved from https://staticsplit.wordpress.com/2012/01/11/author-interview-brian-katcher-almost-perfect/

Lin, C. K. (2014). Queer(ing) literature in the secondary English classroom. *The ALAN Review, 42*(1), 44–51.

Meixner, E. (2006). Teacher agency and access to LGBT young adult literature. *Radical Teacher, 76*, 13–19.

Miller, s. (2015). Reading YAL queerly: A queer literacy framework for inviting (a)gender and (a)sexuality self-determination and justice. In D. Carlson & D. Linville (Eds.), *Beyond borders: Queer eros and ethos (ethics) in LGBTQ young adult literature* (pp. 153–180). New York: Peter Lang.

Munoz-Plaza, C., Quinn, C., & Rounds, K. A. (2002). Lesbian, gay, bisexual, and transgender students: Perceived social support in the high school environment. *The High School Journal, 85*(4), 81–100.

Nangeroni, N., & Gordene, O. (2005, June 25). Program 516. Podcast retrieved from http://www.gendertalk.com/radio/programs/500/gt516.shtml

NCTE. (2012). NCTE/NCATE standards for initial preparation of teachers of secondary English language arts, grades 7–12. Retrieved from http://www.ncte.org/library/NCTEFiles/Groups/CEE/NCATE/Aprroved-Standards_111212.pdf

Ongley, H. (2015). Q&A: Arin Andrews on Laverne Cox, college life, and living on both sides of the gender spectrum. http://www.styleite.com/qa/qa-arin-andrews-on-laverne-cox-college-life-and-living-on-both-sides-of-the-gender-spectrum/

Peters, J. A. (2004). *Luna: A novel.* New York: Little Brown & Company.

Rockefeller, E. (2007). The genre of gender: The emerging canon of transgender-inclusive YA literature. *The Horn Book Magazine, 83*(5), 519–529.

Rockefeller, E. (2009). Selection, inclusion, evaluation and defense of transgender- inclusive fiction for young adults: A resource guide. *Journal of LGBT Youth, 6*(2–3), 288–309.

Schieble, M. (2012). A critical discourse analysis of teachers' views on LGBT literature. *Discourse: Studies in the Cultural Politics of Education, 33*(2), 207–222.

Smith, C. L. (2012). The story behind the story: Julie Anne Peters on *Luna*. (Weblog comment). Retrieved from http://www.cynthialeitichsmith.com/lit_resources/authors/stories_behind/storypeters.html

Sokoll, T. (2013). Representation of trans* youth in young adult literature: A report and a suggestion. *Young Adult Library Services, 11*(4), 23–26.

Toth, L. (2014, February 14). Beyond magenta: SLJ talks to Susan Kuklin about her book on transgender teens. (Interview). Retrieved from http://www.slj.com/2014/02/interviews/beyond-magenta-slj-talks-to-susan-kuklin-about-her-book-on-transgender-teens/#_

Trimmer, C. (2015). Being authentically you: An interview with Katie Rain Hill and Arin Andrews. *Voya, 38*(3), 20–21.

Williams, V. K., & Deyoe, N. (2015). Controversy and diversity: LGBTQ titles in academic library youth collections. *Library Research and Technical Services, 59*(2), 62–71.

Wilson, M. (2011). Martin Wilson writes: An interview with Cris Beam. http://martinwilsonwrites.com/2011/03/28/author-interview-cris-beam/

Wittlinger, E. (2007). *Parrotfish*. New York: Simon & Schuster Children's Publishing.

CHAPTER 13

Puncturing the Silence: Teaching *The Laramie Project* in the Secondary English Classroom

Toby Emert

Queer Literacy Framework Principles:

6. Engages in ongoing critique of how gender norms are reinforced in literature, media, technology, art, history, science, math, and so on; and,
9. Advocates for equity across all categories of (a)gender performances.

FRAMING THE PROJECT THEORETICALLY

In an article that appeared in *The English Journal* in 2009—"What English Can Contribute to Understanding Sexual Identities"—Viv Ellis questions the reasons for a brutal attack on one of her high school students, who, though he did not identify as queer, because of his "love of dancing and singing, his proud status as a Michael Jackson fan, and his close friendship with another boy … was singled out as different" (p. 53). She asks, "How was sexual identity written onto and read off my student's body?" (p. 53). Unpacking Ellis' question is a complex endeavor that invites us to reflect on the semiotics of bodies, the performance of "gendered selves," and

T. Emert (✉)
Agnes Scott College, Decatur, USA

© The Editor(s) (if applicable) and The Author(s) 2016
sj Miller (ed.), *Teaching, Affirming, and Recognizing Trans and Gender Creative Youth*, DOI 10.1057/978-1-137-56766-6_13

the cultural biases that influence how we inscribe meaning onto our own bodies, as well as the bodies of others. Human bodies are theatrical and rhetorical, reflecting and reinforcing the "ruling socio-symbolic order" (Counsell and Wolf 2001, p. 140). We "read" bodies through cultural lenses, and often these "readings" reflect what Judith Butler has called the heterosexual matrix: "the discursive grid that defines bodies in terms of oppositional and hierarchical gender categories" (as quoted in Foultier 2013, p. 769).

As sites of meta-messaging and cultural reproduction, bodies become "the central object over and through which relations of power and resistance are played out" (Counsell and Wolf, p. 141). Bodies that eschew gender or that do not conform to gendered expectations of appearance and behavior are especially vulnerable to expressions of hostility and displays of power. Though schools have traditionally been places where queer and gender-nonconforming youth are "institutionally ignored, silenced, and often targets of harassment" (Payne and Smith 2011, p. 175), the classroom has the potential to become a site of inquiry regarding the politics of the body. Rather than creating classroom spaces that "reinscribe heteronormative and gendertypical realities" (Miller 2015, p. 39), teachers who ascribe to a Queer Literacy Framework (QLF) invite their students to critically question "uni-dimensional perspectives[s] of gender and sexuality" (p. 41). Furthermore, they purposefully encourage a critique of the sociopolitical systems that influence how we conceptualize our own bodies and the bodies of others and that undergird the enactment of heteronormative scripts that may include harassment and violence.

FRAMING THE LESSON(S)

Franklin Thompson and William Austin (2010) point out that "gender role myths are promulgated from the day we are born" and that many of the perceptions that "fuel our practice[s] are rooted in habitual and stereotypical thinking" (p. 427). Consequently, high school students possess a substantial implicit—though often tacit—understanding of the cultural systems that police their bodies. In order to engage them in a dialog that problematizes gender (and sexuality), it is important to offer texts and assignments that provoke the level of self-reflexivity that produces thoughtful discussions. Students must *learn* to "recognize their internalized prejudices and [the] oppressions internalized through cultural messages" (Swartz 2005, p. 143). The language arts classroom across all grade levels, when guided by a humanistic approach to making meaning, can offer a space ripe for interrogating human expression through stories told in literature. However, English teachers are often reluctant to introduce texts that question stereotypic depictions of gender (and sexuality) because while they may believe in advocating for equity, they fear admonishment from administrators, parents, and their own students (Unger 2007).

This chapter offers a brief description of a research initiative developed in the fall of 2013 that addresses this reluctance by providing support for four secondary English teachers who purposefully engaged their students in a critique of gender norms by introducing units on the ethnographic verbatim play[1] *The Laramie Project* for the first time.

Though the focus of each unit was on addressing the violence enacted when people challenge normative expression of gender and sexuality, I highlight only those moments when challenges to gender norms surfaced and how that can inform pathways for teachers to recognize the realities of trans* and gender creative youth.

The script for *The Laramie Project*, developed by Moises Kaufman (2001) and members of the Tectonic Theatre Company,[2] is a documentary-style account of the brutal attack on gay college student Mathew Shepard in Laramie, Wyoming, in 1998. After beating and robbing Shepard, his attackers, Aaron McKinney and Russell Henderson, left him unconscious and tethered to a fence. He was discovered the next morning by a bicyclist who called for medical assistance, but Shepard died of severe head injuries six days later. The story of the assault received international attention, bolstered by McKinney's and Henderson's confessions in court that they targeted Shepard, whom they met in a bar, at least partially because they knew he was gay. The incident spotlighted the issue of violence perpetrated against queer bodies and inspired a national conversation that ultimately led to the passage of the Matthew Shepard and James Byrd, Jr., Hate Crimes Prevention Act,[3] signed into law by President Barack Obama in 2009. The image of Shepard's body tied to a fence—at first mistaken for a scarecrow by the bicyclist who found him—became an international symbol of the call for the "freedom of humans to be self-expressive without redress of social, institutional, or political violence" (Miller 2015, p. 38).

The play, devised entirely from interviews, newspaper and television reports, and notes the company made during their visit to Laramie in the days following the assault, provides a multivoiced portrayal of the incident and the attention it garnered. For the research project, each of the teachers chose a specific language arts focus for the unit: (1) as a text for critique through literary theory; (2) as a text discussed in a literature circle; (3) as a "mentor" text for completing an ethnographic interview assignment; and (4) as bibliotherapy[4] for students in an extracurricular Gay Straight Alliance (GSA) club.

We chose *The Laramie Project* for this initiative for a number of reasons: (1) its thematic focus on the consequences of unchecked bias toward those perceived as "different" invites students to discuss issues of justice and social responsibility; (2) the play, acclaimed for its approach to relating the story of a highly publicized hate crime, has been widely produced in high schools and college theaters across the USA, though it is rarely studied in language arts classrooms; (3) we expected pushback from school authorities about introducing a text with queer content, so the selection of a work of literature grounded in nonfiction sources allowed the teachers to compose rationales that align with standards requiring students to read a substantial amount of nonfiction; and (4) we understood that, in critiques of culture, it is often instructive to begin conversations that invite students to explore complex concepts, such as the performance of gender, through processes that feel accommodating (Jackson 2011). In this case, the length of the script was manageable for the students; the language is narrative, rather than theoretical; the story is biographical, inviting personal connections; the arrangement of the scenes into what the playwrights labeled "moments" that portray a variety of perspectives allowed the students to consider the concept of subjectivity; and the play's collaging of other texts to generate the script offered the students a model for responding to the themes in the play in similarly sophisticated, but novel, ways (by drafting scripts of their own).

For this chapter, I offer only glimpses of the processes enacted by the four teachers and myself as we worked together to construct the units. To this aim I provide (1) an overview of the effort to intentionally invite language arts students into a conversation about gender, gender expression and identity, and the consequences of intolerance; (2) an introduction to one exemplar assignment; and (3) notes about how discussions of the play impacted students.

FRAMING THE PROCESS

The teachers who participated in the project and I met together on alternating Wednesday evenings, beginning in August 2013, to plan the instructional units and to design a protocol for gathering student responses. The meetings also served as a space for feedback, friendly critique, and personal support. I played the role of facilitator, advocate, and lead researcher. At the conclusion of the meetings, we each wrote an entry in a journal that served as a response to the research plan and to the experiences the teachers were having in their schools and classrooms.

The teachers crafted units that addressed objectives within their established curricula, in some cases pairing the play with a text they were already planning to teach. Several of the teachers expected resistance and felt compelled to ask permission to use the text in their classrooms, so we discussed how to develop written rationales for instructional choices and how to explain to parents and administrators the decision to teach a text that might elicit scrutiny. Some of the teachers' apprehensions were founded. Administrators, parents, and even a few students questioned the choice to teach the play, and in one case, the teacher was asked to reconsider its use. All four teachers, however, ultimately incorporated the text into a unit and later reported that, in reading and discussing the play, their students accepted their invitation to analyze the power of cultural norms and the repercussions of social injustice. "They handled it with maturity, compassion, and humanity, and I really think that we grew closer together as a class because we were reading a play that pushed typical boundaries. They were really excited that you believe in them enough to teach a text like this," one of the teachers explained in a debrief meeting. Another added, "That's what I found to be true, suddenly, these ninth-graders matured almost overnight."

We were sensitive to the possibilities of controversy, but we were also unapologetic in our conversations during meetings as we voiced a commitment to illuminating the gender politics that exist in the culture and that filter into high school classrooms. Though we did not have the specific language of the QLF to guide our efforts, we nonetheless embraced two of the axioms explicitly; we wanted the students to understand that (1) binary views on gender (and sexuality) are potentially damaging, and (2) we are all entitled to the same basic human rights (Miller 2015).

Highlighting an Exemplar Lesson

Though each teacher's unit merits discussion, in this chapter I highlight one example lesson in which students interpreted the text through personal lenses and practiced aspects of empathetic perspective-taking, a prerequisite skill for challenging "the taken-for-granted value of hegemonic demarcations of gender and sexuality … hidden within and by curriculum" (Miller, p. 40). As the teachers began writing the units and we began data-gathering, we imagined sharing the story of the project by developing a verbatim readers' theater play of our own, adapting techniques similar to those used by the Tectonic Theatre Company to generate the script of *The Laramie Project*. By weaving together snippets of our conversations, personal accounts, excerpts from the high school students' reflections, and examples of student work, we created the script as a method of analyzing our notes and drawing preliminary conclusions about the initiative. One of the teachers—who was creating a unit for her senior Advanced Placement English students that included an introduction to Reader Response Theory (Rosenblatt 1969)—adapted this idea for the unit's culminating assignment. She scaffolded the assignment by placing her students in small groups to discuss the play's themes, and then she mentored them as they constructed their own scripts to illuminate highlighted themes. The students later performed their "plays" for their classmates. The teacher introduced the unit with an explanation of Reader Response Theory and then asked her students to consider the impact of the text on them in explicitly personal ways, posing the following questions: (1) What does the text have to do with you and with your life (past, present, or future)? (2) How did you learn and how much were your views and opinions challenged or changed by this text? (3) How well does the text address what you care about and consider as important to the world? These guiding questions encouraged the students to develop a running commentary with the play and ultimately led them to discussions of equity, nonconformity, and personal and political responsibility.

Overviewing the Unit

Focusing on Reader Response Theory—which is concerned with "attending to the meaning each reader makes of a text" (Emert and Hall 2015, p. 57; Rosenblatt 1969)—as a frame for the study of the play, the teacher chose not to preview the text. Instead, she instructed the students to read it and reflect on their reading by writing a substantive two- to three-page personal response. Students brought their reflections to class to ignite discussion. She divided the class into five groups and offered each a central question to direct their conversations. The students continued to work in their small groups throughout the two-week unit, meeting frequently to extend the dialog. They managed their exchanges, conducted background research, and continued to interrogate the depictions of Shepard and the other characters in the play from a variety of angles as they worked. To conclude the discussions, the students wrote a second extended personal response and then, with their groupmates, reviewed the wealth of materials they had read and generated throughout the unit, in order to discover themes for further exploration.

The themes became the organizing ideas that guided the creation of the verbatim scripts for performance. The students primarily used language from the texts they encountered in the unit as they quilted together a drama-based response to their study, so the assignment required them to revisit ideas, to grapple with the nuances of language, and to synthesize their thinking creatively, but purposefully. This kind of assignment was new for both the teacher and the students, but it mirrored the work the teachers and I were doing to summarize what we were learning in the research project, and as such, the students' work became an extension of our own process.

The five groups constructed their scripts, rehearsed them, and ultimately staged a readers' theater performance for their peers. In this way, the class had the opportunity not only to engage deeply with a discussion of the text's themes with their group members but also to witness the tone and style of the discussions of the other groups. The plays generated an additional level of critique, as the teacher asked the "audience" to comment on the highlighted themes expressed in the scripts.

Analyzing the Scripts

The groups' scripts addressed issues both explicitly and implicitly related to gender politics and expression of identity. Furthermore, evidence of the breadth of their discussions was noticeable in their responses to themes expressed in the play, such as social responsibility, acceptance of difference, the repercussions of unchallenged bias, cultural constructions of norms, and the critical need for empathetic understanding. The complex thinking the students were doing about these issues was deeply embedded in their work. Their plays include a range of lines that illustrate the students' expanding perspectives and their articulation of the need to honor, rather than ignore or criticize, "differences," especially those differences that transgress expected gender norms. One group's play, for example, features a scene set in a church in which the characters solemnize the fact that they are being compelled to witness gender injustice and to respond.

One character chastises a church leader who calls for his congregants to "maintain the sight of heaven," suggesting that they condemn "the unnatural and the ungodly." The character rebuts with this line: "People are finally opening their eyes! It's what we all have been waiting for. We no longer have to be afraid of you." Later in the scene, a character responds: "People can't ignore us anymore! How can anyone ignore a story like this? Awareness is going to be the first step to redemption." The twinned ideas of awareness and acceptance show up repeatedly in the scripts.

One group of the students drafted a script titled "Distortion" that includes a scene in which the actors scatter around the "stage" and, as they speak their lines, toss a ball of yarn to each other. The effect is a visual "tangle" of sentiments and perspectives.

> *[JASMINE starts with the ball of yarn and expresses an opinion and tosses the yarn to an actor across the room.]*
>
> **JASMINE:** It's easy to point at Laramie and gasp in shock, but doesn't this kind of event reflect on the entire country?
>
> **ERIKA**: Everybody lives in this bubbled up society where love has become something that has to be defined by gender.
>
> **SAMANTHA:** Who are we to judge others?
>
> **AMANDA:** But … at least we're talking about it … ?

The concluding line, "… at least we're talking about it" echoes significantly, as we consider the taboo nature of robust discussions of (a)gender (and sexuality) in the high school classroom.

In another group's play, three characters discuss the national attention that the Shepard attack attracted, disagreeing about the impact of the sensationalized coverage on the verdict in the attackers' trials. The scene draws a conclusion about the impact of noticing: "I do think that the media actually made people accountable. Because they made people think." The last scene of one group's play, titled simply "Finale," features an introspective monolog in which a character shares this conclusion:

> I recognize that Matthew Shepard was not significant in his life, morbid as it sounds; he was significant in his death. He meant something. He stood for something to people. He stood for the countless other victims that remain nameless. The importance of communicating, of awareness, … the power of reaction is astounding.

Other lines extend the theme of awareness, calling for empathy and action. "Feel the pain that directly affects you," one character admonishes the audience. In another group's script, titled "The Laramie Perspective," the students preview the play with this prolog: "Tolerance is different from acceptance. People are a product of their environment, but if we all learn how to see situations from multiple perspectives, then we have a better chance of becoming accepting." The play ends with the characters asking the audience to stand and join hands as the characters offer these lines in unison: "So we all join hands as one to end the chaos and upheaval. Love is kind, love is strong, love will make right of the wrong. So we all join hands as one until everyone feels they belong."

There is a measure of naive idealism in the students' scripts, but there is also clear evidence of their work to interpret the themes of *The Laramie Project* through their adolescent experience of the world. They connote their emerging understanding of the potential harm of possessing limited views of gender and sexuality and their hope for what is possible when we recognize, accept, and respect those who have been othered, ridiculed, and misunderstood. To wit, the last scene of one play includes this unembellished line: "Some say silence is golden, but it isn't when one should speak up." Featuring this line in the script illustrated the group's sensitive response to the play. More importantly, however, the public performance of the line for their peers acknowledged the silence that typically surrounds the injustices suffered by trans*, gender creative, and gender-nonconforming youth, a silence that fuels "the epidemic of anti-LGBT harassment and violence in American schools" (Cianciotto and Cahill 2012, p. 36).

Analyzing the Teachers' Experiences

The students' scripts demonstrated how they were processing topics integral to the play, but the project was also affecting for the teachers who participated. They reported that the units they taught about *The Laramie Project* felt vital and, in some cases, transformative. One of the teachers reflected on her reasons for participating in the project in a debrief conversation:

> I've had transgender students in the course in the past, and I really loved them and cared a lot about them and saw so many of their struggles, so when I found out about the opportunity to teach *The Laramie Project*, I sort

of felt like I owed it to them to try something that was outside of my normal curriculum, to try something that would maybe do some honor to them. I was afraid of the potential controversy if I taught the play, and wondered if I'd be able to handle it, but I wanted to try.

Later she wrote in her research journal: "My students were really, really moved by the play, and it was probably one of the greatest moments of my teaching career, in terms of watching them perform it, and then reading their reader response journals."

Another teacher, after sharing the difficulties she had in getting permission to teach the play, offered these notes about her students' responses to the unit:

Because many trans or gender creative students feel silenced due to fear, offering students opportunities to study in literature circles with any material that brings up issues of gender and sexuality can create a safer space for discussion. Students work in small groups in literature circles, but they journal and reflect to prepare for the discussions. My students wrote passionately about the controversies within the play, and many wrote entries that left me in tears because I kept thinking about how these kids are being silenced. By allowing them some small space where they could communicate, I played a part in giving them a voice.

The teachers noted that though the choice to teach the play felt risky, it paid off. This excerpt from one teacher's journal illustrates the kind of reward she experienced:

It made me feel so alive as a teacher. I took a chance and did something I totally had no idea how it'd go down in the classroom, and it was awesome. That's not to say it wasn't without bumps, but I taught something that was a really risky text and it worked out great, and my students knew it was risky, so that was also part of it too: we were all doing something that maybe other teachers wouldn't do, and that made the kids feel really good.

"The students knew that in this unit, I had high expectations for them intellectually," one of the teachers wrote, "they knew it was a unit about fostering humanity and open-mindedness and compassion, and they responded to that."

As a final comment in our debriefing of the project, one of the teachers said simply, "I'm proud of us." Others agreed. The statement was an acknowledgment of the commitment to do the expedient work of inviting students to question their own assumptions and expectations about gender norms and their responsibility to puncture the silences that allow for the kind of violence perpetrated on Matthew Shepard.

IDENTIFYING IMPLICATIONS FOR TEACHERS, RESEARCHERS, AND THEORISTS

Secondary English teachers, even those who may understand the rationale for introducing texts that feature queer, questioning, trans, and (a)gender creative characters, typically feel underprepared to lead discussions of gender expression and fear they may cross professional boundaries (Russell 2010). These concerns produce a reluctance that is also likely a byproduct of the fact that many teachers have "given little thought to heterosexual privilege or the experiences of those who identify as lesbian, gay, bisexual, or transgender" (Kitchen 2015, p. 128), much less to those who identify as (a)gender or gender creative. Teachers must be advocates for all students, however, and have the responsibility to work against prejudices that "exacerbate already existing divisions and biases" (Mayo 2014, p. 14). English teachers, in particular, have the unique opportunity to initiate reflective conversations through the choices they make about the texts they introduce to their students.

Those teachers who courageously adopt the principles of the QLF challenge themselves to create a teaching practice that explicitly acknowledges the value of every student in the classroom. This kind of pedagogy is, given the penchant of schools to misunderstand diversity, necessarily ambitious but critical to the enterprise of creating learning spaces where all students, regardless of gender expression, feel safe, highly regarded, and intellectually stimulated. The work of establishing a curriculum (especially a language arts curriculum) that honors the spectrum of student identities and experiences need not be onerous; however, it can be greatly aided simply by selecting texts that invite students to self-reflexivity and introspective questioning. Designing classroom experiences that interrogate the culture's biases about trans* and gender creative identities (and all identities for that matter) is key to ensuring that students have opportunities to question, explore, consider, and reflect on how the culture is constructing us all.

NOTES

1. Verbatim theater is both a form and a technique. The term verbatim refers to the origins of the play's text: "the words of real people are recorded or transcribed by a dramatist during an interview or research process, or are appropriated from existing records such as the transcripts of an official inquiry" (Hammond and Steward 2013, p. 9).
2. The Tectonic Theater Company develops innovative playmaking projects designed to elicit an artistic dialog with audiences about social, political, and human issues.
3. See http://www.justice.gov/crt/about/crm/matthewshepard.php.
4. Bibliotherapy is a form of intervention that guides someone's reading "to foster an understanding of self" (Vare and Norton 2004, p. 190). In school settings, it often involves offering students texts that might address sociocultural issues, develop life skills, or enhance self-image.

REFERENCES

Cianciotto, J., & Cahill, S. (2012). *LGBT youth in America's schools*. Ann Arbor: The University of Michigan Press.

Counsell, C., & Wolf, L. (2001). *Performance analysis: An introductory coursebook*. New York: Routledge.

Ellis, V. (2009). What English can contribute to understanding sexual identities. *English Journal, 98*(4), 52–55.

Emert, T., & Hall, M. (2015). Greater satisfaction from the labor: Creative writing as a text response strategy in the teacher education classroom. In G. Harper (Ed.), *Creative writing and education* (pp. 57–67). Bristol: Multilingual Matters/Channel View Publishers.

Foultier, A. P. (2013). Language and the gendered body: Butler's early reading of Merleau-Ponty. *Hypatia, 28*(4), 767–783. doi:10.1111/hypa.12040.

Hammond, W., & Steward, D. (2013). *Verbatim, verbatim: Contemporary documentary theatre*. London: Oberon Books.

Jackson, Y. (2011). *The pedagogy of confidence*. New York: Teachers College Press.

Kaufman, M. (2001). *The Laramie project*. New York: Vintage.

Kitchen, J. (2015). Inqueeries into self-study: Queering the gaze on teacher educator identity and practice. In M. Taylor & L. Coia (Eds.), *Gender, feminism, and queer theory in the self-study of teacher education practices* (pp. 127–141). Boston: Sense Publishers.

Mayo, C. (2014). *LGBTQ youth and education: Policies and practices*. New York: Teachers College Press.

Miller, s. (2015). A queer literacy framework promoting (a)gender and (a)sexuality self-determination and justice. *English Journal, 104*(5), 37–44.

Payne, E. C., & Smith, M. (2011). The reduction of stigma in schools: A new professional development model for empowering educators to support LGBTQ students. *Journal of LGBT Youth, 8*(2), 174–200.

Rosenblatt, L. (1969). Toward a transactional theory of reading. *Journal of Literacy Research, 1*(1), 31–49.

Russell, V. T. (2010). Queer teachers' ethical dilemmas regarding queer youth. *Teaching Education, 21*(2), 143–156.

Swartz, P. C. (2005). It's elementary in Appalachia: Helping prospective teachers and their students understand sexuality and gender. In J. T. Sears (Ed.), *Gay, lesbian, and transgender issues in education: Programs, policies, and practices* (pp. 125–146). New York: Routledge.

Thompson, F. T., & Austin, W. P. (2010). The gender role perceptions of male students at a prestigious, single-gender, Catholic high school. *Education, 130*(3), 424–446.

Unger, N. C. (2007). Teaching "straight" gay and lesbian history. *The Journal of American History, 93*, 1192–1199.

Vare, J. W., & Norton, T. L. (2004). Bibliotherapy for gay and lesbian youth: Overcoming the structure of silence. *Clearing House, 77*(5), 190–194.

CHAPTER 14

Making Space for Unsanctioned Texts: Teachers and Students Collaborate to Trans*form Writing Assignments

Michael Wenk

Queer Literacy Framework Principles:

2. Understands gender as a construct which has and continues to be impacted by intersecting factors (e.g., social, historical, material, cultural, economic, religious);
3. Recognizes that masculinity and femininity constructs are assigned to gender norms and are situationally performed;
4. Understands gender as flexible;
5. Opens up spaces for students to self-define with chosen (a)genders, (a)pronouns, or names; and,
6. Engages in ongoing critique of how gender norms are reinforced in literature, media, technology, art, history,

INTRODUCTION

Britzman (1995) inquires, "What is required to refuse the unremarked and obdurately unremarkable straight educational curriculum?" (p. 151). Teachers today are faced with a proliferation of emerging identities that

M. Wenk (✉)
Dunstan Middle School, Lakewood, USA

© The Editor(s) (if applicable) and The Author(s) 2016   263
sj Miller (ed.), *Teaching, Affirming, and Recognizing Trans and Gender Creative Youth*, DOI 10.1057/978-1-137-56766-6_14

challenge heteronormative conceptions of curriculum (Britzman 1995; Jacobsen et al. 2012; Miller 2016; Thein 2013). To transform curricula, Miller (this volume, Chap. 2) suggests that educators "can reposition youth as agentive subjects within multiple contexts" so that educators and students "collectively become better equipped to unveil and advance shifting discourses" (p. 26). Agentive subjects in a study—a team of seven students and two teachers—met in spring 2014 to critique representations of sexuality and gender found in literacy activities, particularly in school writing assignments. Participants collaborated to construct writing assignments that they felt were more inclusive of queer issues and identities.[1] Though the study focused on both sexuality *and* gender in literacy activities, for purposes related to the book, this chapter will focus on the importance of how choice and modeling as practices employed by Secondary English Language Arts (SELA) teachers can communicate to students that exploring gender is safe. This chapter presents recommendations from a team of students and teachers for how literacy teachers can develop writing assignments that teach, affirm, and recognize all students on a spectrum of (a)gender identities.

SETTING AND PARTICIPANTS

This study occurred in a large, suburban high school in the Rocky Mountain region. With about 2000 students, Coolidge prided itself on its rigorous academic programs. Coolidge's arts and athletics programs have been perennially successful. The school had over 100 teaching faculty, of whom most possessed a master's degree. In many ways, from the sprawling campus to the number of teachers with advanced degrees, Coolidge resembled a small college. While its lack of socioeconomic and ethnic diversity made the school less than ideal for a study, its openness to curricular innovation and empowerment of queer students made Coolidge a promising site for conducting research about queer issues and identities in the curriculum.

The students, who were members of their school's Gay-Straight Alliance, did not constitute a diverse group: all of the students appeared to be white and cisgender, expressing their gender identity with the preferred pronouns of she/her/hers. They represented grades 10, 11, and 12. Most of the diversity was reflected in sexual orientation: three students identified as lesbian, one student identified as bisexual, one student identified as straight, one student identified as demisexual (sexual attraction depends on forming an emotional bond with someone), and one student identified as both queer and questioning (in a state of questioning both sexuality and gender). As for the teachers, Mr. Jones, a straight, white, cisgender man in his mid-thirties, taught social studies and also an elective diversity class, while Ms. Wright, a straight, white, cisgender woman in her late 20s, taught language arts classes. Names are pseudonyms selected by participants at the first Curriculum Design Team meeting.

THEORETICAL FRAMEWORK

Gee (2010) explains that Discourse is *a socially situated practice* that constitutes a *socially situated identity* (p. 30; italics original). The construction of identity within language employed by a social group is central to Gee's notion of Discourse. In schools, curriculum contributes to Discourses that construct heteropatriarchal identities for students while marginalizing queer identities. Books are not taught and issues are not broached due to Discourses that operate in service of "institutionalized masculinity" (Hall 2003, p. 365). A Spanish textbook, for example, depicts a family in the traditional sense: the family tree shows mom and dad, grandfather and grandmother, aunts and uncles—all paired off as heterosexual couples (see, for example, *Puntos de Partida*, 2012, p. 60). Performativity (Butler 1990) as a concept enables young people and adults who are constituted by and contribute to powerful Discourses to question power structures and to denaturalize what is given, or what is considered "common sense." Deconstructing performativity helps to contest Discourses that enforce binaries and perpetuate the essentialization of gender. In schools, curriculum serves as a productive power, where heteropatriarchal identities are materialized and trans* and gender creative youth (Miller 2015) are rendered unintelligible. I employ the *Queer Literacy Framework promoting (a)gender and self-determination and justice* to understand the strategic moves made by students in this study as they collaborated with teachers to create writing assignments that "generate (a)gender self-determination" (Miller, p. 33). Principles 2, 3, 4, 5, and 6 align with recommendations made by the study's participants.

FINDINGS

In spite of Coolidge's progressive reputation for fostering inclusivity, the seven students who participated in this study said they had few opportunities to address queer issues and identities through writing assignments.

Willow, an 11th grader in the study, said, "I feel a lot of other identities are acknowledged, but mine isn't as much." Students in the study didn't fault their teachers for the scarcity of inclusive writing activities; instead, they attributed erasure of queer issues and identities to homophobic and heteronormative Discourses, which influences what is most often taught in schools. Students empirically deduced that queer topics are not built into the curriculum teachers are given. When queer identities and issues materialized in classrooms at Coolidge, often it was because students initiated dialog during open-ended discussions, or pursued a personally meaningful topic in a writing assignment. Willow stated, "Obviously, there are some circumstances where you could choose a topic related to that. For example, if you wanted to do a current event on gay rights, it's not discouraged or anything. But we're never told, look up something … having to do with gay rights." Daisy, a 10th grader, explained that while "transgender students (in Coolidge's Gay-Straight Alliance) say that they feel really accepted … not necessarily everyone understands them." Students in the study promoted reading and writing activities as a way to cultivate understanding in regard to their trans* and gender creative peers.

Using Choice to Queer Curriculum

Writing assignments and literature study, students emphasized, could provide rich resources for exploring and contesting Discourses that construct identities for queer youth. After the Curriculum Design Team convened for its first meeting, the team split for the second and third meetings into English language arts and social studies groups (This chapter will focus primarily on the work of the English language arts group, which included Ms. Wright). The writing assignments developed by both groups emphasized choices for students regarding resources, topics, and genres. Even as they troubled choice, students in the study insisted that engaging with (a)gender identities through curricular choice can strategically mitigate negative repercussions for teachers and schools, while also interrupting pervasive silences.

Choice is often heralded as a strategy for meeting diverse students' needs and sparking interest in activities and assignments (Fletcher 2006; McKenna and Robinson 2014; Quate and McDermott 2009; Tomlinson 2003). Students in the study named choice as a way to satisfy the needs and interests of students as consumers of curriculum, while also placating parents and community members who might not be happy to hear that gender is a topic of study in their child's school. Choice aligns with QLF Principle 5 because it "opens up spaces for students to self-define with chosen (a)genders, (a)pronouns, or names." By expanding choice in writing assignments, student participants saw opportunities for queer youth to explore queer issues and identities, as well as to nurture queer visibility in the classroom.

The SELA group produced a writing assignment (see Appendix) that captured voice and explored identity. Trying to narrow the ideas generated down to a specific, concrete writing assignment, they developed the following prompt: *I am a person and I happen to be* _____. The prompt promoted endless possibilities for students to address. "Just let them run with it," Ms. Wright said during their meeting. "That could be anything. That idea, it's so open anyway. If your teacher has done a good job of giving you sources that cover these documentaries, these movies, these books, as well as ones for different racial issues, gender issues, things like that. Cultural issues. Everybody has something to write on there, right?" The group decided the genre could be personal narrative, poetry, a letter, or something else. Learning activities included a number of writing prompts designed to get students to think about their own identities as well as build empathy for the identities of others. The writing assignment included the possibility of exploring queer identities, but looked at identity through a broader lens, such as how media and pop culture construct identity, which aligns with QLF Principles 2 and 3, framing gender as a construct. To inform the development of the writing assignment, students would not only respond to a number of prompts but also read and view numerous nontraditional texts, paired with canonical course texts. This aspect of the assignment aligns well with QLF Principle 6, in which a class "engages in ongoing critique of how gender norms are reinforced in literature, media, technology, art, history, science, math, etc." The SELA group envisioned their writing assignment unfolding over time, embedded in existing units of study, but with the addition of queer-themed texts and prompts as a way to queer the curriculum.

Discussing Choice in a Curriculum Meeting

In our first Curriculum Design Team meeting, Ms. Wright made a strong claim about choice: "I think yeah, just building in choice and opportunity where if you are interested in this, if you're willing to explore this and actually, a lot of it comes from other kids and just having that opportunity for kids to say, 'Hey, you guys should really check out this book or you should really watch this documentary.'" Casey, a 10th grader, responded to the idea that if choice is offered, students might be "willing" to explore queer topics:

> I've been thinking that you guys were talking and one thing. ... We're all talking about things that are very specifically geared towards these kinds of issues. What I've been thinking up is an easy way for the teachers to work it in without sticking it in their faces is if you're talking about, for example, a persuasive essay. A lot of the teachers will give examples like, "You can do this or you can do that." Give that as one of the examples. So you aren't saying you have to write about this but it either jogs people's memories or it gives them the idea of, "Oh, maybe I should look into that." Also, I know that we'll have things where we have to write an essay and we're given three different prompts we could do.

Casey laid out two possible approaches so that students might choose to write about a queer topic. First, she asserted that a teacher's examples influence what a student chooses to write about. Even if the topic is wide open, students might become aware of the possibility of a queer topic only if the teacher mentions it as an option. But Casey also offered another approach, suggesting teachers build a queer topic into the options for a writing assignment. If there are three prompts, one option could address queer issues.

Aria, a 12th grader, picked up where Casey left off with a qualification about choice:

> In my opinion, I think that in order to even put that as an option, and for people to actually choose it, you need to teach it a little bit because the issue that most kids will look at that and say, "I am going to go with the one that I know." I am going to go with that one, because you just don't know. Maybe before doing in unit like that, you might want to show some things so that everybody has opportunity to at least write about something.

For Aria, mentioning examples is not enough, because "you need to teach it a little bit." Having the freedom to explore queer topics is not the same as having the capacity to explore queer topics. So that students could venture out of their comfort zone and produce knowledgeable pieces of writing, Aria believed a teacher needs to "show some things" in a unit of study, which could entail sharing queer-themed texts for written analysis or discussing queer-themed responses to prompts.

Daisy then directed the conversation to the work of the teacher:

> Linking the whole textbook back to the writing prompts: If kids don't have the information, they're not going to write about it. ... Like, first semester what we did is we would read a book or a few readings—if it was a synthesis essay—and then have a Socratic seminar. Then, we would do timed writing. Most people put out their timed writing on what we talked about in the seminar.

Kate, a 12th grader, concurred, "Right, because that's what you just talked about and it's easy." What makes the assignment "easy" for students is the scaffolding the teacher has done to prepare them to write. By putting students in dialog with texts and with each other, students are more prepared to write on topics that previously may have been out of reach. Daisy concluded, "If it's not in the reading or if it's not in the discussion, people are not going to write about it unless they are really passionate about the issue. They're not actively going to go out and do that." While study participants saw value in choice, their discussions complicated choice as a means to queer curriculum.

Troubling Choice

What happens when offering choice doesn't yield exploration of queer identities and issues? Students portrayed choice as a compromise to full inclusion of queer issues and identities in the curriculum, not a perfect solution but instead a first step toward greater visibility. "Uncomfortable" children and "screaming" parents loomed large as Casey imagined queer writing assignments in schools. According to students in the study, choice gives teachers the ability to manage community concerns, so that an educator might announce to their students, "I'm not saying you have to read *Parrotfish* (Wittlinger 2007), but if you want to read an amazing novel and learn about trans*youth, then it's an option for you." However, Aria maintained that educators shouldn't always worry about alienating their straight students or community members, because teachers don't often worry about alienating queer students. "You have to think about that one assignment versus a hundred assignments that the other side has experienced," she said. "I think it's okay for them to feel uncomfortable and question for once."

Prevalent Discourses around consumer choice informed how students and teachers talked about curricular options. At Coolidge, like schools around the country, choice is increasingly being asserted as a self-evident right of consumers in the educational marketplace. Students who disagree with curriculum can opt out.

> Aria: Again, if you don't feel comfortable like that, you don't have to take that class because you know it's in the curriculum. That's another thing to think about.
>
> Kate: If it was like really like that that you were going to deal for someone. … Like I said, most people I feel like would be fine with it because they have another assignment, but if it was that. You can just tell the teacher, "I don't want to do this."
>
> Aria: Exactly. There's always another assignment.
>
> Kate: You can write a paper or whatever. Yeah.
>
> Leah: You can opt out of anything, Sex Ed.
>
> Kate: Yeah. Literally you can opt out of anything. People can do PE online. You can pretty much get out of anything.

Willow was bothered by the idea that choice might enable students to avoid challenging topics. "That begs the question that I would like to extend," she said. "Should we tolerate intolerance?" She supposed everyone in a classroom—queer or straight—is made uncomfortable when course content turns to issues like race, gender, sexuality, or disability. But Willow continued, "We don't necessarily need to tolerate that intolerance, and it could be a good thing to even open people's minds if it's done in a classroom setting where it's mediated by a teacher." For Willow, a teacher is an expert not just in content but also in practice, and mediation of content is a long-standing teaching practice.

Without teacher mediation, according to Beatrix (a 10th grader), choice will sometimes be met with apathy in regard to queer issues:

> We did *Romeo and Juliet* last year and we were supposed to tackle an issue that is going on currently and I wanted to do LGBTQ issues and my group was like, "We should just go at something easy." I was like, "No, we should do this because this is important." Then, what I found difficult was like, people don't actually care. They are like, "I am not homophobic but I don't care."

When students opt out of exploring queer themes because of ignorance, apathy, religious objections, or consumer preferences, participants in the study proposed the teacher adopt a stronger stance; however, members of the Curriculum Design Team wrestled with how assertive the teacher should be.

Some of the student participants suggested that the value of choice is compromised when teachers do not support students in writing productively or precisely about queer topics. If a teacher does not demonstrate the possibility of selecting queer topics, many students will not consider the possibility of selecting queer topics. For Casey, a health assignment that she described as "entirely open-ended" was frustrating for her: "We didn't really go over anything like that [queer topics]. He just left us on our own, which frankly was a little annoying. It was that open-ended we weren't even given any ideas." Because queer identities and issues have been erased from classroom Discourses via mandated, heteronormative curricula, students rarely consider gender as a topic for writing, unless the possibility arises in a class discussion. Also, some of the student participants described situations where the teacher did not frontload assignments in ways that addressed (a)gender issues, causing students who pursued queer topics to face ridicule from classmates. In addition, student participants suggested that some of their classmates who are granted the option to address queer topics might poorly handle or abuse the opportunity, by misgendering (or oversexualizing) queer people or invoking homophobic viewpoints. Students noted that simply offering choice doesn't always lead to meaningful educational experiences. Students recommended that teachers need to assert a stronger role in framing choice.

Finessing Choice

Student participants—without exception—suggested that modeling by the teacher is necessary when students are given a choice to read and write about queer topics. *Modeling* is an instructional practice in which a teacher demonstrates products or processes and then encourages student imitation (Gee 2012; Kittle 2008; Meichenbaum 1977; Tharp and Gallimore 1988). The way teachers frame writing prompts sends a message to students not only about what topics are actually on the table but also how students might think about them. Modeling is a form of mediation, by which "learners appropriate cultural and practical knowledge through a relationship with more experienced members of their society" (Smagorinsky 2011, p. 52). Without mediation by the teacher, students might not be aware of some of the innumerable options for answering a prompt that addresses diversity.

Modeling ideas for responding to a prompt—asking students to ponder (a)gender scenarios in novels like *Every Day* (Levithan 2012), for example—opens up possibilities for student writing. Many teachers fear that modeling leads to imitation—that is, copying the model—but when combined with inquiry and experimentation, imitation can lead to something "fundamentally new" (Smagorinsky 2011, p. 209). Offering a list of topics or discussing examples for responding to a prompt might seem limiting, but students in this study suggested otherwise. The findings of 1998 study of writing assignments in 61 classrooms by the Educational Testing Service and the National Assessment of Education Progress concur with students in the study, saying that teachers need to strike a balance between boundless choice and no choice at all (as cited in National Writing Project and Nagin 2006, p. 48). Similar to these findings, student participants from Coolidge noted that choice should not exclude examples, but instead show young people that exploring queer identities and issues is both possible and safe.

Crafting Assignments

The way assignments and activities are framed by the teacher is instrumental to how students receive them, as Ms. Wright explained:

> There are ways, I think, that you can have these conversations without saying, "We're going to talk about LGBTQ rights today," but it's, "Today, we're going to talk about people who don't have a voice, maybe, at certain points." And kind of look at the issue. Then, give that as the place to have those conversations.

As evidenced by Ms. Wright, teachers can couch queer identities among many identities and offer (a)gender issues as "matter of fact," part of the documented struggle for human rights or actual ways people are defined and define themselves.

Daisy's framing of queer curriculum, in particular, was nuanced but also subtly disruptive. For her, choice of texts to read wouldn't necessarily isolate students in silos of their own beliefs:

I think it would be better for either people to read a lot of small stuff or for each person or certain groups of people to read different books or something, because then when the class comes together to talk about it, you can get lots of different perspectives, because even if you just have one perspective of *Luna* (Peters 2004), for example, that's great, but I think it drives the point home if there's lots of different examples with lots of different identities, as well.

Even as teachers offer choice, according to Daisy, students will be exposed to multiple perspectives through activities such as class discussions, especially with thoughtful facilitation by the teacher. Options in reading and writing may give parents and students the illusion of avoiding disagreeable topics, but participants in the study carefully constructed their writing assignment so that options in reading and writing resulted in an exchange of ideas throughout the unit of study.

Students in the study viewed texts as the primary way into learning about and writing about queer issues and identities. Students in the study described how they were often asked by teachers to write about what they had read. In English classes, analysis of texts was a common writing task for students at Coolidge, whether they were placed in AP, IB, or regular "tracks." For these assignments, students were expected to produce literary analyses about novels or poems or plays as a summative assessment for a literature unit and draw from texts for information to produce expository or persuasive texts (such as examining authors from the Transcendentalist literary period). Ms. Wright acknowledged the role of literature in an interview prior to the meetings: "Much of the writing we do is dictated by the literature. So if the literature dealt with more of those issues, of course, the writing would, too."

Student participants were eager to educate Ms. Wright about ways the curriculum might move beyond the literary anthology to include queer-themed texts. Affirming students' voices, Miller (in this volume, Chap. 2) writes, "Conventional literacy practices mean myriad forms of communication, and even the yet to emerge, as applied across any discipline that inherently develops students' speaking, reading, writing, and technological skills in order to interact and engage with the self and the world around" (p. 33). I found that students in the study devoted extensive time during their meetings with teachers discussing resources for the writing assignment they constructed. Students described blogs, movies, commercials, TV shows, poems, plays, websites, novels, essays, documentary films, online videos, TED Talks, and stand-up comedy, which they viewed as sources of information for the teacher as well as inspiration and information for the students who might choose to write about a queer topic.

NORMALIZING (A)GENDER IN LITERACY PRACTICE AS BRIDGE TO TRANS* AND GENDER CREATIVE AWARENESS

In clever and disruptive ways, the Curriculum Design Team at Coolidge High School found space in literacy curricula for queer issues and identities. So that young people in schools can "see themselves reflected back in a positive manner" (Miller 2015, p. 40), students in this study recommended choice of texts to produce and consume as a way to pry open curriculum for queer issues and identities. For Moses (2002), choice is crucial for developing autonomy among people who are oppressed. Drawing on a contemporary liberal philosophical framework, Moses (2002) proposes practices that promote "a favorable context of choice" as a means to put students on "the path to autonomy" (p. 22). By opening up spaces for students to self-define through written work (Principle 5), choice has implications for educators who wish to transform their curricula to reflect (a)gender realities.

When Moses (2002) describes "a favorable context of choice" (p. 22), she argues (like the students in this study) that choice is socially situated. To achieve favorable conditions for developing autonomy, teachers must negotiate between "individual choices and community context" (p. 24). Students in this study complicated unmediated choice as problematic: straight students might write stories that essentialize queer people, or they might exercise their legal and consumer privileges to avoid gender altogether. Aria, for example, wanted teachers to "teach it a little bit" so that students would be more willing to venture into texts and topics they knew or cared little about. Modeling must be taken up as an instructional practice for teachers to employ so that choice does not seem daunting or engender bigotry among students.

At the end of the study, Ms. Wright was able to articulate the value that students placed on choice and modeling. She clearly heard student participants when they said they wanted options for writing assignments. "In terms of the writing and LGBTQ issues in writing," Ms. Wright concluded, "One of things I learned is that it is easy … to have open prompts that allow kids to write about anything, and if they wanted identity or

LGBTQ issues, it can be [an option]." Ms. Wright acknowledged that she also needs to model for her students: "I think I will be way conscientious about how open my prompts are, and I think as far as I already do give examples about you could write about this and that," she said. "I will just be more conscientious about throwing in like, 'You could write about identity or you could write about being queer.'" Ms. Wright envisioned choice and modeling as tools that were relatively easy to employ in making writing assignments more inclusive of queer identities and issues.

To expand the repertoire of writing topics, student participants elevated unsanctioned school texts, such as documentaries, young adult novels, nonfiction texts, blogs, and TV shows, as additions to the literary canon (Principle 6). In reflecting on students' contributions in developing more inclusive writing assignments, Daisy said, "A lot of the books we talked about had to do with transgender perspectives, which are definitely important to understand, I think." Drawing from a queer canon, students positioned resources like documentaries or young adult novels as crucial to informing writing assignments as well as to educating the teachers who were charged with offering choices and modeling topics for their students.

By the time I interviewed her at the end of the study, Ms. Wright had already watched a number of documentaries students recommended. As Ms. Wright was sifting through the recommendations the students provided, she began to understand how these noncanonical texts could support her curriculum:

> I have existing curriculum as far as understanding literature or rhetoric or modes of writing, and I teach that through different texts. Why not bring some of this stuff in as another text option? For me what it is, it is just, it is another eye-opening (experience), right? Oh, why not, why would we not read a text about this or watch a documentary about this? ... It is about bringing in texts that have that perspective that will fit with the curriculum I have, which I think is an easy thing to do.

For Ms. Wright, the resources cited by students in the study weren't about promoting a queer mandate; instead, the resources had curricular worth, like any other text she had previously shared with her students.

The practice of involving students in designing curricula that fosters critical perspectives is rare, even when it seems like it would make eminent sense. Without much preparation in curriculum development but with outsider knowledge, students in this study were able to collaborate with teachers, over a five-hour period, to develop writing assignments that they felt were more inclusive of queer themes and topics. They also were able to recommend instructional practices, such as choice and modeling, that they felt would reduce inhibitions and mitigate community reservations about addressing queer issues and identities in the classroom. By including students as agents in the development of curriculum, this study contested the "narrative of adult design" (Talburt 2004, p. 23) that plays out in schools. This study shows agency not as belonging solely to students or to teachers, but instead results from collaboration and dialog among teachers and students.

CONCLUDING THOUGHTS

Much in the same way that people tune into a particular radio station or scan for stations, students in the study tuned into LOGO (a queer-themed TV network) or scanned YouTube, viewing unsanctioned texts (like *RuPaul's Drag Race*) that portray nonnormative sexualities and genderqueer experiences. According to Miller (2015), queer youth also develop attunement to Discourses that frame their identities via "macro-aggressions" (p. 40) that frame nonnormative identities as deviant. Students in this study not only picked up on Discourses that their teachers could not hear, but they also actively and intentionally dialed into different Discourses. The artifice of a student–teacher curriculum team enabled students to convey queer-themed Discourses to teachers in the study.

Miller (2015) writes that students "who are LGBT*IAGCQ or have differential bodied realities … are highly attuned to prevailing gender and sexual norms" (p. 39). Building from the premise that teachers may not be attuned to Discourses that impact their queer students, I offer several recommendations that can support teachers in developing deeper awareness about trans* and gender creative youth. While it may not be feasible for teachers to collaboratively construct curriculum with students, teachers could solicit ideas and feedback from their students prior to and after a unit of study. Teachers might also investigate Discourses found in young adult literature or electronic texts, as well as pay close attention to Discourses with (a)gender themes circulating among students at their school. Because teachers continue to be challenged by "proliferating identities" (Britzman 1995, p. 158) in their classrooms, the Queer Literacy Framework (Miller 2015) becomes an increasingly important tool for transforming dispositions among educators, so that they can more adeptly attune to Discourses that oppress or affirm trans* and gender creative youth. In the absence of a team of students to advise teachers, teachers could study and practice applications of the different principles of the Queer Literacy Framework (Miller 2015) with their colleagues or with their school's Gay-Straight Alliance. Finally, teachers may consider stepping aside to allow guest speakers into their classrooms to speak knowledgeably about issues facing (a)gender and gender creative youth. Many larger communities have resource centers that teachers can contact; in smaller communities, speakers can join classroom discussions electronically.

It takes time, effort, and mindfulness to create spaces for authentic curriculum that truly speaks to and recognizes trans* and gender creative youth—or for any student who experiences difference. No teacher should feel that they have to undertake this consequential work alone. In the same way teachers support learners in their classrooms, more knowledgeable Others—including queer students who might attend their school—stand ready to support teachers in creating and implementing dynamic and inclusive literacy activities for *all* students.

Appendix: Language Arts Writing Assignment Outline

Language Arts—11th grade

Submitted by the Secondary English Language Arts Group as Part of Their Work on the Curriculum Design Team (Spring 2014)
What kind of writing would students produce? (What is the product or performance?)

The goal is to capture *voice* and the human experience/identity, expressing your identity through that voice, whether that's your own identity or taking on somebody else's identity. Students have choice in topics, but would address themes from all of the texts studied during the semester. Possible genres might include: personal narrative, poetry, or a letter.
What topics or themes would be covered?

- Identity; Gender Roles, Minorities in Society; Labels and Social Construction of Identity; Individuality
- A study of identity, including minority identities and more specifically LGBTQ identities but also Chicano and others (Others)
- Queer issues could include transitioning, bullying, daily life, health

What prompt (or prompt choices) would students address?

- I am a person (American), but I also happen to be _____.
- Write about a moment where you experienced your "identity." Did you choose the identity? Was it imposed upon you?
- Write about how it would feel to be given a different identity.
- If you did not have your labels, who would you be?
- What would it be like to wake up in the body of someone who was a different gender, race, or sexual orientation than you?
- Using one of the books we've studied, how do you think the character's life would have been different if s/he had been queer?

What are some essential questions for students to consider during the unit?

- Who am I? How does identity shape us and how do labels help shape our identity?
- How does media/pop culture shape our identity (or, perhaps, perpetuate stereotypes)? Consider stereotypes like the "butch" lesbian, the effeminate gay man, the smart Asian, the athletic black male, etc.
- How does someone else's identity affect your own identity?

What evidence outcomes would be addressed by this writing assignment?

- The student shows increased knowledge, understanding, and empathy of minority identities.
- The student demonstrates control of voice and, through that voice, an understanding of different human experiences.
- The student incorporates various sources to help build understanding of and articulation of various human experiences.

What texts would students read and analyze to learn about the topics?

The following are resources, such as documentaries, books, and essays, that would be paired with existing texts that deal with identities and labels, such as *Black Boy, Kaffir Boy, Angela's Ashes*, etc.:

- *Every Day* (David Leviathan)
- *Luna* (Julie Ann Peters)
- *Bridegroom*
- *And the Band Played On* (Historical text, Documentary/Mini-Series)

- "Late Victorians" (essay by Richard Rodriguez)
- *How to Survive a Plague* (Documentary)
- *Paris is Burning* (Drag Culture Documentary)
- *Don't Ask, Don't Tell* (Documentary)
- *Outrage* (Journalism Ethics)
- *Blue is the Warmest Color* (censor sex scenes, but some GREAT ideas of identity)
- *Will Grayson, Will Grayson* (David Leviathan and John Green)
- *Milk*
- *Philadelphia*
- *Dallas Buyers Club*
- *Brokeback Mountain* (the identity others impose on you)
- YouTube: The Gay Women Channel
- LOGO Channel: One Girl, Five Gays
- YouTube video: do you think I am gay or straight (sociological experiment)
- Nancy Dean: *Voice Lessons*

What texts would students read and imitate to produce the assigned writing?

- "Late Victorians" (Personal Essay—Rodriguez)
- Poems by Shakespeare, Whitman, SLAM poems
- Stand up Comedy (Kate Clinton, etc.)

What activities will support students in their learning and in producing a piece of writing?

- Socratic Seminars
- Viewing films/YouTube videos, etc.
- "Privilege" game
- Writing Invitations
- Offer students choices of what to read OR to read a wide variety of texts

NOTES

1. This study was IRB approved.

REFERENCES

Britzman, D. (1995). Is there a queer pedagogy? Or, stop reading straight. *Educational Theory, 45*(2), 151–165.

Butler, J. (1990). *Gender trouble: Feminism and the subversion of identity.* New York: Routledge.

Dorwick, T., Perez-Girones, A., Becher, A., & Isabelli, C. (2012). *Puntos de partida: An invitation to Spanish.* Boston: McGraw Hill.

Fletcher, R. (2006). *Boy writers: Reclaiming their voices.* Portland: Stenhouse.

Gee, J. (2010). *An introduction to discourse analysis: Theory and method* (3rd ed.). New York: Routledge.

Gee, J. (2012). *Social linguistics and literacies: Ideology in discourses* (4th ed.). New York: Routledge.

Hall, K. (2003). Exceptional speakers contested and problematized gender identities. In M. Meyerhoff & J. Holmes (Eds.), *Handbook of language and gender* (pp. 352–380). Oxford: Basil Blackwell.

Jacobsen, R., Frankenberg, E., & Lenhoff, S. (2012). Diverse schools in a democratic society: New ways of understanding how school demographics affect civil and political learning. *American Educational Research Journal, 49*(5), 812–843.

Kittle, P. (2008). *Write beside them: Risk, voice, and clarity in high school writing.* Portsmouth: Heinemann.

Levithan, D. (2012). *Every day.* New York: Knopf.

McKenna, M., & Robinson, R. (2014). *Teaching through text: Reading and writing in the content areas* (2nd ed.). Boston: Pearson.

Meichenbaum, D. (1977). *Cognitive behavior modification: An integrative approach.* New York: Plenum.

Miller, s. (2015). A queer literacy framework promoting (a)gender and (a)sexuality self-determination and justice. *English Journal, 104*(5), 37–45.

Miller, s. (2016). *Teaching, affirming, and recognizing trans and gender creative youth: A queer literacy framework.* New York: Palgrave Macmillan.

Moses, M. (2002). *Embracing race: Why we need race-conscious education policy.* New York: Teachers College Press.

National Writing Project, & Nagin, C. (2006). *Because writing matters: Improving student writing in our schools.* San Francisco: Jossey-Bass.

Peters, J. A. (2004). *Luna.* New York: Little, Brown Books for Young Readers.

Quate, S., & McDermott, J. (2009). *Clock watchers: Six steps to motivating and engaging disengaged students across content areas.* Portsmouth: Heinemann.

Smagorinsky, P. (2011). *Vygotsky and literacy research: A methodological framework.* Boston: Sense.

Talburt, S. (2004). In M.L. Rasmussen, E., Rofes, & S. Talburt, (Eds.), *Youth and sexualities: Pleasure, subversion, and insubordination in and out of schools.* New York: Palgrave Macmillan.

Tharp, R. G., & Gallimore, R. (1988). *Rousing minds to life: Teaching, learning, and schooling in social context*. Cambridge, MA: Cambridge University Press.

Thein, A. (2013). Language arts teachers' resistance to teaching LGBT literature and issues. *Language Arts, 90*(3), 169–180.

Tomlinson, C. (2003). *Fulfilling the promise of the differentiated classroom: Strategies and tools for responsive teaching*. Alexandria: Association for Supervision and Curriculum Development.

Wittlinger, E. (2007). *Parrotfish*. New York: Simon & Schuster books for young readers.

CHAPTER 15

Using Queer Pedagogy and Theory to Teach Shakespeare's *Twelfth Night*

Kathryn Cloonan

Queer Literacy Framework Principles:

2. Understands gender as a construct, which has and continues to be impacted by intersecting factors (e.g., social, historical, material, cultural, religious);
3. Recognizes that masculinity and femininity constructs are assigned to gender norms and are situationally performed; and,
6. Engages in ongoing critique of how gender norms are reinforced in literature, media, technology, art, history, science, math, and so on.

INTRODUCTION

Many of Shakespeare's works represent the sociohistorical and gender constructions and craftsmanship of the Early Modern era. Consequently, theatrical and gender constructions generated much anxiety in Early Modern England (Charles 1997, p. 127). The irony of its heteropatriarchal culture governed by a childless female monarch epitomizes this. The Early Modern stage, solely featuring male actors, bestowed audiences with same-sex expressions of love, ostensibly disregarding the procreative purpose of romantic love. To address such

K. Cloonan (✉)
University of Rochester's Warner School of Education and
Human Development, Rochester, USA

© The Editor(s) (if applicable) and The Author(s) 2016
sj Miller (ed.), *Teaching, Affirming, and Recognizing Trans and
Gender Creative Youth*, DOI 10.1057/978-1-137-56766-6_15

anxieties and gender construction, I draw from my own experience as a high school teacher when I taught Shakespeare's sonnets and plays, particularly the comedy *Twelfth Night* (2005), during 11th and 12th grades. This chapter, therefore, demonstrates how teaching about gender expressions and performances during the Early Modern era can invite high school students to reflect on how gender constructs have been shaped and inscribed over time.

Education in the school space is tasked with contributing to the development of society's children, seemingly concerning the transmission of knowledge and content. Yet this charge encompasses much more than transmission: as educators, we facilitate students' identity development and their appreciation of other subjectivities, to include "a matrix of (a)genders, gender identities, gender non-conformities, gender creativities, and gender expressions" (Miller 2015a, p. 27). While formal educational settings increasingly explore gender and sexuality, school study often conflates categories and reductively handles these topics, ignoring the aforementioned matrix, not to mention the possibilities of affirmative curriculum (Charles 1998; Miller 2015b). English literature and language arts (ELA) can provide a more comprehensive understanding of the topics by embracing Miller's (2015a) Queer Literacy Framework (QLF), exploring how gender and sexuality are socially and historically constructed, and more importantly, how the human condition resists fixity, to include fixity of gender or sexuality. Reading and analyzing characters and relationships within texts, mutable like their audiences, allows students to understand and develop their own shifting identities and relationships, in addition to appreciating the identities and relationships of others.

This unit embarks on the contextual study of Early Modern English stage conventions as well as the character of Viola/Cesario in *Twelfth Night* (2005). This character's performance of gender—shaped by the Early Modern context—is analyzed within and through queer theory and pedagogy, while also honoring the QLF. This curriculum unit on gender for high school students in 11th and 12th grades could augment a fuller study of Shakespeare's comedy and milieu for students studying the text; however, I firmly believe that any study of Shakespeare's work should include discussions of gender performance on the Early Modern stage. Doing so strives to not only stimulate critical discourse about gender but also help students understand and contour their own gender identities.

My own personal experience in incorporating meaningful discussions surrounding gender and sexuality in the Secondary English Language Arts (SELA) classroom, particularly through robust engagement with Shakespeare's texts, reveals that not only will students feel more informed, safer, and more validated in the classroom, but also that such discussions strengthen teacher–student and student–student relationships. Conversations surrounding texts as well as welcoming classroom atmospheres precipitated past students' disclosure of identity and health issues, to include the oppression caused by a heteropatriarchal society.

RATIONALE: THE CASE FOR QUEER PEDAGOGY

The SELA classroom has been understood as a potentially powerful setting for exploring queer theory, gender and sexual diversity through fictional texts that explicitly explore gender, as well as queer interpretations of conventional ones (Meyer 2010). Educators who mindfully and purposefully explore the explicit and self-conscious role of teaching about (a)gender identity and expression ultimately provide students with possibilities to develop critical awareness about identity and difference. Meyer (2010) applauds examples of teachers who utilize texts and queer readings of traditional texts and notes the necessity of using such texts to create further spaces, particularly for students' self-expression (p. 69). Creative, productive efforts inspired from queer readings can greatly lead to the enactment of queer pedagogy, where "disruption and open discussion of previously silenced issues" empower both educators and students (Meyer 2010, p. 22). Queer pedagogy, demonstrated when we recognize blurring and fluidity in the work of writers such as Shakespeare, can lead to valuable dialog concerning identities as socially constructed and constrained.

By queering curriculum and topics, teachers who discuss privileges that result from racism, heterosexism, and sexism can explore how such privileges are culturally constructed. Queer theory and pedagogy can promote an investigation of identity and culture production and construction (Winans 2006). For instance, Barker and Kamps (1995) assert that Shakespeare exists as Western "culture's most central icon," garnering boundless attention and interpretation (p. i). Through queer pedagogy, teachers can unpack the privilege that Shakespeare enjoyed as an educated, middle-class male, affording him the "centrality" concomitant with heteropatriarchal legacy. For instance, teachers might ask: What opportunities did Shakespeare's contemporaries who identified as female experience? Who has been allowed to review or interpret Shakespeare's work? What constructs still exist in the field of Shakespeare study and performance? Drawing upon queer pedagogy, teachers can support students in their understanding and recognitions about how dangerous normalizations in society can marginalize recognition. Through such challenges then, teachers can open up spaces for students to suspend labels, and challenge constructions of heteronormativity (Blackburn and Buckley 2005; Winans 2006). By investigating and questioning conventions associated with Shakespeare's work and setting, teachers can encourage students to think about how society and culture produce texts, interpretations, and identities. Specifically for trans* and gender creative youth, taking part in classrooms and schools that dismantle conventional gender constructs and activate queer pedagogy affirm their identities. Furthermore, when teachers invite in a queer pedagogy, generative possibilities for *all* students to recognize and understand one another's lived realities can be realized, simultaneously generating possibilities to build relationships with each other, family members, and community members.

Queer pedagogy in the ELA classroom can involve activities such as personal writing (or empathetic writing) as well as dramatic enactment, allowing students to explore their own feelings and desires or the feelings and desires of others (Blackburn and Buckley 2005; Blackburn and Clark 2011; Lipkin 1999, pp. 350–351). Encouraging students to recognize and embody characters who are not explicitly heard in texts communicates the importance of recognizing all voices and alternative viewpoints. Such recognition is central to this unit, sequenced by daily lessons that investigate Shakespeare's *Twelfth Night* (2005) while also showing what it means to teach queerly.

UNIT SEQUENCE

Day and central question	Lesson activities	QLF Principle(s)
Day 1: An Introduction to Gender How does our modern understanding of gender contrast with that of Early Modern England?	1. Have small groups discuss and share out the following questions: A. What do you understand to be the difference between gender identity and biological sex at birth? B. How does our society affect the way we view gender? C. Where do you think views on gender originate? 2. Using the definitions elucidated earlier in this book or from other key resources, establish classroom expectations for terminology surrounding gender. Posting terms on the wall affirms their use 3. Early Modern Gender: Using four to five graphic representations of individuals from websites such as Great Britain's National Portrait Gallery (www.npg.org.uk) or Scotland's National Portrait Gallery (www.nationalgalleries.org/portraitgallery), have students comment on how gender was expressed. Portraits of Queen Elizabeth I and James I of England work well. How was gender expressed? How does expression differ from twenty-first century ones? 4. Gender on Stage: Introduce (or re-introduce) students to the concept that all Early Modern stage actors were male. Encourage them to think about how this related to heteropatriarchy. Did it reinforce it? Oppose it? How does this stagecraft relate to power dynamics? 5. Have students choose to write a script, letter, or diary entry that imaginatively explores the life of an Early Modern individual whose gender identity does not correspond to their biological birth sex	2. Understands gender as a construct, which has and continues to be impacted by intersecting factors (e.g., social, historical, material, cultural, religious) 3. Recognizes that masculinity and femininity constructs are assigned to gender norms and are situationally performed 6. Engages in ongoing critique of how gender norms are reinforced in literature, media, technology, art, history, science, math, etc.

Day and central question	Lesson activities	QLF Principle(s)
Day 2 How is Viola/Cesario presented in the play *Twelfth Night*?	1. Viewing a film version of the first act (particularly scenes ii and iv) of *Twelfth Night*, have students observe and discuss how Shakespeare (and the film producers) presents the character of Viola/Cesario. Director Trevor Nunn's production (Evans and Parfitt 1996), while not conforming to Early Modern theatrical conventions concerning gender, follows the text. How would this relate to Early Modern stage conventions? How might it be received? 2. Next, have students view the final scene (Act V, scene i) of the play, where Viola reveals herself to be female. Encourage students to think about how this confirms and/or opposes conventions	3. Recognizes that masculinity and femininity constructs are assigned to gender norms and are situationally performed 6. Engages in ongoing critique of how gender norms are reinforced in literature, media, technology, art, history, science, math, etc.
Day 3 How does the presentation of gender in the play confirm and subvert Early Modern gender and theatrical conventions?	1. Divide the class into small groups of four to five and have them craft a simplified mimed performance of one of the scenes they saw on Day 2. Promote casting that resists gender constraints 2. Using lines V.i.257-261, I.iv. 121-122, and I.iv.28-33, discuss how the language in Shakespeare's text suggests that Viola/Cesario resists gender conventions 3. Finally, write an alternative ending that refuses to conform to heteropatriarchal norms. Students should be encouraged to demonstrate knowledge of language and character but also show creative flair	3. Recognizes that masculinity and femininity constructs are assigned to gender norms and are situationally performed 6. Engages in ongoing critique of how gender norms are reinforced in literature, media, technology, art, history, science, math, etc.

Shakespeare's comedy *Twelfth Night* and particularly the character of Viola/Cesario serves as an apt example of how gender is constructed and performed, reminiscent of Butler's (1988) insistence that gender is not only performed, and moreover a series of repeated "acts." Butler's notion of gender as performance denies gender as a fixed, continuous state aligns with Viola/Cesario's shifts in her demonstration of gender over the play's trajectory. Viola/Cesario performs as male and female at various points during the play—even referring to herself as "all the daughters of my father's house,/And all the brothers too" (Shakespeare 2005, I.iv.121-122), evoking gender nonconformity and instability. Discussions surrounding Queen Elizabeth I and her reign during the first lesson can certainly prompt students to consider the relative agency, or "successful masquerading of masculinity" that an initially female Viola demonstrates (Hutson 1996, p. 141). Students should be prompted to think about reception and the identities of audience members, including Queen Elizabeth I during the play's enactment in 1602 (Holland 2011, p. 390).

Yet ultimately, just as James I ultimately secures the English throne in 1603, so too is heteropatriarchy reinstated in Shakespeare's play as audience members witness Viola capitulate to her female, subservient identity and a heterosexual union by the end of the play (DiGangi 1996; Holland 2011). Introducing students to the ambiguities of Early Modern gender dynamics on the first day of this unit—that a female wielded sovereign power in a heteropatriarchal society and that male actors performed female roles in the theater—starts to dismantle binaries surrounding gender and gender norms.

Gender norms, defined by Butler (1999) as "ideal dimorphism, heterosexual complementarity of bodies, ideals and rule of proper and improper masculinity and femininity, many of which are underwritten by racial codes of purity and taboos against miscegenation" (p. xxiii), may have changed somewhat since the Early Modern era; however, teachers and students can draw parallels between the two societies, interrogating and dismantling binaries. For instance, DiGangi (1996) insists that the enduring nature of Shakespeare's work testifies to the fact that his work does not present same-sex desire as frequently as that of other Early Modern playwrights, more readily accepted during sexually repressive, heteronormative times. Shakespeare's plays do often reinforce patriarchal, nuclear family structures and silence same-sex relationships with plays resolving in heterosexual unions.

This resolution of the play, viewed on the second day of the unit, not only witnesses heterosexual unions but also the revelation of Viola/Cesario's twin brother, Sebastian. Students should grapple with this plot device—the reintroduction of a twin once thought dead—as relating to the heteropatriarchal impulse associated with Shakespeare's popularity. The final assignment to write an alternative ending could incorporate language conventions of the time such as second-person pronoun formality (you/thou), rhetorical devices, the use of blank verse, and limited stage direction as well as speech and action consistent with the characterization developed in *Twelfth Night* prior to the V.i. Assessment of the assignment should match the attention paid to language and dramatic conventions. Additionally, students who illustrate the ability to imagine alternatives and disassemble Early Modern gender constructs should be rewarded, as they will effectively exhibit the queer reading and writing that this unit promotes.

IMPLICATIONS AND SUGGESTIONS

As a consequence of the presumed heteronormative and homophobic nature of many pre-K-12 settings, a queer pedagogy is clearly needed (Blackburn and Clark 2011). Researchers, literary critics, and practitioners continue to illuminate and queer readings of texts and bodies. Theory is being generated, as evidenced by this book and others, yet that research must be translated into praxis through curriculum plans and units.

A quick perusal of Internet and textual resources for teaching Shakespeare, in fact, reveal that numerous perspectives and curricular units exist; however, rarely do they address queer readings of Shakespeare's work. Shakespeare's popularity, evidenced by continued study of his texts in the SELA classroom and performance of his plays on the modern stage, demonstrates the connection that Western students, teachers, and audience members feel toward Shakespeare's work. While plots and characters seemingly reflect imagined settings and plots, these characters and their interactions have resonated with audiences over time. Associated with "the invention of the human," Shakespeare and his plays reflect emotions, desires, and motivations that reflect the human condition (Menon 2011, p. 11). Characters who invoke hatred, laughter, love, and a host of other reactions from readers and playgoers not only reflect the era in which they were created but also speak to the subsequent periods during which these characters have been staged and understood. As windows into the Early Modern era, Shakespeare's plots and characters also reflect on the eras in which they are performed. Viewers and readers can investigate the original performances that Shakespeare's acting company originally produced as well as dramatic interpretations over time. Audience members, including contemporary ones, understand literature through their own experiences. Fostering discussions about how character and (a)gender is performed in Shakespeare's plays leads to investigation into how we, as audience members, are reflecting and projecting our own perceptions of gender onto his texts.

By using the work of Shakespeare to illustrate how gender constructs during the Early Modern era were both subverted and reinforced, teachers can point to ambiguities that exist in twenty-first century American society. In particular, Viola/Cesario's powerful performance of both masculinity and femininity juxtaposes the play's heteropatriarchal resolution, as well as the exclusion of actors who identify as female from the Shakespearean stage. The complicated staging of gender in the Early Modern era certainly differs from how modern theater and film operates; however, in other ways, the heteropatriarchal resolution of *Twelfth Night* shares many similarities with modern U.S. cultural expectations and norms. With their students, teachers can draw parallels between Shakespeare's plot and modern film plot resolutions in order to highlight notions of "happily ever after." Equally, a discussion of how modern films present gender norms—and how the modern film industry rewards these norms—can prompt students to think about the perpetuation of gender norms and the heteropatriarchal resolution.

Ultimately, having students view policies and performances of gender relating to the Early Modern era can lead to fruitful discussions concerning gender constructs that have endured, both in theatrical production as well as in wider society. Studying Shakespeare's works, writ large, offers students a window through which to view another era—as well as a mirror in which to view their own.

Bibliography

Barker, D., & Kamps, I. (1995). *Shakespeare and gender: A history*. New York: Verso.

Blackburn, M. V., & Buckley, J. F. (2005). Teaching queer-inclusive English language arts. *Journal of Adolescent & Adult Literacy, 49*(3), 202–212.

Blackburn, M. V., & Clark, C. T. (2011). Analyzing talk in a long-term literature discussion group: Ways of operating within LGBT-inclusive and queer discourses. *Reading Research Quarterly, 46*(3), 222–248.

Butler, J. (1988). Performative acts and gender constitution: An essay in phenomenology and feminist theory. *Theatre Journal, 40*(4), 519–531.

Butler, J., & ebrary Inc. (1999). *Gender trouble: Feminism and the subversion of identity*. New York: Routledge.

Charles, C. (1997). Gender trouble in twelfth night. *Theatre Journal, 49*(2), 121.

Charles, C. (1998). Was Shakespeare gay? Sonnet 20 and the politics of pedagogy. *College Literature, 25*(3), 35–51.

Clark, C., & Blackburn, M. (2009). Reading LGBTQ literature with young people: What's possible? *The English Journal, 98*(4), 25–32.

DiGangi, M. (1996). Queering the Shakespearean family. *Shakespeare Quarterly, 47*(3), 269.

DiGangi, M. (2007). Queer theory, historicism, and early modern sexualities. *Criticism, 48*(1), 129–142.

Evans, S., Parfitt, D. (Producers), & Nunn, T. (Director). (1996). *Twelfth night: Or what you will* [Motion picture]. London: BBC Films.

Holland, S. (2011). Twelfth night: Is there an audience for my play? In M. Menon (Ed.), *Shakesqueer: A queer companion to the complete works of Shakespeare* (pp. 385–393). Durham: Duke University Press.

Hutson, L. (1996). On not being deceived: Rhetoric and the body in twelfth night. *Texas Studies in Literature and Language, 38*(2), 140–174.

Lipkin, A. (1999). *Understanding homosexuality, changing schools*. Boulder: Westview Press.

Menon, M. (2011). *Shakesqueer: A queer companion to the complete works of Shakespeare*. Durham: Duke University Press.

Meyer, E. (2010). *Gender and sexual diversity in schools: An introduction*. New York: Springer.

Miller, s. (2015a). Why a queer literacy framework matters: Models for sustaining (a)gender self determination and justice in today's schooling practices. In s. Miller (Ed.), *Teaching, affirming, and recognizing trans and gender creative youth: A queer literacy framework*. New York: Routledge.

Miller, s. (2015b). A queer literacy framework promoting (a)gender and (a)sexuality self-determination and justice. *English Journal, 104*(5), 37–44.

Shakespeare, W. (2005). *Twelfth night* (B. Mowat & P. Werstine, Eds.). New York: Simon & Schuster.

Winans, A. (2006). Queering pedagogy in the English classroom: Engaging with the places where thinking stops. *Pedagogy, 6*(1), 103–122.

CHAPTER 16

The Nonconclusion: Trans*ing Education into the Future—This Cannot Wait

sj Miller

For Blue, and all of the youth these amazing authors have written for, trans*ing education cannot afford to wait any longer than it already has. Statistics of bullying, drop-out rates, truancy, lowered grade point averages, mental health issues (Kosciw et al. 2014), and suicidal ideation, including attempts and completion, for trans* and gender creative youth (Ybarra et al. 2014), continue to surpass *any* population of teens to date. If the schooling system were to include curriculum that addressed, broadly speaking, (a)gender from early on in schooling experiences, it could disrupt the continuance of macroaggressions, and instead, support them to develop a positive self-image.

While this book includes examples about how to teach, affirm, and support the recognition of trans* and gender creative youth for uptake by literacy educators, pre- and in-service teachers for only a *few* disciplines, a hope is for other disciplines across all grade levels to also apply the QLF to math, science, the humanities, technology, history, physical education, art, and so on.

sj Miller (✉)
Santa Fe, New Mexico, USA

© The Editor(s) (if applicable) and The Author(s) 2016   293
sj Miller (ed.), *Teaching, Affirming, and Recognizing Trans and Gender Creative Youth*, DOI 10.1057/978-1-137-56766-6_16

There are several cobeneficiaries of this research (see Fig. 16.1), which include researchers, teacher educators, pre- and in-service teachers, classroom students, and society writ large. As students develop (a)gender self-determination, their lived and embodied recognitions by self and other, has immeasurable potential to be spatialized into contexts and the indeterminate. Over time, as more trans* and gender creative youth impact spaces, opinions can change—they *must* change. Though change has been happening for decades, just less visibly, consider this—trans* and gender creative youth will continue to age, some may marry, some will become parents, some grandparents, and even great grandparents. Some may become laborers, professionals (e.g., teachers, professors, doctors, therapists, lawyers, dentists), CEOs, and yes, even politicians. Their presence (across continents) will occur within myriad socioeconomic, cultural, ethnic, religious/nonreligious, spiritual, and linguistic spaces. They will comprise different national origins, (a)sexual orientations, (a)gender expressions, philosophies, genetic information, HIV status, veteran status,

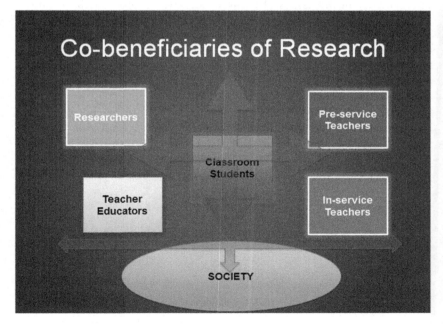

Fig. 16.1 Co-beneficiaries of this research

body sizes, heights, and mental and physical abilities. For the authors of this book and the many others who support the psychosocial-emotional development of trans* and gender creative youth, we know and believe deeply that they are *no* different than any other being and are thereby entitled to the same inalienable rights and to be treated with *dignity*.

Beyond what these authors have shared, findings from this book reveal large holes within curriculum that are trans* positive. To that end, future research *must*—not could or should—but *must* take up how to mediate schooling experiences for all trans* and gender creative youth across all identities and intersectionalities. Districts and schools *must* commit to such efforts in order for them to become both sustainable and a normalized part of the schooling experience for *all* trans* and gender creative youth; and, pre-K-12th grade curriculum *must* change in order to advance a future recognizability for these youth. To these aims, it is recommended that,

- Researchers *must* address ongoing gaps in teacher education and work closely to continue to deepen and develop the efficacy of a theory of trans*ness into trans* pedagogical strategies that affirm and recognize the intersectional realities facing trans* and gender creative youth.
- Preservice teacher education *must* introduce (a)gender identity topics in early childhood education and throughout elementary, middle, and secondary coursework and across disciplinary programs. Programs should decide in which courses such uptake would fit best.
- Teacher educators *must* work closely with school districts to develop professional development models that can support curriculum specialists and teachers in their ongoing awareness about how to meet the needs of trans* and gender creative youth.
- Because no district faces identical issues nor has identical student bodies, district curriculum specialists *must* work alongside classroom teachers and educate each other about the classroom and schooling experiences of *their* trans* and gender creative youth. Collectively they can develop curriculum that develops internal and external safety, is inclusive, and affirming, and generates both recognizability and visibility to self and other.
- Districts and schools *must* work closely with community organizations that address (a)gender and gender violence (e.g., rape crisis centers, LGBT or gender identity nonprofits, doctors, mental health

and health care practitioners) to develop a deeper understanding of the issues facing trans* and gender creative youth.

- Districts and schools *must* work alongside families so as to learn from, and with, their experiences and to develop support groups.
- Districts and schools *must* work to change and update district and school policy, codes of conduct, to enumerate bullying policies, to create safe bathrooms and locker rooms, to consider issues about participation in sports and physical education classes—typical spaces for extreme harassment, and to reflect on how to create a schooling environment that can help to foster external safety.
- Teacher educators, districts, schools, community organizations, and families *must* caucus with legislatures to change state policy about trans* rights to be more inclusive of health care needs, identification changes, and bullying policies.

Change is possible. The double consciousness, or psychic split that many trans* and gender creative youth experience, can be alleviated as all of these constituents work to support one another in sustainable ways. For those who will be impacted by the collective lessons described throughout this book, and as compassion and mindsets are expanded and deepened, the development of even more resources to teach, affirm, and recognize our trans* and gender creative youth, makes (a)gender self-determination no longer just a possibility, but, a *reality*.

THE FUTURE IS NOW—THE POST TRANS*

So, what might a proleptic trans*/post trans* schooling system look like, and how might that potentially change humanity? As trans* becomes part of the fabric of the schooling system and woven into the mainstream of society, we enter into a trans* space. A post trans* space, though indeterminate, would demonstrate how contexts have become sustainable to hold and care for the commonplace normalization of the trans* and gender creative body. In these myriad spaces (e.g., school, jobs, families, etc.), trans* and gender creativity would no longer incur macroaggressions nor marginalization, but for those who embody these glorious identities they would experience the same dignities entitled to any other human. In this post trans* space, the possibility for the unknown and for new knowledges to continue to emerge would become part of social and interpersonal discourses. On a macroscale then, by accepting that the unknown is part and parcel to its larger normalization, a post trans* space becomes accepted without redress. In post trans* contexts, therefore, while people will always *see* difference, the prior systemic misrecognition dysphoria of trans* and gender creativity collapses.

If indeed this post trans* space were realized, a space where trans*ness blends but doesn't blend in, and as trans* and gender creative youth and all people for that matter experience these expanding contexts, humanity might not only see more trans*gentleness, they might also see and experience more trans* and gender creative *justice*. In the wake of such justice then, for schools, curriculum would include trans* and gender creative narratives, books of all genres and story lines, histories, political victories, trailblazers, photos and pictures, and media icons. Students would have ample options for names, (a)pronouns, and (a)gender. There would be no fear of bullying or harassment related to bathrooms, locker rooms, and physical education classes, and most important, school would no longer be about *survival*, it would be about *success, thriving*, and *fulfillment*. The noise and emotional labor once tolerated finally fades away into the distance. No longer would they experience a double consciousness or have to be validated through another's gaze. *When*, not if, the post trans* happens, the Blues of the world needn't remain Blue anymore, nor would they need nearly half a lifetime to discover their true selves—*they would just be free to be themselves in a world better prepared to embrace, accept, love, and recognize them from birth.*

REFERENCES

Kosciw, J. G., Greytak, E. A., Palmer, N. A., & Boesen, M. J. (2014). *The 2013 National School Climate Survey: The experiences of lesbian, gay, bisexual and transgender youth in our nation's schools.* New York: GLSEN.

Ybarra, M. L., Mitchell, K. J., & Kosciw, J. G. (2014). The relation between suicidal ideation and bullying victimization in a national sample of transgender and non-transgender adolescents. In P. Goldblum, D. Espelage, J. Chu, & B. Bognar (Eds.), *Youth suicide and bullying: Challenges and strategies for prevention and intervention* (pp. 134–147). New York: Oxford University Press.

Erratum to: Teaching, Affirming, and Recognizing Trans and Gender Creative Youth

sj Miller

Erratum to:

Teaching, Affirming, and Recognizing Trans and Gender Creative Youth

DOI 10.1057/978-1-137-56766-6

The book was published prematurely, missing some of the author corrections and additional errors were inserted during production process. The version supplied here has been corrected and approved by the editor.

The online version of the original book can be found under

DOI 10.1057/978-1-137-56766-6

---

sj Miller (✉)
University of Colorado Boulder, Boulder, USA

Correction to: Teaching, Affirming, and Recognizing Trans and Gender Creative Youth

sj Miller

CORRECTION TO:

sj Miller (ed.), *Teaching, Affirming, and Recognizing Trans and Gender Creative Youth*, https://doi.org/10.1057/978-1-137-56766-6

The following changes are done in the book.

1) The affiliation of all 3 series editors' are updated.
2) International Advisory Board details are updated in the series information text page.
3) The volume editor affiliation is updated.

The updated original online version of the book can be found at
https://doi.org/10.1057/978-1-137-56766-6

© The Author(s) 2019   C1
sj Miller (ed.), *Teaching, Affirming, and Recognizing Trans and Gender Creative Youth*, https://doi.org/10.1057/978-1-137-56766-6_18

GLOSSARY OF TERMS: DEFINING A COMMON QUEER LANGUAGE

Agender Rejecting gender as a biological or social construct altogether and refusing to identify with gender.

(A)gender Justice or Queer Autonomy These interchangeable terms each ideologically reflect an actualized freedom of humans to be self-expressive without redress of social, institutional, or political violence. See also **queer autonomy.**

(A)gender Self-determination This is the inherent right to both occupy one's (a)gender and make choices to self-identify in a way that authenticates self-expression. It is also a type of self-granted or inherited permission that can help one refute or rise above social critique; it presumes choice and rejects an imposition to be defined or regulated; it presumes that humans are entitled to unsettle knowledge, which can generate new possibilities of legibility; and, it means that any representation of (a)gender deserves the same inalienable rights and the same dignities and protections as any other human. This de 'factoness' grants individuals ways of intervening in and disrupting social and political processes because one's discourse and self-determined ways of being demonstrate placement as a viable stakeholder in society, revealing that no one personhood is of any more or less value than any other.

Ally Any non-lesbian, non-gay man, non-bisexual, or cisgender person whose attitude and behavior are anti-heterosexist and who is proactive and

© The Editor(s) (if applicable) and The Author(s) 2016   299
sj Miller (ed.), *Teaching, Affirming, and Recognizing Trans and Gender Creative Youth*, DOI 10.1057/978-1-137-56766-6

works toward combating homophobia, transphobia, and heterosexism on both a personal and institutional level.

Apronoun Refusal of using pronouns when self-identifying.

Aromantic One who lacks a romantic orientation or is incapable of feeling romantic attraction. Aromantics can still have a sexual orientation (e.g., "aromantic bisexual" or aromantic heterosexual"). A person who feels neither romantic nor sexual attraction is known as an aromantic asexual.

Asexual/Ace A person who does not experience sexual attraction to another person. Individuals may still be emotionally, physically, romantically, and/or spiritually attracted to others, and their romantic orientation may also be LGBTQIA (A in this case meaning ally). The prefixes of homo-, hetero-, bi-, pan-, poly-, demi- and a- have been used to form terms such as heteroromantic, biromantic, homoromantic asexual, and so on. Unlike celibacy, which people choose, asexuality is intrinsic. Some asexual people do engage in sexual activity for a variety of reasons, such as a desire to please romantic partners or to have children.

Assigned Gender The gender one is presumed or expected to embody based on assigned sex at birth.

Assigned Pronouns The commonly accepted pronouns that others use to describe or refer to a person based on actual or perceived gender.

Assigned Sex The sex one is assigned at birth based on genitalia.

Bigender Refers to those who have masculine and feminine sides to their personality. This is often a term used by cross dressers. It should not be confused with the term two-spirit, which is specifically a term used by Native Americans.

Bisexuality/BI A sexual orientation in which a person feels physically and emotionally attracted to both genders.

Butch An identity or presentation that leans toward masculinity. Butch can be an adjective ("she's a butch woman"), a verb ("he went home to butch up"), or a noun ("they identify as a butch"). Although commonly associated with masculine queer/lesbian women, it's used by many to describe a distinct gender identity and/or expression, and does not necessarily imply that one identifies as a woman.

CAFAB and CAMAB Acronyms meaning "Coercively Assigned Female/Male at Birth." Sometimes AFAB and AMAB (without the word "coercively") are used instead. No one, whether cis- or trans, has a choice in the sex or gender to which they are assigned when they are born, which is why it is said to be coercive. In the rare cases in which it is necessary to refer to the birth-assigned sex of a trans person, this is the way to do it.

Chosen Gender The gender one feels most comfortable embodying and how one sees the self.

Chosen Pronouns or Preferred Gender Pronouns The pronouns that one feels most comfortable being used when spoken or referred to. Examples might include: 'ze', 'per,' they, 'or 'hir'.

Cisgender or Cissexual A person who by nature or by choice conforms to gender based expectations of society (Also referred to as gender straight or 'Gender Normative'). A prefix of Latin origin, meaning "on the same side (as)." Cisgender individuals have a gender identity that is aligned with their birth sex, and therefore have a self-perception and gender expression that match behaviors and roles considered appropriate for their birth sex: for example, a person who is femininely identified that was born female. In short, cisgender is the opposite of transgender. It is important to recognize that even if two people identify as men (one being cis and the other being trans*), they may lead very similar lives but deal with different struggles pertaining to their birth sex.

Cissexism Synonymous with transphobia, this definition is associated with negative attitudes and feelings toward transgender people, based on the expression of their internal gender identity. Cissexism is also the belief that cisgender individuals are superior to transgender people and that a cisgender lifestyle is more desirable to lead.

"Coming Out" Also, "coming out of the closet" or "being out," this term refers to the process in which a person acknowledges, accepts, and in many cases appreciates her or his lesbian, gay, bisexual, or transgender identity. This often involves sharing of this information with others. It is not a single event but instead a life-long process. Each new situation poses the decision of whether or not to come out.

Crip Increasingly used to refer to a person who has a disability and embraces it, rather than feeling sorry for themselves. Historically used as a disparaging term for a person who is partially disabled or unable to use a limb or limbs. It is similar to the word queer in that it is sometimes used as a hateful slur, so although some have reclaimed it from their oppressors, be careful with its use.

Cross-Dressing (CD) The act of dressing and presenting as the "opposite" binary gender. One who considers this an integral part of their identity may identify as a cross-dresser. Transvestite is an obsolete (and sometimes offensive) term with the same meaning. Cross-dressing and drag are forms of gender expression and are not necessarily tied to erotic activity, nor are they indicative of one's sexual orientation. Do NOT use these terms to describe someone who has transitioned or intends to do so in the future.

Demisexual A demisexual is a person who does not experience sexual attraction unless they form a strong emotional connection with someone. It's more commonly seen in, but by no means confined to, romantic relationships. The term demisexual comes from the orientation being "halfway between" sexual and asexual. Nevertheless, this term does not mean that demisexuals have an incomplete or half-sexuality, nor does it mean that sexual attraction without emotional connection is required for a complete sexuality. In general, demisexuals are not sexually attracted to anyone of any gender; however, when a demisexual is emotionally connected to someone else (whether the feelings are romantic love or deep friendship), the demisexual experiences sexual attraction and desire, but only toward the specific partner or partners.

Drag Stylized performance of gender, usually by female-bodied drag kings or male-bodied drag queens. Doing drag does not necessarily have anything to do with one's sex, gender identity, or orientation.

Femme An identity or presentation that leans toward femininity. Femme can be an adjective (he's a "femmeboy"), a verb (she feels better when she femmes up"), or a noun ("they're a femme"). Although commonly associated with feminine lesbian/queer women, it's used by many to describe a distinct gender identity and/or expression and does not necessarily imply that one identities as a woman.

Gay A common and acceptable word for male homosexuals, but used for both genders.

Gender Socially constructed roles, behaviors, and attributes considered by the general public to be "appropriate" for one's sex as assigned at birth. Gender roles vary among cultures and time continuums.

Gender Affirmation/Confirmation Surgery Having surgery as means to construct genitalia of choice. Surgery does not change one's sex or gender, only genitalia. Gender/genitalia reassignment/reconstruction surgeries affirm an essentialist perspective of being born in the wrong sex from birth and are less frequently used in a lexicon.

Gender Binary A system of viewing gender as consisting solely of two categories (termed woman and man) which are biologically based (female and male) and unchangeable, and in which no other possibilities for gender or anatomy are believed to exist. This system is oppressive to anyone who defines their birth assignment, but particularly those who are gender-variant people and do not fit neatly into one of the two categories. *See also* *non-binary gender.*

Gender Creative Expressing gender in a way that demonstrates individual freedom of expression and that does not conform to any gender.

Gender Expression/Presentation The physical manifestation of one's gender identity through clothing, hairstyle, voice, body shape, and so on, typically referred to as feminine or masculine. Many transgender people seek to make their gender expression (how they look) match their gender identity rather than their birth-assigned sex.

Gender Fluid Individuals who are between identifying with a gender or who do not identify with a gender. This term overlaps with genderqueer and bigender, implying movement between gender identities and/or presentations.

Gender Identity One's personal sense of his or her correct gender, which may be reflected as gender expression.

Gender Non-conforming A term for individuals whose gender expression is different from societal expectations related to gender.

Gender Role/Expression How one performs gender in the world as it relates to social expectations and norms.

Genderqueer Those rejecting binary roles and language for gender. A general term for non-binary gender identities. Those who identify as genderqueer may identify as neither woman nor man; may see themselves as outside of the binary gender boxes; may fall somewhere between the binary genders; or may reject the use of gender labels. Genderqueer identities fall under the "trans" umbrella. Synonyms include androgynous.

Gray-Asexual Asexuality and sexuality are not black and white; some people identify in the **gray** (spelled **"grey"** in some countries) area between them. People who identify as **gray-Asexual** can include, but are not limited to, those who: do not normally experience sexual attraction, but do experience it sometimes; experience sexual attraction, but a low sex drive; experience sexual attraction and drive, but not strongly enough to want to act on them; **and** people who can enjoy and desire sex, but only under very limited and specific circumstances. A person can be gray-heterosexual, gray-homosexual, and/or gray-bisexual.

GSM Gender and Sexual Minority is a term used to describe those who fall outside of dominant gender and sexuality identities.

Hate Crime Any act of intimidation, harassment, physical force, or threat of physical force directed against any person, or their property, motivated either in whole or in part by hostility toward their actual or perceived age, disability, gender identity, ethnic background, race, religious/spiritual belief, sex, sexual orientation, and so on.

Heteroflexible Similar to bisexual, but with a stated heterosexual preference. Sometimes characterized as being "mostly straight." Commonly used to indicate that one is interested in heterosexual romance but is "flexible" when it comes to sex and/or play. The same concepts apply to homoflexible.

Heteronormative/Heteronormativity A culture or belief system that assumes that people fall into distinct and complementary sexes and genders and that heterosexuality is the normal sexual orientation. A heteronormative view is one that involves alignment of biological sex, sexuality, gender identity, and gender roles.

Heterosexism The assumption that all people are or should be heterosexual. Heterosexism excludes the needs, concerns, and life experiences of lesbian, gay, and bisexual people while it gives advantages to heterosexual people. It is often a subtle form of oppression which reinforces realities of silence and invisibility.

Heterosexuality A sexual orientation in which a person feels physically and emotionally attracted to people of the opposite gender.

Homonormative/Homonormativity The assimilation of heteronormative ideals and constructs into LGBTQIA culture and identity. Homonormativity upholds neoliberalism rather than critiquing monogamy, procreation, normative family social roles, and binary gender roles. It is criticized as undermining citizens' rights and erasing the historic alliance between radical politics and gay politics, the core concern being sexual freedom. Some assert that homonormativity fragments LGBTQIA communities into hierarchies of worthiness: those that mimic heteronormative standards of gender identity are deemed most worthy of receiving rights. Individuals at the bottom of the hierarchy are seen as an impediment to this elite class of homonormative individuals receiving their rights. Because LGBTQIA activists and organizations embrace systems that endorse normative family social roles and serial monogamy, some believe that LGBTQIA people are surrendering and conforming to heteronormative behavior.

Homophobia The fear, dislike, and/or hatred of same-sex relationships or those who love and are sexually attracted to those of the same-sex. Homophobia includes prejudice, discrimination, harassment, and acts of violence brought on by fear and hatred. It occurs on personal, institutional, and societal levels.

Homosexual A person who is physically, romantically, emotionally, and/or spiritually attracted to a person of the same gender. Many prefer "gay," "lesbian," and so on because of the term's origins as a medical term at a time when homosexuality was considered a disorder.

Homosexuality A sexual orientation in which a person feels physically and emotionally attracted to people of the same gender.

Inclusive Language The use of non-identity specific language to avoid imposing limitations or assumptions on others. For example, saying "you all" instead of "you guys" in order to not impose assumptions regarding a person's gender identity.

In the Closet To be "in the closet" means to hide one's homosexual identity in order to keep a job, a housing situation, friends, or in some other way to survive. Many GLBT individuals are "out" in some situations and "closeted" in others.

Intersex Describes a person whose natal physical sex is physically ambiguous. There are many genetic, hormonal, or anatomical variations which can cause this (e.g., Klinefelter Syndrome, Adrenal Hyperplasia, or Androgen Insensitivity Syndrome). Parents and medical professionals usually assign intersex infants a sex and perform surgical operations to conform the infant's body to that assignment, but this practice has become increasingly controversial as intersex adults are speaking out against having had to undergo medical procedures which they did not consent to (and in many cases caused them mental and physical difficulties later in life). The term intersex is preferred over "hermaphrodite," an outdated term which is stigmatizing and misleading.

Internalized Homophobia The fear and self-hate of one's own homosexuality or bisexuality that occurs for many individuals who have learned negative ideas about homosexuality throughout childhood. One form of internalized oppression is the acceptance of the myths and stereotypes applied to the oppressed group. Internalized oppression is commonly seen among most, if not all, minority groups.

Invisibility The constant assumption of heterosexuality renders gay and lesbian people, youth in particular, invisible and seemingly non-existent. Gay and lesbian people and youth are usually not seen or portrayed in society, and especially not in schools and classrooms.

Label Free Individuals who shirk all labels attached to gender and reject the gender binary.

Lesbian A femininely identified individual who is emotionally, physically, romantically, sexually, and/or spiritually attracted to femininely identified individuals.

Monosexual/Multisexual Umbrella terms for orientations directed toward one's gender (monosexual) or many genders (multisexual).

Non-binary Gender Non-binary refers to (a)gender as broader, less defined, more fluid, and a more imaginative and expressive matrix of ideas. It challenges power differentials, by deconstructing and reconstructing ideas, reflecting on disjunctures, unpacking gender, gender identities, and gender expressions, and providing opportunities for new knowledges to emerge.

Pansexual/Omnisexual "Pan," meaning "all." Someone who is emotionally, physically, romantically, sexually, and/or spiritually attracted to all gender identities/expressions, including those outside the gender-conforming binary. Similar to bisexual, but different in that the concept deliberately rejects the gender binary. Polysexual people are attracted to "many," but not necessarily all, genders.

Passing A term used by transgender people to mean that they are seen as the gender with which they self-identify. For example, a transgender man (born female) who most people see as a man. Also a term used by non-heterosexual people to mean that they are seen as or assumed to be heterosexual.

Polyamory Having more than one intimate relationship at a time with the knowledge and consent of everyone involved. It is distinct from both swinging (which emphasizes sex with others as merely recreational) and polysexuality (which is attraction toward multiple genders and/or sexes). People who identify as polyamorous typically reject the view that sexual and relational exclusivity are necessary for deep, committed, long-term loving relationships.

Preferred or Chosen Gender Pronouns Self-selected pronouns for how an individual prefers to be referenced. While there is an emerging lexicon or pronouns, it is best to ask the individual how one self-references.

QPOC "Queer People of Color" or "Queer Person of Color."

Queer Despite the negative historical use of this term, it has been embraced in the last decade, particularly by younger members of the GLBT community. It is an umbrella term that many prefer, both because of convenience (easier than 'gay, lesbian, etc.) and because it does not force the person who uses it to choose a more specific label for their gender identity or sexual orientation. Queer also refers to a suspension of rigid gendered and sexual orientation categories and is underscored by attempts to interrogate and interrupt heteronormativity, reinforced by acknowledging diverse people across gender, sex, and desires, as well as to foreground the sexual. It embraces the freedom to move beyond, between, or even away from, yet even to later return to, myriad identity categories. Queer is not relegated to LGBT*IAGCQ people, but is inclusive of any variety of experience that transcends what has been socially and politically accepted as normative categories for gender and sexual orientation.

Queer Autonomy or (A)gender Justice These interchangeable terms each ideologically reflect an actualized freedom of humans to be self-expressive without redress of social, institutional, or political violence. See also **(*a*)*gender justice***

Romantic Orientation A person's enduring emotional, physical, romantic and/or spiritual—but not necessarily sexual—attraction to others. Sometimes called affectional orientation. "Romantic orientation" is often used by the asexual community in lieu of "sexual orientation."

Safe Space A place where people who identify within the LGBTQIA communities feel comfortable and secure in being who they are. In this place, they can talk about the people with whom they are involved without fear of being criticized, judged, or ridiculed. Safe spaces promote the right to be comfortable in one's living space, work environments, and so on. It is focused toward the right to use the pronoun of a significant other in conversation, and the right to be as outwardly open about one's life and activities as anyone else.

Same-Gender Loving A term created by the African-American community that some prefer to use instead of "lesbian," "bisexual," or "gay" to express attraction to and love of people of the same gender. SGL is an alternative to Eurocentric homosexual identities, which may not culturally affirm or engage the history and cultures of people of African descent.

Self-determined Presumes the right to make choices to self-identify in a way that authenticates one's self-expression and self-acceptance, rejects an imposition to be externally controlled, defined, or regulated, and can unsettle knowledge to generate new possibilities of legibility.

Sex Sex refers to the biological traits, which include internal and external reproductive anatomy, chromosomes, hormones, and other physiological characteristics. The assignment and classification of people at birth as male or female is often based solely on external reproductive anatomy. Related terms: intersex, female, male.

Sexual Orientation A person's emotional, physical, and sexual attraction and the expression of that attraction. Although a subject of debate, sexual orientation is probably one of the many characteristics that people are born with.

Sexual Minority A term used to refer to someone who identifies their sexuality as different from the dominant culture (i.e., heterosexual), for example, homosexual, gay, lesbian, bisexual, transsexual, transgender, or transvestite.

Sexual Affirmation/Alignment Surgery Establishing one's affirmed sex via legal and medical steps.

Stealth Going stealth means for a trans* person to live completely as their gender identity and to pass in the public sphere; when a trans* person chooses not to disclose their trans* status to others. This can be done for numerous reasons including safety, or simply because the person doesn't feel others have the right to know. For transsexuals, going stealth is often the goal of transition.

*Trans** Prefix or adjective used as an abbreviation of transgender, derived from the Greek word meaning "across from" or "on the other side of." Many consider trans* to be an inclusive and useful umbrella term. Trans (without the asterisk) is most often applied to trans men and trans women, and the asterisk is used more broadly to refer to all non-cisgender gender identities, such as agender, cross-dresser, bigender, genderfluid, gender**k, genderless, genderqueer, non-binary, non-gendered, third gender, trans man, trans woman, transgender, transsexual, and two-spirit.

Transgender (TG) The experience of having a gender identity that is different from one's biological sex. A transgender person may identify with the opposite biological gender and want to be a person of that gender. A transgender person may or may not be pre- or postoperative; if they are, they are likely to refer to him/herself as transsexual. This has become an umbrella term for non-conforming gender identity and expression.*

Transphobia Irrational fear of trans* people through active prejudice and active discrimination by institutions, communities, and/or individuals that diminishes access to resources throughout mainstream society.

Transition Adopting one's affirmed, non-biological gender permanently. The complex process of leaving behind one's coercively assigned birth sex. Transition can include: coming out to one's family, friends, and/or co-workers; changing one's name and/or sex on legal documents; hormone therapy; and possibly (though not always) some form of surgery. It's best not to assume that someone will "complete" this process at any particular time: an individual's transition is finished when they are finally comfortable with how their gender identity is aligned with their body and may not include going through all of the aforementioned steps.

Trans* Woman or Trans Man Informal descriptors used relative to one's affirmed gender. Variants include T*, trans person, and trans folk.

Transsexual People (TS) Typically those taking all available medical and legal steps to transition from their assigned sex to their affirmed sex. Transitioning across the sexual binary can go from female to male (FTM) or male to female (MTF). Some go stealth, hiding their transsexual history.

Two-Spirit A contemporary term that references historical multiple gender traditions in many First Nations cultures. These individuals were sometimes viewed in certain tribes as having two spirits occupying one body; two-spirit indicates a person whose body simultaneously manifests both a masculine and a feminine spirit. Many Native/First Nations people who are LGBTQIA or gender non-conforming identify as Two-Spirit; in many Nations, being two-spirit carries both great respect and additional commitments and responsibilities to one's community.

When Discussing or Having Conversations with People, It Is Best to Avoid

- She-male, tranny, transie, sex change, he-she, shim
- Sexual preference (suggests choice)
- Hermaphrodite (an outdated clinical term)
- Putting the affix "ed" on the end of transgender, (a)gender, and so on, because the affix implies something that has "happened" to a person rather than state what a person is

Notes on Contributors

Jill Adams is Associate Professor of English at Metropolitan State University of Denver. She teaches composition, young adult literature, and English education methods courses.

Cathy A.R. Brant is Assistant Professor at University of South Carolina in the Early Childhood Education program in the Department of Instruction and Teacher Education. She holds a Ph.D. in Teaching and Learning from the Ohio State University, an M.Ed. in Elementary/Early Childhood Education from Rutgers University, and a B.A. in Sociology from Douglass College at Rutgers University. After spending six years as an elementary school teacher, she realized her passion and commitment to issues of equity in teacher training. Brant's research focuses on the integration of sexuality and (a)gender issues in teacher preparation.

Karina R. Clemmons is Associate Professor of Secondary Education in the School of Education at the University of Arkansas at Little Rock, where she researches and teaches graduate and undergraduate teacher education courses. She taught English Language Arts for Speakers of Other Language (ESOL) in middle and high school, and to adults in the USA and abroad. She researches, publishes, and presents in the areas of young adult literature, teacher education, social justice, technology in education, and literacy in the content areas.

Clemmons has presented her work at the American Educational Research Association, the International Literacy Association, the National Council of Teachers of English, the National Science Teachers Association, as well as other regional, national, and international conferences. One recent publication with her colleague Heather Olvey is a book chapter titled "Graphic Texts as a Catalyst for Content Knowledge and Common Core Content Literacy Standards in STEM classes", in J.A. Hayn, A. L. Nolen, & J. Kaplan (Eds.), *Young Adult Nonfiction: Gateway to the Common Core*. Clemmons recently presented "Attitude Adjustment: Using YAL to Encourage Social Justice" at the annual meeting of the International Literacy Association with her colleagues Judy Hayn and Heather Olvey.

Kathryn Cloonan graduated from Swarthmore College in Pennsylvania and then packed her books, put her field hockey stick into a rolling suitcase while clutching a one-way ticket to London, UK. Following ten years of teaching English in secondary schools there, Katie returned to her hometown of Rochester, New York, in order to pursue a Ph.D. in Teaching, Curriculum, and Change at the University of Rochester's Warner School of Education and Human Development. Active in the university's David T. Kearns Center for Leadership and Diversity in Arts, Sciences and Engineering as a pre-college writing instructor and graduate assistant, Katie helps coordinate writing classes for the Center's Upward Bound summer program. At the Warner School, Katie serves as an adjunct instructor and research assistant on a study of teacher candidates' experiences with early edTPA implementation, funded by the Spencer Foundation. An avid reader, athlete, listener, and teacher, Katie loves learning from others' stories and lives most of all.

Katherine Mason Cramer is Associate Professor of English Education at Wichita State University, Kansas. She teaches young adult literature and English methods courses.

Toby Emert is Associate Professor of English Education and Chair of the Department of Education at Agnes Scott College, a liberal arts school for women near Atlanta, Georgia. He teaches courses in young adult literature, language arts pedagogy, social justice education, and the fine and performing arts. He has also taught at the University of Kentucky, Kennesaw State University, and the University of Virginia, where he completed his doctoral work. He chairs the Lesbian, Gay, Bisexual, and Transgender Issues in Academic Studies Committee for the National Council of Teachers of English (NCTE) and writes about queer YA literature as a guest columnist for *The ALAN Review*. He is past president of the Pedagogy and Theatre of the Oppressed, an international organization, and serves on its board of directors. His scholarship focuses on issues of marginalization, including the education of the children of refugees and the potential impact of the arts-based instructional interventions. His articles have appeared in *English Journal*, *Voices from the Middle*, *Language Arts*, and *Intercultural Education*, among others.

Hidehiro Endo is Assistant Professor of the Faculty of International Liberal Arts at Akita International University, Akita, Japan. He has taught Japanese and teacher education courses at the undergraduate level, English at the high school level, and is teaching teacher education courses in the Teacher's License Program. His research interests include social justice issues in education, English language teaching and learning, and teaching and teacher education. His peer-reviewed articles have appeared in *Teaching and Teacher Education*, and he was guest coeditor for a special LGBT issue of the *International Journal of Critical Pedagogy*. He is also coeditor of the book series, *Research on Queer Issues*. His research involves examining how English language teachers in high schools in Japan are interpreting and implementing new curricular laws put into effect in 2014. This research will result in instructional materials to help English teachers teach in English.

Paula Greathouse is Assistant Professor of English Education at Tennessee Technological University. Prior to entering the collegiate forum, she was a secondary English and Reading teacher for 16 years. Paula has won several awards for her teaching, including the Florida Council of Teachers of English High School Teacher of the Year in 2011 and the National Council of Teachers of English Teacher of Excellence Award in 2012. Paula has received awards for her advocacy in the LGBTIQ community including the Pride Award from the University of South Florida in 2013. Paula continues to share her experiences including LGBTIQ texts in her classroom with teachers from around the country through presentations at local and national conferences and has made a commitment to improving the schooling experiences of LGBTIQ students through her membership in NCTE's LGBT Issues in Academic Studies Advisory Committee.

Judith A. Hayn taught 15 years in the public schools and is the Interim Associate Dean of the College of Education and Health Professions at the

314 NOTES ON CONTRIBUTORS

University of Arkansas at Little Rock. Her research focuses on social justice issues in YAL; she has published numerous reviews, articles, and teacher curriculum materials. She coedited three texts focused on using YAL in the English language arts classroom. Her books *Young Adult Nonfiction: Gateway to the Common Core* was published in 2015 while *Teaching Young Adult Literature: Integrating, Implementing, and Re-Imagining the Common Core* will be published in 2016. A revision of the text *Teaching Young Adult Literature Today: Insights, Considerations, and Perspectives for the Classroom Teacher* (2012) is in production.

benjamin lee hicks is an artist, an activist, and an out, trans* elementary school teacher. They have been teaching kindergarten to grade six students in the Toronto District School Board, Ontario, Canada, for the past eight years. They are a student at The Institute of Traditional Medicine, studying Contemplative Psychotherapy, as well as an M.A. candidate in Curriculum Studies and Teacher Development at the Ontario Institute for Studies in Education (OISE), University of Toronto. They are interested in the ways that we prepare teachers to address topics of queerness and gender identity in elementary school classrooms from an antioppressive framework, and their research will focus on how faculties of education can learn to do this more holistically in order to improve teacher follow-through and sustainability of practice in classrooms.

Kate E. Kedley is a doctoral student in the Language, Literacy, and Culture program at the University of Iowa. Kedley's research focuses on English education abroad, teacher movements in Central America, and queer identities in Language Arts classrooms. Kedley's article "Queering the teacher as a text in the English language Arts classroom: beyond books, identity work and teacher preparation" has appeared in the journal *Sex Education: Sexuality, Society and Learning*.

Aryah O'Tiss S. Lester is a trans* woman of color from New York and Georgia who has been a Miami-Dade, Florida, resident since 2005. She is the Chair for the State of Florida Health Department's Transgender Work Group and a member of the Miami-Dade HIV/AIDS Partnership and the Prevention Committee and County Trans Work Group. She also sits as a member on the National Alliance of State and Territorial AIDS Directors (NASTAD) Transgender Networking Group. In 2013, Lester opened the

Trans-Miami Center and extended her National Alliance of Transgender Advocates and Leaders (NATAL) network. She was most recently named to the 2015 Trans 100 List.

Cris Mayo is Professor and Associate Head in the Department of Education Policy, Organization and Leadership Studies and Director of Online Learning at the College of Education at the University of Illinois at Urbana-Champaign. Her books in queer studies, gender and sexuality studies, and philosophy of education include *LGBTQ Youth and Education: Policies and Practices* (2013), *Disputing the Subject of Sex: Sexuality and Public School Controversies* (2004, 2007), and her articles have appeared in journals such as *Educational Theory, Studies in Philosophy and Education, Policy Futures in Education, Review of Research in Education*, and *Sexuality Research and Social Policy*.

Paul Chamness Miller is Associate Professor of the Faculty of International Liberal Arts at Akita International University, Akita, Japan. He teaches writing and composition courses in the English for Academic Purposes program as well as courses for the Teacher's License Program. One of his primary areas of research is LGBT issues in K-12 public school settings. His peer-reviewed articles have appeared in journals such as *Teaching and Teacher Education*, and he was guest coeditor for a special LGBT issue of the *International Journal of Critical Pedagogy*. He is also coeditor of the book series, *Research on Queer Issues*. In addition to his research on LGBT issues, he also researches intersections of social justice and language studies. He serves as the editor of the book series *Readings in Language Studies* and serves as editor of the international journal *Critical Inquiry in Language Studies*.

sj Miller is Associate Professor of Literacy at the University of Colorado, Boulder. sj is Executive Committee member of the Conference on English Education (CEE), coeditor of *English Education*, coeditor of the book series *Social Justice Across Contexts in Education*, Lambda Literary Board Member, and advisory board member for *Critical Studies in Gender and Sexuality in Education, Journal of Adolescent and Adult Literacy*, and CU's Chancellor's LGBT Committee.

Most notably, sj won the 2005 Article of the Year Award from the *English Journal* for "Shattering Images of Violence in Young Adult

Literature: Strategies for the Classroom" and coauthored *Unpacking the Loaded Teacher Matrix: Negotiating Space and Time Between University and Secondary English Classrooms*, which received the Richard A. Meade award from NCTE. sj helped draft the *Beliefs Statement about Social Justice in English Education* and helped pass the *NCTE Resolution on Social Justice in Literacy Education*, which informed the newly vetted CAEP Social Justice Standard 6. sj's coauthored *Generation BULLIED 2.0: Prevention and Intervention Strategies for Our Most Vulnerable Students* and has been awarded "Essential Book for Professionals Who Serve Teens," by *Voices of Youth Advocate Magazine*. sj was named the 2015 recipient of the Joanne Arnold Courage and Commitment Award for contributions to advocacy and education in the lives of LGBTQ people at CU and beyond and is the newly appointed Chair for AERA's Queer Special Interest Group. sj's articles have appeared in a number of journals, including *English Education, English Journal, Alan Review, Teacher Education and Practice, Scholar-Practitioner Quarterly, Journal of Curriculum Theorizing, International Journal of Critical Pedagogy*, and *Educational Leadership Quarterly*. This is sj's fifth book.

Heather A. Olvey was a graduate research assistant for the Teacher Education Department of the University of Arkansas at Little Rock. She earned her Master's in Education in 2015. She has presented her research in Young Adult Literature at the International Literacy Association Conference and has made contributions to several professional publications. She teaches English language arts in the Little Rock area.

Summer Melody Pennell is a doctoral candidate in education at the University of North Carolina, Chapel Hill, and a former high school English teacher. Her research interests include English methods, teacher education, critical literacy, intersectionality, and qualitative methods. She is dedicated to creating welcoming spaces for LGBTQIA students and teachers.

Stephanie Anne Shelton is a Ph.D. candidate in the Language and Literacy Education Department at the University of Georgia. She is a teaching assistant at the Institute for Women's Studies and serves as the managing editor of the *Journal of Language and Literacy Education*. She received the Carol J. Fisher Award for Excellence in Research and Genelle

Morain Award for Excellence in Graduate Teaching from her department, and the Graduate Student Diversity Engagement Award from the university. She serves as the co-chair of the Literacy Research Association's Gender and Sexualities Innovative Community Group.

Ashley Lauren Sullivan is Assistant Professor of Early Childhood Education at Penn State Erie, The Behrend College. Her research focuses on social justice and equity in early childhood education, LGBTQ children and families, transgender children's literature, poverty studies, and literacy development from ages two to five. Prior to her position at Behrend, Sullivan worked as a kindergarten teacher, curriculum writer, and professional development facilitator for Hartford Public Schools in Connecticut. She has presented her research locally, nationally, and internationally at conferences, including those held by the America Educational Research Association, the International Reading Association, and Reconceptualizing Early Childhood Education. She has taught a variety of courses including those centering on young children's play, parental involvement, foundations of early childhood education, LGBTQ studies, diversity, and nutrition, health, and safety. Sullivan is thrilled to contribute to this book as it combines her passions for education, transgender children, and literacy.

Michael Wenk holds his Ph.D. in Curriculum and Instruction (Literacy) from the University of Colorado Boulder, where he taught undergraduate and graduate language and literacy courses for elementary and secondary teacher candidates. He also is a graduate of the University of Michigan (B.A. English, 1990) and the University of Colorado Denver (M.A. Information and Learning Technologies, 2000). Since 1988, Michael has worked in public schools as a secondary English teacher, instructional coach, and curriculum specialist. He has been honored by both students and colleagues for his work in the classroom, which was highlighted by giving a commencement address at Red Rocks Amphitheater in Morrison, Colorado. He presents on as well as writes about cross-content literacy instruction, cross-generational literacies, instructional technologies, reading and writing workshop, and critical literacies. Michael is an active member of the Colorado Language Arts Society (a state affiliate of the National Council of Teachers of English), serving over the past ten years as president, webmaster, and affiliate journal editor.

INDEX